The economics of labour

Edited by John Creedy and Barry Thomas

Butterworth Scientific

London Boston Durban Singapore Sydney Toronto Wellington

First published 1982

© Butterworth & Co (Publishers) Ltd 1982

British Library Cataloguing in Publication Data
The Economics of labour.
  1. Labor supply – Great Britain
  I. Creedy, John   II. Thomas, Barry
  331.12′0941   HD5765.A6

  ISBN 0-408-10827-4
  ISBN 0-408-10826-6 Pbk

Typeset by Butterworths Litho Preparation Department
Printed in Great Britain by Thomson Litho Ltd, and bound by
Hunter Foulis Ltd

Acknowledgements

We should like to thank the staff of Butterworths for their interest in this book, and for helpful advice, particularly at the early stages of its development. Although each chapter has been contributed by a different author, our objective was to produce an integrated text, using a consistent style of presentation and level of approach. This would not have been possible without the considerable cooperation of the contributors, to whom we are very grateful. We should especially like to thank Margaret Hayes, who dealt cheerfully and efficiently with a considerable amount of typing.

John Creedy
Barry Thomas

The economics of labour

Contributors

J. Creedy is Professor of Economics and Head of the Department of Economics at the University of Durham. He has previously lectured at Reading University, and has worked at the National Institute of Economic and Social Research. His main research interests are concerned with the distribution of income, public policy, and the history of economic thought. He is the author of *State Pensions in Britain* (1982), and the editor of *The Economics of Unemployment in Britain* (1981).

B. Thomas is Senior Lecturer in Economics at Durham University. He was previously lecturer at Salford University and was a Research Fellow at the SSRC Industrial Relations Research Unit at the University of Warwick. His main research interests are in the operation of labour markets. He is co-author, with David Deaton, of *Labour Shortage and Economic Analysis* (1977).

D. Deaton is a Research Fellow in the SSRC Industrial Relations Research Unit at the University of Warwick. His main research interests are concerned with unemployment and labour market segmentation. He is co-author, with Barry Thomas, of *Labour Shortage and Economic Analysis* (1977) and, with John Bowers and Jeremy Turk, of *Labour Hoarding in British Industry* (1982).

J. Ashworth is Lecturer in Economics at Durham University. He was previously a Research Fellow at the University of Stirling, working on the Taxation and Labour Supply project. His main research interests are in the econometric analysis of individuals' labour supply, and in the macroeconomic analysis of the determinants of wage and price inflation.

R. M. Lindley is Director of the Institute for Employment Research at the University of Warwick. His main research interests are in macroeconomics and labour economics. He is editor and co-author of *Britain's Medium-Term Employment Prospects* (1978), *Economic Change and Employment Policy* (1980) and *Higher Education and the Labour Market* (1981).

R. Disney is Lecturer in Economics at the University of Kent at Canterbury. He has previously lectured at the University of Reading and the University of Addis Ababa. His research interests include the economics of underdeveloped countries, labour economics and social policy.

K. Whitfield is Lecturer in the Department of Industrial Economics at the University of Sydney. His main research interests are in the economics of professional labour markets. He has been involved with longitudinal surveys of professional scientists in both Britain and Australia.

B. Chiplin is Senior Lecturer in industrial economics at the University of Nottingham. His main research interests are in industrial and labour economics. His most recent books include *The Economics of Advertising* (with Brian Sturgess, 1981), and *Tackling Discrimination at the Workplace* (with Peter Sloane, 1982).

List of tables

List of figures

Contents

Chapter 1

Introduction

The economics of labour is concerned with the complex set of factors that affect the demand for and supply of different types of labour service, and the operation of different kinds of labour market. It deals with the role of labour services in the production process, and with the structure of pay in the economy where pay represents both a price and a distributive share[1].

Many of the central ideas of labour economics have been familiar to writers from Adam Smith onwards but they were not fully integrated into a coherent and distinctive field of study until the present century[2]. In its early days as a special subject area there was a major concern with labour market institutions. This tradition has now developed into the more formalized study of industrial relations while modern labour economics has become a direct interest of mainstream economists. During the 1960s and 1970s there has been the development of an active emphasis on theory, drawing on and adapting orthodox theory and developing alternatives where appropriate, and also an emphasis on measurement. The purpose of this book is to reflect these interests, and to provide an outline of modern labour economics which is useful to students and to non-specialists. While each chapter has been contributed by a separate author, every attempt has been made to produce an integrated text which provides a coherent analysis of labour markets, with special reference to Britain where appropriate. This introduction is not intended to provide a substantive analysis of particular issues, but aims to draw attention to a number of important aspects of the economics of labour which are examined in more detail in the following chapters. First, the role of economics in the study of labour is briefly considered. Some general descriptive features of the labour market in Britain are then presented in section 1.1. Some important aspects of labour services and the markets for labour which must be recognized by the economist are then discussed in section 1.2. A plan of the book is provided in section 1.3.

The importance of labour economics as a separate area of study derives from the crucial position of labour in a complex industrial society like Britain. Except in times of war there is now little 'compulsion' in the allocation of labour to different occupations, and in the direct allocation of the resulting supply of particular goods and services to different households. Thus the household as an economic unit plays a crucial role in both supplying labour and in appropriating resources with its earnings.

The role of labour economics in the study of such an individualistic society, with a considerable amount of specialization, is of course much greater than it would be in a society where a large proportion of the work is carried out by individuals who have very little freedom over their choice of work, location of residence and consumption pattern. The labour markets used today have been developed comparatively recently. The transition between different types of societies, for example between those using slave labour and feudal systems and the present, provides a fascinating subject of study; but the present book is concerned exclusively with the economics of advanced industrial societies[3].

The development of labour markets has necessarily involved the development of a number of important economic institutions, concerning for example organizations of employers and employees, different methods of wage payment[4], and arrangements for training individuals in particular skills. Many of these institutions are considered in this book, but it must be stressed that their economic analysis necessarily excludes many aspects which are of direct interest to those concerned with political or sociological *processes*[5]. While it must be fully recognized that many fundamental relationships and causes involved in the distribution of income from employment are ignored, there is nevertheless a special role for the labour economist. Thus

> whatever their causes, the movements of the labour market are knit up with those of prices, incomes, and output generally, in a system whose static and dynamic connections have been explored only by economic analysis. (Phelps Brown, 1962, p. 8)[6].

1.1   The labour market in Britain

At the beginning of the 1980s the total population of the UK was about 56 million people, of whom about 26 million were in the labour force. The population was distributed among approximately 19.5 million households, so that on average there were roughly

1.3 workers per household. These aggregate data obviously conceal a great deal of detail; there is a wide dispersion in the number of individuals and workers within each household[7]. Not all of the labour force are employed at any particular time. Many individuals are sick (often because of accidents at work), but a disturbing feature of the late 1970s and early 1980s has been the large increase in unemployment. In late 1981 there were about three million people on the unemployment register; approximately 11½% of the labour force.

It must be stressed that these figures give only a static view of the labour market. Obviously many of those who are not working (such as young children, and those in full-time education) will work at a later stage in their life cycle. Similarly many others (in particular the retired and a large proportion of married mothers) will have worked in the past. There is also a continuous flow of individuals through the unemployment register, so that many more than the 'stock' of unemployed will suffer from its effect at some stage in their life, while some will do so repeatedly.

When considering differences in labour force participation over the life cycle, it is worth examining different demographic groups. About 92% of men in the age group 16–64 years are in the labour force, of whom only 10% are self-employed[8]. About 60% of married women in the age group 16–59 years are economically active (a rise of 10% since the early 1970s), and about 70% of non-married women are economically active[9]. Not all of those in employment work full-time, however. In the late 1970s about 20% of all employees were part-time, and about 85% of these were women (most were married with dependent children). An important feature of the first half of the 1970s was that the number of part-time workers increased by almost 30%.

The principal institutions in the labour market are trade unions, employers associations and the government. The latter appears as a major employer, and as the source of labour market policies. Such policies take the form of legislation, for example to regulate pay, training and the behaviour of employers and trade unions, and also the sponsoring of bodies such as The Advisory Conciliation and Arbitration Service and the Manpower Services Commission. Most workers have their pay set by collective bargaining, and trade unions are obviously an essential part of this process. Union membership is more than 13 million, that is over half the labour force. Most of this membership is concentrated in a small number of very large unions which span several industries. Some overall authority and coordination of the trade union movement is provided by the Trades Union Congress.

Turning to the distribution of the labour force among different sectors of the economy, approximately 70% are employed in the private sector, and this figure has fallen from 76% in the early 1960s. There are approximately 9.2, 12.4, and 8.4% of the labour force employed respectively in central government, local government and public corporations. In fact much of the formal analysis of labour markets applies to situations in which a marketed commodity or service is produced, within organizations pursuing limited objectives.

It is also useful to consider the proportion of total personal income that is derived from employment. Wages and salaries comprise about 60% of total personal income, while income from self-employment is just over 9%. The figure of 60% has to be viewed in conjunction with the fact that employers' national insurance contributions and social security benefits comprise 8.6 and 7.1% respectively of total personal income[10]. The former are of course directly related to wages and salaries (though there is some dispute about their incidence), and some of the largest components of the latter (for example pensions, unemployment and sickness benefits) are conditional on previous earnings of individuals. The figures above relate to the personal sector of the economy and include private non-profit making bodies such as universities, trade unions, churches and charities. For households, income from employment is even more important. Of average weekly household income 72% is from wages and salaries and 5% from self-employment.

The subject of the division of total income between 'wages' and 'profits' has of course aroused much interest in the past, and much of this interest derived from the view that this reflected a division between different 'classes' of the community: between those who were dependent only on wages (and owned no property) and those who received all of their income from 'profits'[11]. However, most households now receive income from a variety of sources whose relative importance varies over the life cycle.

1.2   The economics of labour

The fact that labour economics deals with the activities of human beings who not only compete against each other but recognize the necessity for and advantages from cooperation in a highly independent system, indicates that labour cannot be analysed in the same way as the exchange of ordinary commodities. As Phelps Brown has stated the job a man does carries with it relations with other people that go far beyond the relation of buyer and sellers . . . [it] is likely to carry with it particular ways in which he behaves toward other people, and they toward him (1962, p. 30).

The work ethic, which has come to occupy a major role in the value systems prevailing in most advanced capitalist societies, means that 'people build much of their lives around their jobs' (Donovan Commission, 1968, p. 142). A person's position in society and his or her income and prospects are based on their jobs and the expectation that the job will continue. Unemployment for individuals is often more than just an economic problem.

The labour market is thus a special market and has a number of distinctive features. The employment of labour involves a continuing personal relationship between employers and employees whereas transactions in commodity markets are usually brief and impersonal. The nature of the labour contract is frequently a relationship in which the employee agrees to accept the authority of the employer within some range. The terms of the contract are rarely, if ever, defined in full detail; their terms are implicit[12].

One reason why the contract cannot be specified completely is that there is some uncertainty about the future demand for the commodity or service being marketed, so that circumstances affecting the nature of the job may well change after initial agreement has been reached. There is also uncertainty about the abilities of the individual concerned. Some jobs may involve a willingness on the part of the employee to undertake a programme of training, and neither party has full information about the future outcome. The need to maintain the goodwill of employees, and the costs of making adjustments to unforeseen changes in product demand, affect employers' behaviour in important ways[13].

A further crucial feature of the labour contract is that, in the absence of slavery, the worker agrees to provide labour services in return for an agreed wage, but still retains property rights in himself. An implication of this simple fact is that any skills which are acquired by the employee in carrying out the prescribed work, or from formal training provided at the expense of the employer, remain the 'property' of the employee. He has some control over how his skills are used at the place of employment, and these abilities cannot be appropriated by the employer even when the worker leaves the job[14]. This aspect of the labour contract reduces the element of authority (tasks must be carried out with a large amount of mutual agreement)[15] and significantly affects the operation of labour markets in which individuals need to undertake extended training.

Whereas the ownership of property rights in the worker is fairly well agreed the ownership of such rights in *jobs* is a less certain matter. 'We have to decide to whom, in modern society, jobs really belong.' (Wedderburn, 1971, p. 55). The answer is of importance for policy questions such as whether workers should be compensated for the loss of jobs (for example, in the form of redundancy payments) in addition to receiving the usual benefits paid to the unemployed.

An obvious characteristic of labour which does not apply to most commodities (though it also applies to many personal services) is that it is not normally transferable. The person selling labour services must 'deliver' them himself and be present when they are applied[16]. An important implication of this is that it is necessary to live within reasonable distance of the place of employment, and the labour market opportunities of members of a household may be seriously constrained by the need of one member of the household to work in a particular location. The ability and willingness of individuals and households to move their place of residence is often severely restricted by a variety of factors, and this affects the way in which labour markets adjust to changing circumstances.

Not only is labour difficult to 'transport', and cannot be 'transferred', but another feature, which is to some extent linked to the latter aspect, is that labour services cannot be 'stored'. If labour services are not used during one particular day, it is clearly not possible to use them on a later occasion (as would be the case with storable fuel, for example)[17].

Another very important characteristic of labour is that the acquisition of special skills involves a fairly lengthy process of training. This training may take the form of extended education prior to entry into the labour market, and of further training 'on the job'. The process of training itself is usually rather costly, involving direct costs of training as well as forgone earnings for individuals and forgone output for employers. The institutions that are devised for providing the required training, and the methods used to 'shift' the costs of training, will have important implications for the operation of labour markets. Indeed, it is helpful to differentiate between markets for education and training, and the more familiar markets for labour services. The recognition that training involves an investment in skills which yield a source of future income (and output) naturally leads to the concept of 'human capital'[18].

Technological change may also lead to skill obsolescence, which has several effects. It may lead to a reduction in the growth of real earnings (relative to average real earnings) in the older age groups[19]. Further, the limited span of a 'working life' means that the time and other costs involved in retraining considerably reduce the incentives to make such investments later in life. Mobility between occupations after entry into the labour force is generally limited to alternatives where a substantial transfer of skill is possible. Occupational choice tends to be an 'all-or-nothing' decision. It is difficult to engage in several trades simultaneously. As Meade noted:

> while property owners can spread their risks by putting small bits of their property into a large number of concerns a worker cannot easily put small bits of his effort into a large number of different jobs. This presumably is the main reason why we find risk-bearing capital hiring labour rather than risk-bearing labour hiring capital. (1972, p. 426).

The need for extensive training in some occupations also imposes constraints on occupational choice, depending on whether the costs are borne directly by individuals, firms or by government expenditure[20]. Constraints may not only be imposed in the market for education, but also in the labour market itself where entry restrictions are sometimes imposed by those already in the occupation. These points are some of the reasons giving rise to the possibility that the labour market may be composed of groups for which the competitive model is not appropriate; what are called 'non-competing' groups. However, as will be seen in later chapters of this book, it is extremely difficult empirically to assess the competitiveness of labour markets.

1.3 Plan of the book

It has been seen that the majority of working people are employed by firms or other organizations, such as public corporations, in the production of goods and services for which there is an anticipated demand. Chapter 2, by David Deaton, considers employers' demand for labour. The chapter begins by examining the basic theory of the derived demand for factor services under different market conditions by firms who are assumed to maximize profits. The theory is framed in terms of labour services, but it is often required to investigate the relationship between output and the *number* of individuals employed; that is, the employment function. This requires the decision regarding the hours worked by employees, along with the costs of adjusting to unforeseen changes in product demand, to be considered explicitly in the specification of the employment function. The chapter examines the problems raised by, and limitations to, the traditional analysis of labour demand.

Chapter 3, by John Ashworth, then turns to the subject of the supply of labour; in particular the relationship between the supply of hours and the real net wage[21]. Chapter 3 presents the basic economic theory of labour supply, and examines the problems of specifying and estimating labour supply schedules. This issue is given particular importance by the fact that any government policy, for example to raise additional tax revenue or to influence the distribution of net income, may be frustrated by changes in labour supply as a direct result. Supply responses, what are often called 'incentive effects', may therefore place constraints on the taxable capacity of a country or the ability to redistribute incomes. The problem is severely complicated by the considerable number of interdependencies involved. For example changes in both direct and indirect taxes will affect the real net wage (though in different ways), and the existence of numerous non-employment sources of household income will also affect labour supply.

It has been seen that entry into the labour market and occupational and educational choices are part of a very complex process consisting of a number of separate stages. Chapter 4, by Robert Lindley, examines some of the economic aspects of these processes. The chapter stresses the importance of considering separately the 'markets' for education and for labour, and argues that successful research in this area requires the collection and analysis of more detailed data relating to the flows of individuals among various educational and occupational categories. Some of the major results of British studies are presented. The difficulties of using (and adequately testing) the theory of human capital in its modern form, to estimate supply schedules for individuals entering education and labour markets, are examined. The need to isolate demand and supply elements is also stressed. Finally the problems facing government policy aimed at stimulating the supply of appropriately trained manpower are discussed.

Chapter 5, by Richard Disney, is concerned with the economic analysis of the pay structure. At the most general level the structure of pay within and among occupations may be regarded as arising from the interaction of the many demand and supply elements. However, partly because the latter models are insufficiently well developed for such a rigorous exercise, analysis of the structure of pay has concentrated on a number of wide-ranging issues connected with pay inequalities. There is a large number of theories which attempt to provide an explanation of pay inequalities, and this chapter outlines the important elements of those theories. These theories are concerned, for example, with the role of education, the extent of competition in labour markets, the (sometimes discriminatory) methods used by employers to select workers, and the unequal incidence of unemployment experience. The various attempts to discriminate empirically between competing theories are also examined.

One of the most important labour market institutions is that of the trade union. The role of unions in the labour market is examined in Chapter 6, by Barry Thomas. The chapter examines economic models of unions, in terms of their objectives and the determinants of bargaining power. There has been much debate concerning the possible effects of unions on wages. Issues include the ability of unions to raise the relative wages of their members, and their effects on the overall dispersion of wages. A further question concerns the possible effects of trade unions on the efficiency of resource allocation, through the use of bargaining power (including, for example, strikes).

The important characteristics of labour which were discussed briefly in section 1.2 (concerning, for example, property rights, the need for lengthy training, and factors affecting the nature of competition in labour, and educational markets) all become relevant in the discussion of professional labour markets. There has been an increase in the number of professional workers, such as scientists and engineers, who are employed by firms or other institutions rather than being self-employed (the classic example of the latter is that of the medical professions). It has been argued that an important institution, the 'internal labour market' has developed in order to try to deal with the special problems raised. The wide variety of issues raised in the analysis of professional markets is discussed in Chapter 7, by Keith Whitfield. Particular attention is given to the examination of the career structure of professional workers in a life cycle context.

The final chapter, by Brian Chiplin, is concerned with the many issues which are raised by unemployment. The way in which labour markets operate, concerning for example the hiring and firing behaviour of employers and the labour supply behaviour of individuals and households, has important implications for the nature of flows through the unemployment register and is best examined in dynamic terms. The nature and determinants of flows onto and off the register must be appreciated; the total number of unemployed at any particular time reflects only one dimension of unemployment. The chapter also discusses the role of labour market policies in the context of unemployment.

Notes

1. There is of course an intimate relationship between 'exchange' and 'distribution' in general (see, for example Edgeworth, 1925, p. 13, and Marshall, 1961, p. 83), but it is much more obvious in the case of labour services.
2. See McNulty (1980). In this introduction several references are made to these early writers.
3. The conditions for the widespread use of labour markets involving contracts are discussed clearly in Phelps Brown (1962, p. 11). 'The first is law and order. The second is the presence of a market, in which the wage earner can exchange his pay for houseroom and consumables. The third is the availability of free training for a trade.' For a detailed discussion of slavery by an economist see Cairnes (1863).
4. Some idea of the large variety of methods of remuneration that have been used in the past may be obtained from Schloss (1892). Alternatives to the basic wage system include co-partnerships and profit-sharing schemes, though these are not discussed in the present book. An important aspect of the development of the present system involves factory legislation, the early history of which is discussed in Hutchins and Harrison (1907).
5. The role of a limited economic theory is sometimes questioned. Rees (1971, p. 1), for example, argues that the behaviour of trade unions is very different from that of households or firms and therefore cannot be deduced from the main body of microeconomic theory. Internally, labour organizations vary enormously, justifying a non-exclusive theory.
6. The following point, made by Phelps Brown (1962, p. 7), is also well worth bearing in mind. 'The test of the labour economist's ability to stop short at the boundary of someone else's field is his capacity to advise.'
7. High household income is of course positively related to household size and the number of workers. For example in 1979, of households with weekly household income in the range £80–90, there were on average 2.6 persons and 1.2 workers per household. In the group with more than £250 per week there were on average 3.9 persons and 2.6 workers per household (*Social Trends*, 1981, p. 97).
8. The participation rate of men in the 'prime' age groups has declined slightly in recent years.
9. About 12% of non-married women in the age group 16–59 are in full-time education, reflecting the low average age of the

group. In 1961 married women comprised roughly half of the female labour force, but by 1979 this had risen to two-thirds.

10. Further, imputed rent of owner-occupiers and grants from public authorities amount to 3.7 and 5.4% respectively of total personal income (*Social Trends*, 1981, p. 86).

11. Concentration on the 'factor' distribution has led to a number of claims for labour's right to 'the whole produce of labour'. The classic discussion of this literature is Menger (1899). This phrase must not be taken literally because even in a purely socialistic system some provision would need to be made for investment and for 'social insurance' purposes.

12. For an examination of different types of contract, such as recurrent spot contracts, contingent-claims contracts, authority relationships, and discussion of their appropriateness for describing the labour contract, see Williamson (1975). The charactertistics and consequences of the implicit contracts have been the subject of considerable analysis; see Azariadis (1981).

13. This is not meant to suggest that goodwill and problems of information in commodity markets are not important, indeed much interesting work has been carried out in recent years. On labour market adjustments, see Thomas (1981), and Chapters 2 and 8 of the present book.

14. For example, Freeman (1971, p. 2) notes that in non-slave societies there is no market for human assets operating in the same way as the market for financial assets.

15. There have of course been long periods when labour was in an extremely weak position relative to the employer, and early forms of apprenticeships explicitly gave the employer a great deal of authority. The relative weakness of labour in the past has been emphasized by most writers on the subject; see for example the well-known statement of Smith (1776; reprinted in 1976, p. 75).

16. Marshall (1961, p. 566) provides a colourful example of this property. 'It matters nothing to the seller of bricks whether they are to be used in building a palace or a sewer: but it matters a great deal to the seller of labour . . . whether or not the place in which it is to be done is a . . . pleasant one, and whether or not his associates will be such as he cares to have.'

17. Marshall (1961, p. 567) notes that the worker may nevertheless be refreshed by rest. He suggested that this property is one reason why labour has no 'reserve fund', leading to a disadvantage in bargaining.

18. The concept of human capital is of course very old. Indeed, it could be claimed that it is as old as modern economics itself, since an attempt to measure the value of the human capital of Britain was made by Sir William Petty around 1691 (see Hull, 1899). A useful survey of the roots of human capital theory is given by Kiker (1966).
19. The pattern of investment in education and training, followed by returns which accrue in later years, with perhaps some 'obsolescence' in old age, gives rise to a characteristic age-earnings profile. For a statistical analysis, and further references to the literature, see Creedy (1974).
20. A lively discussion of the effects of different kinds of support for education on the supply of different types of skill (and consequently on earnings in different professions) is provided by Smith (1976). The importance of education also means that family background can have a significant effect on attainment, and much research has been carried out into inter-generational mobility. Pigou (1952, p. 493) has observed that, 'Fathers who invest in their sons' activities unremuneratively are not expelled by bankruptcy from the profession of fatherhood.'
21. Labour supply is of course affected by retirement behaviour, and will also depend on the health of the population (though registered sickness may depend on economic factors), and unemployment benefits (which are examined further in Chapter 8 of this book). It is obviously very difficult to measure the supply of 'effort', or the amount of labour supplied to the so-called 'black economy'.

References

Azariadis, C. (1981). Implicit contracts and related topics: a survey. In *The Economics of the Labour Market* (ed. by Z. Hornstein, J. Grice, A. Webb). London; HMSO

Cairnes, J. E. (1863). *The Slave Power*. London; Macmillan. (Reprinted in 1968 by Augustus M. Kelley)

Creedy, J. (1947). Income changes over the life cycle. *Oxford Economic Papers* **26,** 405–423

Donovan Commission (1968). *Report of the Royal Commission on Trade Unions and Employers' Associations 1965–1968*. London; HMSO

Edgeworth, F. Y. (1925). *Papers Relating to Political Economy*, Vol. I. London; Macmillan for the Royal Economic Society

Freeman, R. B. (1971). *The Market for College Trained Manpower.* Cambridge, Mass.; Harvard University Press

Hull, C. R. (ed.) (1899). *The Economic Writings of Sir William Petty,* Vol. 1. Cambridge; Cambridge University Press

Hutchins, B. L. and Harrison, A. (1907). *A History of Factory Legislation.* London; P. S. King and Son

Kiker, B. F. (1966). The historical roots of the concept of human capital. *Journal of Political Economy* **74,** 481–499

Marshall, A (1961). *Principles of Economics* (ed. by C. W. Guilleband). London; Macmillan for the Royal Economic Society

McNulty, P. J. (1980). *The Origin and Development of Labour Economics.* Cambridge Mass.; MIT Press

Meade, J. (1972). The theory of labour-managed firms and profit sharing. *Economic Journal* **82,** 402–428

Menger, A. (1899). *The Right to the Whole Produce of Labour.* (Translated by M. E. Tanner with an introduction and bibliography by H. S. Foxwell). London; Macmillan

Pigou, A. C. (1952). *The Economics of Welfare.* London; Macmillan

Phelps Brown, E. H. (1962). *The Economics of Labour.* New Haven; Yale University Press

Rees, A. (1971). The current state of labour economics. Industrial Relations Centre, Queen's University at Kingston, Ontario

Schloss, D. F. (1892). *Methods of Industrial Remuneration.* London; Williams and Norgate

Smith, A. (1976). *An inquiry into the Nature and Causes of The Wealth of Nations.* (ed. by E. Cannan). Chicago; University of Chicago Press

Thomas, R. B. (1981). Labour market adjustments. In *The Economics of Unemployment in Britain* (ed. by J. Creedy), pp. 17–47. London; Butterworths

Wedderburn, K. W. (1971). *The Worker and the Law.* Harmondsworth; Penguin

Williamson, O. E. (1975). *Markets and Hierarchies: Analysis and Antitrust Implications.* New York; The Free Press

Chapter 2

Employers' demand for labour

2.1 Introduction[1]

Most British workers are not self-employed, but work for employers who combine their services with those of other factors of production to produce goods and services that consumers wish to buy. Hence only for a small proportion of the labour market can the theory of consumer demand directly provide a theory of labour demand. This chapter is concerned with the bulk of the labour force which sells its labour power to an employer. For a theory of labour demand it is therefore appropriate to look to the theory of the firm and the behaviour of employers.

But the fact that the demand for labour is a derived demand is not its only peculiarity. If so, labour could be treated in exactly the same way as the demand for capital goods, raw materials or semi-finished goods which are not bought directly by consumers. Unlike sellers of other factors, the worker must be present when the services he supplies are used in the production process. He retains some control over how his services are used after the 'exchange' has taken place. His services are highly perishable. Moreover, the organization of production in most enterprises means that the sellers of labour are brought together, thereby providing much greater scope for combining and taking collective action than exists for suppliers of any other factor.

It is these peculiarities which give the analysis of labour markets its own distinctive flavour. Those who have sought to discredit the application of economic analysis to labour delight in quoting the opening two sentences of Hicks's (1963) *Theory of Wages*.

> The theory of the determination of wages in a free market is simply a special case of the general theory of value. Wages are the price of labour; and thus, in the absence of control, they are determined, like all prices, by supply and demand.

They take this as an indication of the apparent naîvety of economists though, as Crossley (1973, p. 213) has pointed out, they rarely quote the second half of the paragraph which suggests that[2]

> The need for a special theory of wages only arises because both the supply of labour, and the demand for it, and the way in which demand and supply interact on the labour market, have certain peculiar properties, which make it impossible to apply to labour the ordinary theory of commodity value without some further consideration.

In this chapter both the theory of labour demand and some of its applications are discussed. Section 2.2 provides an outline of that part of the theory of the firm which leads to the basic theory of labour demand. The way this theory can be applied to help forecast employment is considered next in section 2.3. Section 2.4 then deals with the role of labour demand and the employer's position more generally in determining the structure of wages. Finally section 2.5 takes up the issue of *jobs* and examines the implications of employment continuity and its effect on the labour market.

2.2   The basic theory of labour demand

The general problem

The conventional 'textbook' theory of the demand for labour is derived directly from the theory of the profit-maximizing firm. This theory, and the derivation of the short-run demand for labour, is presented in this section and some of its principal limitations are examined.

The typical profit-maximizing firm in the private sector of a capitalist economy is assumed to be trying to combine the services derived from labour and capital in an optimal way to produce a saleable output. It has to decide on how much to produce and the quantities of factor services to use, and also how much to pay for its factors' services. Its decisions of course will be constrained in a number of ways. The amount it can produce from any combination of factor inputs is governed by the set of known techniques for producing a particular good. The formal statement of this constraint is called the production function. The firm must also set a price for its product at which the quantity produced can be sold. Under certain conditions, namely those of perfect competition, there will be a market price for the product at which the firm can sell as much as it wishes. For the moment, however, it is assumed that the product demand function, the relationship between the price and the quantity that can be sold, is such that once a given quantity for sale is chosen the firm has to accept the price, and if a larger quantity is to be sold a lower price has to be accepted. Finally, the availability of factor services acts as a constraint on the firm. In view of the differences between labour and other factors it is reasonable to assume that the cost of capital services is independent of the quantity purchased by the firm, whereas the greater the quantity of labour services the firm wishes to purchase, the higher the wage it has to offer[3]. The relationship between the wage offer and the amount of labour services available at that wage is described by the labour supply function.

If one considers a hypothetical firm which faces unchanged conditions over time, the optimization problem can be set out in terms of a standard constrained maximization problem which can be solved using simple calculus. The firm is assumed to be trying to maximize profits (π), which are defined as the difference between sales revenue and factor costs

$$\Pi = pQ - wL - rK \tag{2.1}$$

where p is the product price
        Q is the quantity produced
        w is the wage rate per unit of labour services
        L is the input of labour services
        r is the cost per unit of capital services
and K is the input of capital services.

Of these r can be taken as exogenously given (it is a parameter). The firm has to decide on the values of the other variables. The firm cannot produce more than permitted by the production function, $Q_S (K, L)$, so that

$$Q \leqslant Q_S (K, L) \tag{2.2}$$

Nor will it produce more than the product demand function $Q_D(p)$ allows it to sell

$$Q \leqslant Q_D(p) \tag{2.3}$$

And its ability to secure labour services is limited by the labour supply function $L_S(w)$, so that

$$L \leqslant L_S(w) \tag{2.4}$$

Two remarks are in order at this stage. First, when both labour services and output are homogeneous and when conditions in the product and labour market remain unchanged over time, it is a necessary condition of profit-maximization that (2.2), (2.3) and

(2.4) are equalities. The firm will not produce less than is technically feasible given the production function, nor charge less for its product than it needs to given the product demand function, nor offer a higher wage than it needs in order to secure a given labour supply. The second point is that the product demand curve implies that the firm cannot choose both its output *and* product price, and the labour supply curve means that it cannot choose both the wage offer *and* the labour supply. In some formulations of this problem the wage and the product price are taken as parameters; but r is the only parameter in this presentation.

It is convenient to re-write the product demand and labour supply functions as price and wage equations

$$p = p(Q) \tag{2.5}$$
$$\text{and} \quad w = w(L) \tag{2.6}$$

which can then be inserted in (2.1) giving

$$\Pi = p(Q)Q - w(L)L - \bar{r}K \tag{2.7}$$

where $\bar{r}$ is the exogenously given value of r. The profit-maximizing firm is then concerned to maximize (2.7) subject to the production function in (2.2). Inserting (2.2) in (2.7) gives a function which shows that profits depend on the levels of capital services and labour services and the parameter $\bar{r}$. The first-order profit-maximizing conditions are given by setting the partial derivatives to zero

$$\partial\Pi \partial K = \partial\Pi/\partial L = 0$$

and solving to yield optimal values of K and L, given the parameter $\bar{r}$. Once these optimal values of K and L are known they can be used to determine the optimal level of output, from (2.2). The consequent optimal product price and wage offer are found from (2.5) and (2.6).

This approach shows how a firm might in principle compute the optimum values of its decision variables if it had sufficient knowledge of product and factor market conditions and of all its production possibilities. But such information is itself a costly item and it is likely that only those firms already producing in the market possess a reasonably clear picture of market conditions. Such firms are of course rarely in a position to exploit that information fully for they do not start from a position of complete flexibility. Thus if predictions about the behaviour of the firm are to be derived, it would be more appropriate to assume that its decision-making is sequential. The firm may for instance take a prior decision on the amount of capital to employ in the light of long-run expected values of the product and factor prices and subsequently take a series of short-run decisions on the level of output and the employment of labour services. It is these short-run decisions which provide a theory of labour demand.

The short run

With the level of capital stock already determined, the firm's short-run problem is to maximize profits by setting L, Q, w and p subject to the constraints of the short-run production function (which is the same as the long-run function but with a fixed level of capital services)[4], the labour supply function and the product demand function. Under these circumstances a relatively simple rule can be derived for profit maximization: the firm should take on labour until the costs of doing so equal the benefits derived from it. The mechanics of this rule are shown in terms of marginal costs and benefits in *Figure 2.1*. The firm faces an upward-sloping

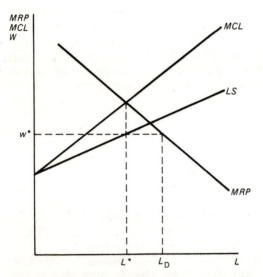

Figure 2.1 Short-run profit-maximization for a firm facing an upward-sloping labour supply curve

labour supply curve, *LS*. Thus the marginal cost of labour, *MCL*, defined as the increase in the firm's total wage bill as the level of labour services increase, comprises both the wage paid to additional units of labour and the cost of increasing wages (for all labour employed) in order to attract the additional labour. The marginal revenue product, *MRP* (defined as the revenue derived from selling the output produced by an additional unit of labour), tends to decline as more labour is employed for two reasons. First, the law of diminishing returns suggests that adding more labour to a fixed capital stock yields successively smaller additions to output. Secondly, in order to sell the extra output the product price must be reduced. The firm maximizes profits by employing L^* units of labour so that the marginal cost, *MCL*, and the marginal revenue product, *MRP*, are equated. To recruit the required amount of labour, the firm needs to pay a wage of w^* which is less than the marginal revenue product of labour. A firm in this position may give the impression of being short of labour because at a wage of w^* it would be prepared to employ L_D units of labour.

The analysis of labour demand is further simplified if one assumes perfect competition in either the labour market or the product market. The essential feature of competition for these purposes is that the firm being small relative to the market takes rather than sets prices and wages. This means that by charging anything less than the market price the competitive firm loses revenue and that by charging more than the market price it cannot sell any of its output. Similarly, in the labour market, by paying above the market wage the firm reduces its profits and by offering less than the market wage the firm finds it imposible to attract labour. Thus if there is perfect competition in both the labour and product markets then w and p are given. The short-run optimization problem is to maximize

$$\Pi = pQ - wL \tag{2.8}$$

subject to $Q = Q(L, \bar{K}) \tag{2.9}$

where w and p are parameters and $\bar{K}$ is the fixed level of capital services. Putting (2.9) into (2.8) and deriving the first order conditions gives

$$\partial \Pi / \partial L = p \partial Q / \partial L - w = 0$$

so that $w/p = \partial Q / \partial L \tag{2.10}$

Equation (2.10) implies that the real wage is equal to the marginal product of labour; a notion which once dominated labour demand theory. Many economists subscribe to the view that the notion of marginal productivity has been more confusing than it has been helpful. This view is examined below. However, if marginal productivity theory is treated simply as a convenient way of summarizing the result of differential calculus applied to a model with fairly restrictive assumptions it may still have its uses.

The elasticity of derived demand

One of the most useful applications of marginal productivity is the formulation of the rules of derived demand. Under conditions of perfect competition and constant returns to scale, factors will be paid their marginal products. Hicks (1963, pp. 242–243) has shown that the elasticity of demand, ρ, for one factor is a function of the elasticity of substitution, σ, the elasticity of demand for the product, ε, the elasticity of supply of the other factor, η, and the proportion of total costs attributable to the factor, κ. This can be expressed as

$$\rho = \{\sigma(\varepsilon + \eta) + \kappa\eta(\varepsilon - \sigma)\} / \{\varepsilon + \eta - \kappa(\varepsilon - \sigma)\} \qquad (2.11)$$

From (2.11) Marshall's four rules of the elasticity of derived demand may be deduced. They are stated here in terms of the demand for labour but of course they also apply to the derived demand for any factor.

(1) The elasticity of demand for labour will be greater, the greater is the elasticity of demand for the product. Thus the degree to which a wage rise leads to a fall in employment depends on the degree to which a rise in price reduces product demand.

(2) The elasticity of demand for labour will be greater, the greater is the elasticity of substitution between labour and other factors. Thus the effect of a wage rise on employment is greater if employers can readily substitute capital for labour.

(3) The elasticity of demand for labour will be greater, the greater is the elasticity of supply of other factors. Thus for the effect of a wage rise to be great, employers must be able to substitute other factors without driving up the price of those factors.

(4) The elasticity of demand for labour will be greater, the greater is the proportion of production costs due to labour, but only if $\varepsilon > \sigma$; that is, only if the elasticity of demand for the final product is greater than the elasticity of substitution. The latter condition usually holds for capital–labour substitution but not for substitution between two similar categories of labour. (See Hicks, 1963, pp. 376–378.)

These rules are useful not only for analysing the effect of a change in supply in a competitive market but for any conditions where the wage can be treated as exogenous[5]. For instance, they can be used to predict the effect of an increase in wages negotiated by trade unions on the level of employment in a particular industry, and further, if one knows something about the relative preferences of trade unions for employment increases and wage increases to predict the bargaining behaviour of trade unions.

The use of labour demand theory

The present discussion differs from many expositions of labour demand theory in that it does not treat the concept of marginal productivity as central, but merely as one way of expressing the labour demand curve under competitive market conditions. In what he calls 'A do-it-yourself guide to marginal productivity', Thurow (1976, Appendix A) poses a series of questions which anyone proposing to apply marginal productivity must ask. Is it meant to apply to individuals for a single point in time, to groups of workers or at the level of the industry? What happens under conditions of oligopoly? How should disequilibrium be treated? In short, the apparent elegance and precision of marginal productivity when used as an empirical tool raises more questions than it answers.

The applied labour economist may therefore choose to discard the concept of marginal productivity, but even as a theoretical basis for labour demand its applicability is doubtful. In his commentary on the first edition of *Theory of Wages* Hicks says

> There are several things that are wrong in that chapter ['Marginal Productivity and the Demand for Labour']; marginal productivity . . . is one of them. . . . There is, however, one thing that is right. This is the division of the effect of a factor–price change into an effect on the scale of output and an effect on the method of production (or on the proportions in which factors are combined). This, which appears . . . as a way of 'explaining' marginal productivity, is in fact a more powerful and more general approach than marginal productivity. . . . The original marginal productivity theory can be to some extent rehabilitated; but how much is the rehabilitation worth? Something: but not, in my present view, a great deal. As a theory of the demand for labour it is much inferior to the 'scale-proportions' theory. . . (1963, pp. 322 and 334).

But whatever its theoretical basis, the usefulness of the basic 'textbook' model of labour demand is itself limited by the things it fails to consider. In particular, little heed has been paid to the peculiarities of labour as a factor of production, the time dimension has not been satisfactorily considered, and the important difference between hours and employment dimensions of labour services has been neglected. This means that the empirical estimation of labour demand involves much more than simply estimating the downward-sloping labour demand curve. This is not to say that the *ceteris paribus* labour demand curve is wrong, merely that the other things which it assumes to be equal are in reality often more interesting than the wage level.

But if one asks economists a hypothetical policy question concerning the effects of a wage subsidy, or of equal pay legislation, they will immediately reach for their labour demand curve. For example, in discussing the likely effects of a 35-hour week on employment, Hughes does just that, suggesting that the policy 'will result in an increase in employment if the elasticity of demand for manual hours is less than 1.1 while that for non-manual hours is less than 1.3, assuming of course that there is no substitution of overtime hours for normal hours' (1980, p. 292).

The fact that the elasticity is now known is not necessarily the fault of the economics profession, but may simply reflect the fact that wages have not shown sufficient variation to enable a reliable estimate to be made.

Thus the usefulness of labour demand curves varies according to the context. In theoretical questions thay can scarcely be avoided but in most empirical analysis they tend to be ignored. The reason for this is apparent if the process whereby wages affect employment levels is considered. Hicks's 'scale-proportions' theory in which the elasticity of demand is decomposed into an output effect and a substitution effect is extremely useful for this purpose. A wage increase will lead to a price increase which affects the demand for the product which in turn affects the demand for labour. At each stage of the process exogenous factors may have an effect: on prices, product demand, or labour demand. In addition, the wage increase may affect the firm's choice of the capital intensity of the production process, but if wages have also increased in the capital goods sector the net effect would be negligible. In theoretical reasoning the argument assumes *ceteris paribus* and hence the exogenous factors at each stage are ignored. Neither do the time lags matter if one if concerned with long-run changes. Thus the process can be contracted to foretell the effect of wages on employment. In empirical analysis the exogenous factors and the time lags do matter, so labour demand has to be estimated as a function of product demand and whatever exogenous factors are relevant.

2.3   Employment forecasting

This section considers how the theory of labour demand may be used to estimate what are generally known as employment functions. So far the demand for labour has been taken to mean the demand for labour services. In order to specify an employment function the employer's choice between the employment level and the hours worked per employee must be considered. Furthermore, one must allow for the fact that it is costly for the employer to adjust the level of employment to meet short-run variations in product demand.

Since the original work of Brechling (1965) and Ball and St Cyr (1966) on short-term employment functions, a vast literature on the subject has developed. But although the studies which have been carried out differ in their detailed specifications, the underlying construction is sufficiently uniform to allow a basic model to be outlined.

The specification of an employment function

The first step in specifying an employment function is to assume that the production function takes a particular mathematical form. One very convenient form is the Cobb-Douglas production function, written as

$$Q_t = AL_t^{\alpha} K_t^{\beta} e^{gt} \tag{2.12}$$

where Q_t is an index of output at time t, L_t is a measure of labour services, and K_t is a measure of capital services. The exponential time trend is a continuous shift in the function resulting from technical progress, whereby output grows at the constant proportional rate, g, and A, α, β, and g are parameters. It is usually assumed that in the short run, capital stocks and the state of technology are taken as given and that output is exogenously determined by demand. Under these conditions, the desired level of labour services, L^* is found by solving (2.12) to give

$$L_t^* = \{Q_t^{-1} A K_t^{\beta} e^{gt}\}^{-(1/\alpha)} \tag{2.13}$$

To transform (2.13) from an equation in labour services to an equation in employment, it is necessary to specify how the firm chooses its optimum combination of workers, E, and hours per worker, H. If all combinations of hours and workers are equally productive, then labour services can be measured in terms of total man-hours, L (equal to EH), and the choice of the worker–hours mix depends on the costs of various combinations. Labour costs can be thought of as comprising three elements: the fixed cost of employing workers, such as national insurance contributions; the cost of man-hours paid at the basic hourly wage rate; and the cost of deviating from standard hours, namely the costs of overtime and short-time working. It is convenient to express these deviation costs in a quadratic form; that is, depending on the square of the difference between actual and standard hours[6]. Successive deviations of hours below their normal level lead to an increased likelihood of the firm having to pay short-time working compensation and incurring costs associated with worker dissatisfaction. Increasing amounts of overtime become increasingly costly if, at low levels of overtime, the cost benefits of increased worker satisfaction modify the cost of paying the overtime premium. However, at high levels of overtime the dissatisfaction of having to work overtime adds to the costs of the overtime premium. The labour costs, C, can then be expressed as

$$C = wEH + fE + cE(H - \bar{H})^2 \tag{2.14}$$

where w represents the basic hourly wage rate, f the fixed costs of employing workers, $\bar{H}$ standard hours, and c is a parameter affecting the costs of deviating from standard hours. Cost minimization then requires that (2.14) is minimized, subject to $L = EH$. The solution gives the optimal level of hours H^* as

$$H^* = \{(\bar{H}^2 + f/c)\}^{1/2} \tag{2.15}$$

Thus the optimal level of hours will equal the standard level of hours only if fixed labour costs are zero. If standard hours and the cost parameters are unchanged over the period, then since by definition $L = EH$, the optimum level of employment E^* is obtained simply by dividing L^* in equation (2.13) by H^* in equation (2.15). It is convenient to write this as

$$E^* = B \{Q_t^{-1} K_t^\beta e^{gt}\}^{-(1/\alpha)} \tag{2.16}$$

where $B = A^{-(1/\alpha)}/H^*$

If capital is always fully utilized then variations in K_t are attributable entirely to variations in the level of capital stock. By assuming that changes in the capital stock are sufficiently smooth to be represented by the time trend, K_t can be eliminated. Taking the logs of (2.16) and eliminating K_t gives

$$\text{Log } E^*_t = \log B + (1/\alpha) \log Q_t - (g/\alpha)t \qquad (2.17)$$

Equation (2.17) is an expression for the desired level of employment rather than the actual level. These will differ if the process of adjusting the level of employment involves a cost. Increasing the level of employment will be costly because the firm has to pay for recruitment, selection, and training of new workers. Reducing the level of employment may involve the firm in the cost of redundancy payments or the less tangible cost of worker resistance or reaction. To capture the effects of these costs a slow adjustment process can be postulated. This can be formulated in a number of ways, for example

$$(E_t/E_{t-1}) = (E^*_t/E_{t-1})^\lambda \qquad (2.18)$$

with $0 \leqslant \lambda \leqslant 1$.

This shows that the change in employment is some fraction of the desired employment change in any period. The speed of adjustment, λ, increases as the costs of adjustment fall.

Taking the logs of equation (2.18) and substituting into (2.17) gives

$$\log E_t = \lambda \log B + (\lambda/\alpha) \log Q_t - (\lambda g/\alpha)t + (1-\lambda) \log E_{t-1}$$
$$(2.19)$$

Employment is dependent on its past value, the level of output and the time trend. This can be transformed into an estimating equation by the addition of an error term.

Empirical estimation of the employment function

The estimating form of the employment function specified in equation (2.19) was used with quarterly data for British manufacturing industry over the period from the second quarter of 1970 to the first quarter of 1981. The following result, with t-statistics given in brackets, were obtained:

$$\log E_t = 0.880 + 0.188 \log Q_t - 0.0096t + 0.805 \log E_{t-1}$$
$$(1.429) \quad (6.653) \qquad (-2.7667) \quad (10.787)$$
$$R^2 = 0.992$$

The result initially appears to be quite successful. The output variable and the lagged employment variable are statistically significantly different from zero. The time trend is also significant at the 5% level and the multiple correlation coefficient R^2 is very high. However, there are two major problems. The first relates to the values of the structural parameters λ and α. These can be derived from the estimated coefficients on $\log E_{t-1}$ and $\log Q_t$. The values from the estimated equation are $\lambda = 0.195$ and $\alpha = 1.037$. This suggests that the speed of adjustment, measured by λ, is rather low, with less than a fifth of the desired adjustment being achieved in the period of a quarter of a year. But while this seems low there are no grounds for regarding it as 'incorrect' since any value between zero and unity is permissable. The estimate of α does however create problems[7]. The law of diminishing returns suggests that α, which from the production function represents the output–employment elasticity, should be significantly less than unity. The result shown here of a value greater than unity seems also to be a common result of studies which have attempted to estimate this kind of demand function. When the same equation was estimated for 14 manufacturing industries by Bowers and Deaton (1980, p. 167), the estimated value of α lay between zero and unity in only two cases. But to infer that the results disprove the law of diminishing returns would seem rather drastic. A more reasonable conclusion would be that one or more of the assumptions made in order to specify the equation does not hold. This point will be considered below.

The second problem is revealed when the equation was estimated using data for sub-periods. The results for the period up to the last quarter of 1975 are

$$\log E_t = 1.115 + 0.165 \log Q_t - 0.0014t + 0.792 \log E_{t-1}$$
$$\quad\quad (1.198) \quad (4.083) \quad\quad (-2.6561) \quad (7.654)$$

$$R^2 = 0.968, \text{ with } \alpha = 1.26$$

and for the period beginning with the first quarter of 1976 are

$$\log E_t = 0.349 + 0.181 \log Q_t - 0.0011t + 0.869 \log E_{t-1}$$
$$\quad\quad (0.347) \quad (2.732) \quad\quad (-2.9442) \quad (6.044)$$

$$R^2 = 0.989, \text{ with } \alpha = 0.724$$

Thus the estimated parameters differ somewhat between estimation periods, which suggests that using the equation for the first sub-period would not have produced very good forecasts for employment in the second sub-period.

Such an equation represents the most basic form of the short-run employment function, and since the original work of Ball and St Cyr (1966) and Brechling (1965) there has been a large number of studies that elaborate the basic model. Such elaborations, which are surveyed by Hazledine (1981), include the explicit use of a capital stock variable, the inclusion of price and wage variables, full interrelated demand functions for all factors and their utilization rates, different adjustment processes and different specifications of the production function.

However, the difficulty which is illustrated in the above equations seems to pervade employment forecasting. In a recent review of the state of employment forecasting, Henry has observed:

> when estimating employment–output relationships with simple dynamics, quite radically different parameter values are obtained when the employment function is estimated over different sample periods. This failure implies two things. First, that it is difficult to forecast either employment or unemployment, sometimes even over relatively short periods of time. Second, policy implications for the medium term become highly uncertain. (1981, p. 288).

Tarling has argued that, 'the *ad hoc* amendments of the past, such as bending productivity trends, changing lag structures and adding new variables have all been short-lived' (1981, p. 313). He suggests that the way forward is to reconsider the basic assumptions of the models and that a major limitation of employment function work has been, 'the tenacity with which we hold on to the assumption of an atomistic market with homogeneous labour'. Hence more attention should be paid to the degree of market control exercised by firms and the different strategies employers devise to deal with different sections of the workforce.

In analysing the employment–output relationship outside the conventional employment function framework, Bowers, Deaton and Turk (1982) argue that the tendency for employment to fluctuate less over the cycle than output is particularly problematical in view of the high observed rates of voluntary labour turnover. Why do employers retain labour when they could reduce employment by natural wastage? This phenomenon is only partially explained by the heterogeneity of labour. Their survey findings suggest that firms experience considerable technical inflexibility inhibiting the adjustment of employment levels in response to output variation, particularly where work is organized on an assembly line basis. However in addition to this source of employment stability the process of plants opening and closing adds to employment variation. If the labour market is viewed in this way it is hardly surprising that employment functions that build on the notion of the representative firm fail to predict very well.

2.4   Wage structure and labour demand

The first impression gained from orthodox economic theory is that wages, like the prices of commodities, are determined by the interaction of supply and demand. However, if labour were perfectly mobile between industries, and responded rapidly to wage differentials, then it may be thought that employers' demands for labour affect the geographical and industrial distribution of manpower rather than the distribution of wages. The latter would be determined by the structure of supply of different types of labour, according to their abilities and training.

In the long run, by which is meant a time scale sufficiently long to permit mobility between occupations, the supply curve to a particular occupation is elastic and supply prices are determined by supplies of particular skills. In the short run, however, supply curves are upward sloping and an increase in demand is likely to bid up wages, encouraging entry into occupations where demand has risen. The importance of labour demand for wage structures therefore depends on two questions: are long-run supply curves in fact sufficiently elastic to ensure the irrelevance of demand patterns for long-run wage structure[8] and is labour allocation in the short-run achieved by wage adjustments?

A number of studies, such as Reddaway (1959) and Crossley (1966), have demonstrated a positive relationship between wage changes and employment changes in the short run, but no such relationship over longer periods. This evidence is consistent with the competitive theory which suggests that demand has only a short-run influence on wage structure. It does not, however, mean that wage adjustments are the sole or even the main mechanism in the allocation of labour or that the employers' position is irrelevant to the long-run wage structure[9]. There is evidence to suggest that the demand for labour may play an important role. For example, analyses of the distribution of income typically show a large unexplained variation in earnings after taking account of personal characteristics (see Atkinson, 1975, Chapter 5). Further, studies of inter-industry wage structure suggest that after controlling for differences in supply-side characteristics, the degree of monopoly power in the product market is a significant determinant of the level of wages (Weiss, 1966; Mulvey, 1976). Thus the firm's ability to pay may be crucial in accounting for the wages paid in a particular firm.

This statement is not as tautological as it might initially appear. If the firm can recruit as much labour as it requires at the market wage rate, is there any reason why it should offer higher wages simply because it can afford to do so? The argument that a firm's wage offer is influenced in the long run by its ability to pay could mean one of three things. First, the firm may be seeking to maximize something other than profit, such as an objective function in which the wages of its employees is one factor. Secondly, the extent to which the threat of sanctions by the workforce is successful in raising wages depends on the firm's product market power. Thirdly, the firm may seek better quality workers or better motivation of existing workers by offering higher wages. The first of these ideas is developed in the literature on labour-managed firms and is not further pursued here[10]. The other two ideas are now developed in the context of a firm in a competitive labour market.

The firm's wage strategy in the presence of worker sanctions

Where workers are able to impose sanctions which would reduce profits the firm has to decide whether to pay wages above the competitive level in order to prevent such sanctions being used. Its ability to pay higher wages will depend on product market conditions. Consider a firm which is a monopolist or oligopolist in its product market but which faces a competitive labour market with wage w_c and an organized workforce which is prepared to impose sanctions which reduce the firm's profits to a proportion s

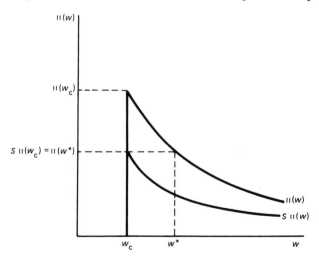

Figure 2.2 The effect of sanctions on the profits of an oligopolist facing a competitive labour market

of their original level in response to particular wage offers[11]. Its profit function $\Pi(w)$ before and after sanctions are applied is shown in *Figure 2.2*.

Because it is recruiting from a competitive labour market, the firm cannot recruit labour at a wage below the competitive level w_c. Any wage higher than w_c leads to an erosion of profits. The union organization is assumed to be sufficiently in control of its members to allow it to 'turn on' or 'off' sanctions at will up to a maximum level of $(1-s)\Pi(w)$. The optimum strategy for the union is to select a sanctions profile such as to secure a wage offer of w^*, which is the solution to

$$\Pi(w^*) = s\Pi(w_c) \tag{2.20}$$

This will induce the firm to buy-off the union's sanction by offering a wage w^*, because any wage offer of less than w^* invokes sanctions which reduce its profits.

In order to solve for w^*, the profit function $\pi(w)$ must be specified. It will depend on the elasticity of the product demand curve facing the firm, ε, which is assumed to be constant. The firm's product demand curve can then be expressed as

$$pQ = AQ^\beta \tag{2.21}$$

where $\beta = 1 - (1/\varepsilon)$, p is the price of the product, Q the quantity of the product produced and sold, and A is a constant[12]. Assuming there is capital input and that there are constant returns to scale the units can be so chosen that $Q = L$.

The firm's profits are the difference between sales revenue and labour costs, thus

$$\Pi = pQ - wL \tag{2.22}$$

Substituting for pQ in (2.22) gives

$$\Pi = AL^\beta - wL \tag{2.23}$$

The first order condition for profit-maximizing is

$$\partial\Pi/\partial L = \beta AL^{\beta-1} - w = 0 \tag{2.24}$$

$$\text{Then } w = \beta AL^{\beta-1} \tag{2.25}$$

Substituting (2.25) into equation (2.23) gives profits in terms of the labour input:

$$\Pi = AL^\beta(1-\beta) \tag{2.26}$$

Taking the logs of (2.20) and substituting for π from (2.26) gives

$$\log s = \beta(\log L^* - \log L_c) \tag{2.27}$$

Applying the competitive and optimal positions to the log form of (2.25) gives

$$\log L^* = (\log w^* - \log \beta A)/(\beta - 1) \tag{2.28}$$

$$\log L_c = (\log w_c - \log \beta A)/(\beta - 1) \tag{2.29}$$

Substituting (2.28) and (2.29) into (2.27) gives

$$\log w^* = \log w_c + (\beta - 1)(\log s)/\beta \tag{2.30}$$

From the definition of β, equation (2.30) becomes

$$\log w^* = \log w_c + (\log s)/(1 - \varepsilon) \tag{2.31}$$

Equation (2.31) implies that the union can induce the firm to offer a wage which exceeds the competitive market wage by a factor which depends on the sanctions which the union can impose and on the firm's elasticity of product demand. Thus the union's power to raise the wage depends not only on its ability to impose effective sanctions but also on the firm's market power. If the firm is a perfect competitor in the product market and therefore its product demand curve is infinitely elastic, the union cannot influence the wage paid. The cost to such a firm of deviating from the market price is so great as to make the threat of sanctions by the workforce negligible in comparison. If, however, the firm has a certain amount of market power, it can raise its product price with only a modest erosion of profits and therefore it is more susceptible to sanctions imposed by the workforce. Thus in the presence of union sanctions the firm's ability to pay is a crucial influence on the wage that it offers.

The firm's strategy where productivity depends on wages

A firm's market power is not the only determinant of its ability to pay. It may also be able to pay higher wages if by doing so it can secure better quality workers or better motivation from its existing workforce. It is assumed here that the firm is operating in a competitive market in the sense that it can recruit as much labour as it wishes. However the productivity of workers is positively related to the wage paid in the way described by the curve in *Figure 2.3*. In other respects the firm is similar to the one in the previous example. Hence profits can be expressed as

$$\Pi = AQ^{\beta} - wL \tag{2.32}$$

and output is a function of both the labour input (L) and the wage (w) so that

$$Q = Lh(w) \tag{2.33}$$

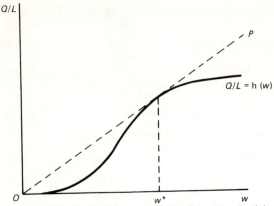

Figure 2.3 The firm's optimum wage when labour productivity is a function of the wage

Profit-maximization requires that marginal revenue is equal to the marginal cost of increasing output through increasing wages, and therefore productivity, and also equal to the marginal cost of increasing output through increasing employment. Thus

$$\beta A Q^{\beta-1} = L/(\partial Q/\partial w) = w/(\partial Q/\partial L) \qquad (2.34)$$

The values of partial derivatives in (2.34) are found by differentiating (2.33) so that

$$\partial Q/\partial w = L(\partial h/\partial w) \text{ and } \partial Q/\partial L = h(w) \qquad (2.35)$$

and the substitution of these into the last equality in (2.34) yields

$$h(w)/w = \partial h/\partial w \qquad (2.36)$$

The optimum wage (w^*) is that which satisfies equation (2.36). It is interesting to note that w^* is independent of the elasticity of the demand for the product. Equation (2.36) implies a necessary condition for profit maximization; the marginal effect of wages on productivity must be equal to the ratio of productivity to wages. This condition is met in *Figure 2.3* when the ray from the origin (which has a slope of $h(w)/w$) is tangential to the productivity curve (which has a slope of $\partial h/\partial w$). The firm is thus prepared to increase wages so long as the benefits in terms of increased productivity exceed the costs of increasing wages. In doing so the firm minimizes its unit labour costs. If firms in the same labour market differ in the technology they use or the degree to which a higher quality of labour can be used to increase productivity, their productivity functions will be different. The implication of this is that the wage offered to workers will vary among firms in the same competitive labour market.

This section has examined the argument that the wage structure is determined almost exclusively by supply-side factors. The orthodox theory of labour demand in which employers passively transmit market forces tends to lead to this conclusion. If however the market power of firms is considered, along with the sanctions that the workforce can inflict on the employer, and the likelihood that wages influence the level of labour productivity which a firm can achieve, a different picture emerges. The employer is no longer a purely passive agent; both his ability to pay and the way he uses labour are important considerations. What happens on the demand side of the labour market does matter though the conventional applications of labour demand theory may not reveal this.

2.5   The demand for labour and the creation of jobs

The conventional view of the demand for labour is that employers hire workers who possess various skills. A view with a different emphasis is that employers *create jobs* and then train workers to fill them. This latter view, together with the allied idea of employment continuity, is used in this section as a context for discussing employers' wage and non-wage adjustments to changes in market conditions.

It was shown in section 2.1 that the demand for labour differs from the demand for commodities in a number of important respects. The demand for labour services is a derived demand, and the amount traded between individual buyers and sellers of labour, that is the hours worked per week, is much more restricted than the amount traded between individual buyers and sellers of a commodity. But there is another important difference: in advanced industrial societies, in particular, labour is not bought and sold on a casual day-to-day basis. The typical arrangement is that workers seek to supply labour on a semi-permanent basis and employers seek a workforce whose composition is relatively stable.

The employment relationship is a continuing one and some of the implications of this for the working of the labour market in the short run are now considered. For many purposes it is more realistic to think of employers trying to fill a particular set of job vacancies rather than simply recruiting purveyors of given labour services. This distinction can be seen by considering the behaviour of the firm. Before hiring labour it must decide how it will produce its output, the amount and type of machinery to use and how to organize the work. It is likely to use some degree of labour specialization creating jobs that require a variety of skills. Instead of considering whether it can use the labour services on offer, the firm establishes job slots which it tries to fill. Many of these jobs require some sort of training which is not readily available on the market but which can be supplied by the firm. Often the productivity of the worker depends as much on the design of the job as on his own abilities. Continuity of employment is therefore the norm. Having decided on the way the work is to be organized the firm then has to decide how best to fill those jobs that become vacant or are newly created, or how to dispense with jobs that for reasons of output reduction or technical or organizational change are no longer required.

The implications of this view that firms try to create and fill job slots are twofold. First, the notion of a labour demand curve is problematic. The institution of *jobs* breaks the direct link between wages and labour demand and one can no longer say that the demand curve represents a firm recruiting labour up to the point where marginal cost equals marginal revenue product. It may still be legitimate to use the concept as an abstraction in long-run analysis, but it is highly suspect if used indiscriminately, for instance to predict the short-run effect of a wage reduction on employment.

Secondly, the concept of the labour supply to an individual firm changes under employment continuity. Earlier, the distinction was made between a firm in a perfectly competitive labour market where there is an elastic labour supply and the firm takes the wage from the market, and a monopsonist with an upward sloping supply curve. These ideas are useful but do not make explicit the fact that the firm's contact with the external market is entirely in terms of the flows of new recruits and leavers. The supply of labour is the current employment plus applicants less quits and other leavers. Applicants and retained employees may well respond to different signals. The incumbents are likely to respond more to wages and other conditions whereas applicants respond more to vacancy notification, and are subject to hiring standards in the way that the incumbent labour force is not. The firm has therefore considerable discretion in responding to the market. It may use different forms of adjustment and two major alternatives, wages and hiring standards, are now examined.

Consider first the case where wages are the only adjustment device which the firm uses. It can increase the flow of applicants prepared to accept jobs and reduce the turnover of employees by increasing its wage rate relative to other firms in the labour market. The firm's optimization problem involves balancing the costs of a higher wage against benefits of faster recruitment and reduced labour turnover. The firm will respond to an increase in product demand by increasing its wage offer, and to an increase in labour supply by reducing its wage offers. Under these conditions unemployed workers are engaged in the process of searching for a job with an acceptable wage. Unless they are new entrants to the market they will have become unemployed because they were not prepared to accept a wage cut; they could find a job if they were prepared to accept a low enough wage. In this sense unemployment is voluntary in a market where firms pursue a flexible wage policy, though to some extent unemployment results from workers being 'fooled'. Those who subscribe to such a view of the labour market (such as Phelps *et al.*, 1970, p. 7) argue that unemployment in a depression results from workers interpreting a general decline in wages as a decline specific to their own firm. They quit and search for their true wage until they realize the generality of the decline.

In the case where wages are fixed, and the firm responds to demand changes and changes in labour market conditions by varying its hiring standards, a different picture emerges. If such a firm wishes to increase the number of applicants it must relax its hiring standards by accepting workers who are (or who it suspects to be) of lower ability, more difficult to train, or less reliable. If, however, it is faced with a flood of applicants it can respond by tightening up those hiring standards. The optimization problem for a firm with this fixed-wage policy is to balance the gains from recruiting more efficient or more easily trainable workers against the costs of waiting longer to recruit and the consequential loss of output. The firm will respond to a fall in product demand by raising its hiring standards, either reducing its intake and running down by natural wastage or by making some of its employees redundant (in effect applying the new hiring standards to its incumbent labour force). The unemployed job searchers differ from those in the flexible-wage market. They will tend to be new entrants to the labour force or those who have been made redundant. They will be searching not so much for a better wage but for jobs in firms that are recruiting and whose hiring standards they can exceed. They are therefore involuntarily unemployed.

These two competing models of the labour market, based on alternative assumptions about firms' adjustment behaviour, have different implications for the way labour markets work and in particular the nature of unemployment[13]. The question naturally arises as to which model is the more appropriate. On the face of it the model of fixed wages seems to fit the current British labour market much better than the flexible-wage model. It can account for the observed pattern of labour market behaviour such as the cyclical pattern of quits, the existence of redundancies and other evidence of involuntary unemployment, the concentration of unemployment amongst new entrants and, not least, what is known of the actual behaviour of employers. However, the fixed-wage model is not entirely satisfactory for wages are not completely inflexible. While money wage cuts are rare there have sometimes been significant reductions in real wages as, for example, in 1980–1981. Moreover, there are sections of the labour market where negotiation over wages is at the point of hiring and where workers quit and then search for a better job while unemployed. Thus a more general model might allow for some intermediate position between fixed wages and wage flexibility.

It is, of course, interesting to ask why there should be fixed wages anyway. Under what conditions are they the norm? There are several possible reasons for such inflexibility. It is tempting, particularly in the British context, to attribute it to the institution of collective bargaining in which wages are adjusted periodically rather than continuously. But to argue along these lines implies that unemployment would be voluntary were it not for the intervention of trade unions. It is much more plausible to argue that wage inflexibility is the product of employment continuity. Indeed there is a growing literature that argues that an employer will in his own interests seek to stablize wages rather than adjust them, so that he never pays more than the minimum required to attract the workforce he requires[14]. Thurow, for instance, sees the elimination of wage competition as an employer strategy designed to facilitate training and the acceptance of technical change:

> If workers feel that they are training potential wage or employment competitors every time they show another worker how to do their job, they have every incentive to stop giving such informal training. In that case each man would seek to build his own little monopoly by hoarding skills and information to make himself indispensable. Wage and employment insecurity also means that every man has a vested interest in resisting any technical change that might reduce his wages or employment opportunities. (1976, p. 81).

Others, such as Azariadis (1975), see wage stability as the outcome of an implicit contract between employer and employee. Workers who are assumed to be risk-averse prefer a guaranteed wage to an uncertain wage with the same expected value. Employers who are assumed to be risk-neutral will offer a lower but stable wage and thus increase profits overall but accept some variation in them. Both employers and workers therefore gain by the arrangement which stabilizes wages. While the particulars of these two arguments differ they both suggest that where the employment relationship is a continuing rather than a casual one wages are unlikely to be sufficiently flexible for labour markets to clear continuously. The pursuit of profits by employers leads them to use strategies which significantly alter the way the labour market operates. These strategies are likely to vary between employers in different circumstances and employers may well use different strategies for different groups of workers.

Once the analysis changes from that of employers demanding labour services to that of firms creating jobs which they seek to fill, the picture of the way the labour market works takes on a new dimension. Employers are no longer passive transmitters of market forces but active participants whose decisions and strategies are crucial. For some purposes, such as the analysis of long-run changes in the labour market, it is legitimate to abstract from these details but when analysing short-term issues their importance cannot be ignored.

2.6   Conclusions

The services which labour can provide are sometimes desirable in themselves but more frequently they are bought by employers who by combining them with the services of other factors can produce a saleable commodity or service. The demand for labour can therefore be said to be a derived demand. This means that the employer when deciding how much labour to recruit will tend to follow a relatively simple rule: recruit labour until the marginal benefit equals the marginal cost. In competitive markets this rule is particularly straightforward: hire labour up to the point at which the value of the output produced by the last worker employed just equals the wage the employer must pay. By assuming that employers observe this optimizing rule, a schedule of the demand for labour can be derived whereby the numbers employed increase as the wage declines.

Viewed in this way the employer has very little discretion when employing labour. In reality he has a much more complex set of decisions to make. Much of this complexity arises from the peculiar characteristics of labour as a factor of production. Because the seller of labour services has to be present when those services are actually used, and because workers vary in the quality and in their tastes, the demand for labour is very different from the demand for other factors of production. Even in an otherwise competitive labour market the employer has a certain amount of discretion in setting wages. He must pay heed not only to the effects of different wage levels on the supply of labour but also to the effect on worker motivation and the likelihood of workers applying sanctions. He must consider the effects not only of his wage levels but also of their variability. The employer must decide on how to allocate labour to different tasks, what sort of labour to recruit to fill the various jobs he creates, whether to train workers and if so how to retain the workers he has trained. In short the employer in the real world cannot simply apply mechanistic rules in determining his demand for labour, he has to devise strategies to recruit, control, and retain workers for the various tasks he requires them to undertake.

This chapter has argued that it is necessary for the economist to move beyond the mechanistic models of labour demand in order to answer questions about the labour market. In considering the problem of employment forecasting it was argued that models based on the representative firm were limited in their usefulness. In examining wage structures it was shown how important it is to look not only at labour supply but also at various aspects of the firm's ability to pay. In trying to understand adjustment processes in the labour market the importance of employer strategies and decisions was demonstrated. When building models of employer behaviour greater realism is required not merely for its own sake but in order to provide a better understanding of the labour market and the way it works.

That is not to say that the economist should seek to interpret all labour market phenomena in terms of the behaviour of the particular employers involved and avoid building abstract models of the labour market. The implications of what has been said in this chapter are that such models should take account of the complex role that employers play in the labour market. In particular the degree of product market power which firms have and the extent to which firms seek to create stable employment relationships are central to questions of manpower allocation, wage structure and the nature of unemployment.

Notes

1. I am grateful to Peter Nolan for helpful comments and suggestions.
2. A recent example of quoting only the first two sentences of Hicks is Hyman and Brough (1975, p. 110).
3. The justification for treating the supply of labour and capital differently rests on the peculiarities of labour as a factor of production. Because the supplier of labour has to be present when his services are used the geographical size of the labour market on which the employer can draw will be smaller than that of the market for capital goods. The firm can therefore be large relative to the labour market but small relative to other factor markets. Moreover, variations in taste between workers mean that they value non-pecuniary aspects of the job differently. Both these considerations imply that the firm has some discretion in the wages it can pay. Where the firm faces an upward sloping supply curve for labour it takes on the characteristics of a monopsonist.
4. The assumption is also made that the level of capital utilization is constant.
5. Under conditions other than perfect competition these rules still apply but the formula for ρ will be different.
6. This expression for the costs of different levels of hours is taken from Hughes and Leslie (1975).
7. The estimation of this kind of employment function raises some statistical difficulties which cannot be discussed here. These involve, for example, the properties of the error term (complicated by the autoregressive nature of the function) and the estimation of the standard error of α.
8. Under certain conditions long-run labour supply curves will be upward sloping. If for instance people differ in their tastes, so that a certain job is liked by some but not others a higher wage will have to be offered to attract the latter to it. Also, if some jobs require certain natural abilities the supply of labour to those jobs is limited and therefore not perfectly elastic even in the long run.
9. Thurow (1976) argues for instance that hiring standards form the major adjustment mechanism. For evidence of non-wage adjustments see Thomas and Deaton (1977), and for further discussion of adjustment processes see Thomas (1981).
10. For an analysis of labour-managed firms see Vanek (1975).
11. This is a simplified version of the framework used by Wood (1978).

12. If the firm's product demand curve has constant elasticity, ε, then

$$dQ/Q = -\varepsilon(dp/p)$$

Integration gives $\log p + (1/\varepsilon)\log Q = \log A$.

Therefore $\log p + \log Q = \log A + \beta \log Q$, where $\beta = 1 - (1/\varepsilon)$.

Hence $pQ = AQ^{\beta}$

13. For a more analytical treatment of the two different models and their effects see Pissarides (1976).
14. This literature is reviewed by Okun (1981).

References

Atkinson, A. B. (1975). *The Economics of Inequality*. Oxford; Oxford University Press

Azariadis, C. (1975). Implicit contracts and underemployment equilibria. *Journal of Political Economy* **83**, 1183–1202

Ball, R. J. and St Cyr, E. B. A. (1966). Short-term employment functions in British manufacturing industry. *Review of Economic Studies* **33**, 187–216

Bowers, J. and Deaton, D. (1980). Employment functions and the measurement of labour hoarding. *Manchester School* **48**, 157–186

Bowers, J., Deaton, D. and Turk, J. (1982). *Labour Hoarding in British Industry*. Oxford; Basil Blackwell

Brechling, F. P. R. (1965). The relationship between output and employment in British manufacturing industries. *Review of Economic Studies* **32**, 187–216

Crossley, J. R. (1966). Collective bargaining, wage structure and the labour market in the United Kingdom. In *Wage Structure in Theory and Practice* (ed. by E. M. Hugh-Jones), pp. 156–235. Amsterdam; North-Holland

Crossley, J. R. (1973). A mixed strategy for labour economists. *Scottish Journal of Political Economy* **20**, 211–238

Hazledine, T. (1981). 'Employment functions' and the demand for labour in the short run. In *The Economics of the Labour Market* (ed. by Z. Hornstein, J. Grice and A. Webb), pp. 149–181. London; HMSO

Henry, S. G. B. (1981). Forecasting employment and unemployment. In *The Economics of the Labour Market* (ed. by Z. Hornstein, J. Grice and A. Webb), pp. 283–309. London; HMSO

Hicks, J. R. (1963). *The Theory of Wages* (2nd edn.). London; Macmillan

Hughes, B. and Leslie, D. (1975). Hours of work in British manufacturing industries. *Scottish Journal of Political Economy* **22,** 293–304

Hughes, J. J. (1980). The reduction in the working week: a critical look at *Target 35. British Journal of Industrial Relations* **18,** 287–296

Hyman, R. and Brough, I. (1975). *Social Values and Industrial Relations.* Oxford; Basil Blackwell

Mulvey, C. (1976). Collective agreements and relative earnings in U.K. manufacturing in 1973. *Economica* **43,** 419–427

Okun, A. M. (1981). *Prices and Quantities.* Oxford; Basil Blackwell

Phelps, E. S. (ed.) (1970). *Microeconomic Foundations of Employment and Inflation Theory.* New York; Norton

Pissarides, C. A. (1976). *Labour Market Adjustment.* Cambridge; Cambridge University Press

Reddaway, W. B. (1959). Wage flexibility and the distribution of labour. *Lloyds Bank Review* **54,** 32–48

Tarling, R. J. (1981). Forecasting employment and unemployment: Comment. In *The Economics of the Labour Market* (ed. by Z. Hornstein, J. Grice and A. Webb), pp. 313–315. London ; HMSO

Thomas, R. B. (1981). Labour market adjustments. In *The Economics of Unemployment* (ed. by J. Creedy), pp. 17–47. London; Butterworths

Thomas, B. and Deaton, D. (1977). *Labour Shortage and Economic Analysis.* Oxford; Basil Blackwell

Thurow, L. C. (1976). *Generating Inequality.* London; Macmillan

Vanek, J. (1975). *The General Theory of Labour-Managed Market Economics.* Ithaca. N.Y.; Cornell University Press

Weiss, L. W. (1966). Concentration and labor earnings. *American Economic Review* **56,** 96–117

Wood, A. (1978). *A Theory of Pay.* Cambridge; Cambridge University Press

Chapter 3

The supply of labour

3.1 Introduction

There has been considerable interest in the supply of labour in recent years and a substantial research effort has been devoted to the estimation of labour supply functions. This work is not only of theoretical interest but is significant from a policy point of view. Overall management of the economy requires knowledge of the determinants of labour supply, and problems of regional imbalance, for instance, are most effectively tackled if the authorities are aware of labour supply elasticities.

For most discussions of labour supply the relevant wage variable is the net wage after allowing for the effects of direct taxes and income transfers. Many government policies may have an effect on labour supply through their impact on net wages. Redistributive tax and transfer policies (including proposals for negative income taxes), or policies to index tax brackets to counteract fiscal drag in an inflationary economy, may have incentive or disincentive effects on the supply of labour.

In popular discussions of taxation and work effort it is commonly believed that rises in income tax rates will have a disincentive effect on the supply of effort. Supporters of this view are to be found in all political parties. It is a view which requires careful examination since the merits of many government policies, of the type mentioned above, depend crucially on its validity. Due weight will be given to this question in this chapter.

The analysis of labour supply is most usefully undertaken within the framework of price theory, and it is convenient to follow the usual procedure of considering; first, the objects of choice, secondly the constraints upon the choice, and thirdly, the tastes that govern that choice. In the case of labour supply the object of choice is work against leisure. The constraints are first the physical constraint that limits the number of hours of leisure which are available and secondly the fact that work is not the only source of income. In addition, there are tastes relating to whether it is considered that work is a 'good' or 'bad', and other outside influences such as whether the individual is making the decision alone or whether this decision is being made as a member of a household. Consideration of these factors, particularly tastes, will determine how much an individual or members of a household are willing to participate in the labour force, and this also depends on whether participation is constrained to being in one job or more than one job.

Section 3.2 provides a theoretical discussion of the individual's labour supply decision. It also considers what changes must be made to the model if the individual is included in a household unit. Section 3.3 deals with the budget constraint and its construction and section 3.4 examines the analytical problems involved in attempting to collect data to estimate the model. Some of the results of questionnaire studies are presented in section 3.5 and some econometric results for men are to be found in section 3.6. (A summary of the econometric results is presented in the Appendix to this chapter.) Section 3.7 deals with the incorporation of participation rates into the models and looks, in particular, at the labour supply of women and hence at the household. Finally section 3.8 gives some tentative conclusions and possible lines of advance.

3.2   The theory of labour supply

The individual decision

This section outlines the main features of the basic neoclassical model of labour supply, in which the individual is entirely free to vary the number of hours worked. While this assumption may initially appear to be very unrealistic, since many individuals are constrained by contractual agreements, it may be thought to apply in a long run context where the variation in hours worked may be achieved by mobility between jobs which offer, for example, different lengths of standard working week.

In the conventional theory of consumer demand the individual is assumed to maximize utility by allocating a fixed income over a set of commodities, where the price of each commodity is taken as given (or regarded as 'parametric'). The analysis of labour supply uses the techniques of demand analysis to examine the allocation by an individual of his available time between the activities of work and leisure. The benefits from work are summarized by the resulting real income, represented by the variable C. (The model therefore involves a strict dichotomy between the decision concerning the acquisition of income, or *total* consumption, and the allocation of that income *among* different commodities.) The hours spent in leisure, denoted by the variable L, are of course by definition not used to obtain further income from market activities involving self-employment.

Thus the individual's preferences are represented by a utility function:

$$U = U(C,L) \tag{3.1}$$

showing the utility derived from various quantities of total consumption (real income) C and leisure L. The characteristics of this utility function may be depicted by a family of indifference curves as shown by I_1, I_2 and I_3 in *Figure 3.1*. Each indifference curve, as

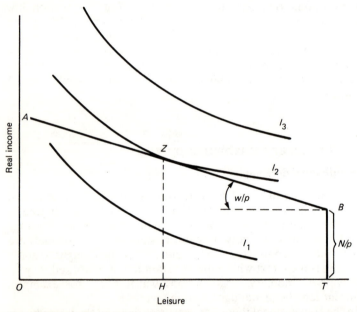

Figure 3.1 The utility function and the budget constraint

in the standard analysis of consumer demand, represents different combinations of total consumption and leisure that yield the same level of satisfaction. The negative slope of each indifference curve indicates that it is possible to hold the level of utility constant while substituting leisure for goods in consumption. The convexity is the result of imperfect substitutability between leisure and goods, so that the indifference curves display decreasing marginal rates of substitution. It is of course assumed that the individual prefers more of both leisure and goods to less, so that indifference curves further away from the origin represent higher levels of utility. This idea may be objected to on the grounds that the first few hours of work may actually be a pleasant alternative to leisure and thus there would be indifference curves which are actually upward sloping at higher levels of leisure. Examples are shown in *Figure 3.2,* but as this complication adds little to the argument which follows it is ignored here.

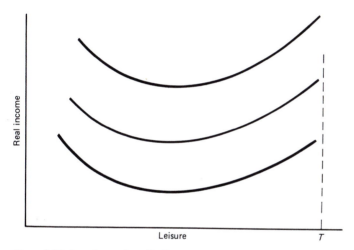

Figure 3.2 Leisure becoming a 'bad'

It is then necessary to consider the constraints on utility maximization. First, there are only a finite number of hours (168) in the week, which imposes an obvious time constraint. It is in fact the construction of the budget constraint which marks the major difference between the conventional analysis of consumer demand and that of labour supply. In the former case the problem is simplified by the assumption of fixed income and prices. But in examining labour supply there is the greater complexity caused by the fact that total consumption (one argument in the utility function) is constrained by income, which is in turn affected by the choice concerning hours worked (or conversely, hours of leisure; another argument in the utility function). It is convenient to begin by assuming that the individual faces fixed prices, represented by the index number p, and can work for a fixed money wage of w per hour.

In addition to market earnings, it is usual to consider the existence of non-market (unearned) income. This income includes on the positive side things such as rent, interest and profits, and on the negative side debt which the consumer has to meet before he can begin to consume (such as hire purchase commitments). Clearly there is nothing to preclude this unearned income, denoted by N, being negative[1]. Therefore it can be seen that the individual can consume any combination of real income and leisure provided neither of them is negative, and the amount of leisure does not exceed a maximum, denoted by T hours[2]. This basic budget constraint is also shown in *Figure 3.1*. If the individual consumes T hours of leisure (does not work), then his real income (total consumption) cannot exceed the real value of his non-wage income; that is N/p. As the individual begins to work, his consumption can be increased at a rate which depends on the real wage, w/p. The budget constraint is therefore ABT in *Figure 3.1*. The section AB of this constraint can be written algebraically as

$$pC = (T-L)w + N \qquad (3.2)$$

In order to compare this with standard consumer theory it is only necessary to write (3.2) in terms of real income, C; so that

$$C = (T-L)w/p + N/p \qquad (3.3)$$

The slope of the straight line AB in *Figure 3.1* is therefore given by w/p, the real wage. This is the intuitively obvious result that the real wage is the rate of exchange between leisure and work.

Maximization of utility, subject to this budget constraint, is therefore a standard problem and involves choosing a particular bundle of real income and leisure that is both on the budget line and also on the highest indifference curve. The optimal combination is shown in *Figure 3.1* as point Z, where the indifference curve I_2 is tangential to the constraint AB. At this point the marginal rate of substitution between real income and leisure is equal to the real wage w/p. Thus it is possible to apply standard demand theory to the analysis of labour supply. Notice however that the result given above and shown in *Figure 3.1* implicitly assumes that the individual is participating in the labour market, so that the solution gives the number of hours worked. But in fact non-participation is easily handled within this framework, in the form of the familiar 'corner solution'. This is illustrated in *Figure 3.3* where the highest indifference curve which may be reached is the curve I_2 which

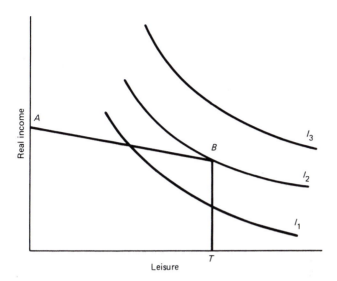

Figure 3.3 Non-participation

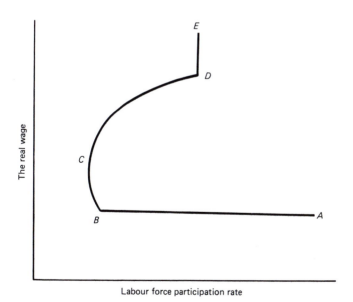

Labour force participation rate

Figure 3.4 The supply curve and economic development

touches the 'corner' of the budget constraint at point B. Notice that even large variations in the real wage would not induce the individual to begin working.

It has often been suggested that participation decisions are related to economic development. Thus, in *Figure 3.4* the section AB shows the situation where every member of the population is required to work in order to survive. The section BC reflects the case where incomes have risen but tastes have remained stable, so that fewer members of society work. Then CD corresponds to the case where tastes change, and DE tends to be characteristic of fully industrialized societies[3]. As in the analysis of consumer demand, it is instructive to consider the comparative statics of changes in the budget constraint.

The effect of a change in non-wage income

The immediate effect of an increase in non-wage income, N, is to shift the section AB of the budget constraint of *Figure 3.1* upwards. This is shown in *Figure 3.5*, where the new budget constraint is given as $A'B'T$. The optimal position shifts from E_1 to E_2, implying an increase in leisure from H_1 to H_2. The income effect of the increase in non-wage income is therefore shown as a decrease in hours worked of $H_2 - H_1$, so that leisure is here a 'normal good'. However, there may be circumstances in which leisure is an 'inferior good'.

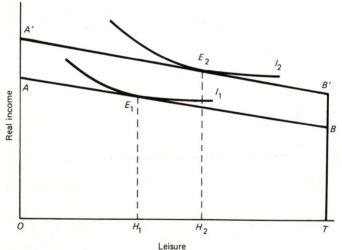

Figure 3.5 The income effect

The effect of a change in the wage rate

Consider next the effect of an increase in the wage rate facing the individual. This may arise for a variety of reasons, but a factor which applies to all individuals and which results from government policy is the marginal rate of income tax. Indeed, the effect on labour supply of a change in the tax structure has been, and continues to be, an important subject of research. The following analysis assumes that the wage rate changes by a fixed amount, so that if it is considered to arise from a change in taxes it is implicit that the marginal tax rate is constant at all income levels.

The change in the wage rate will of course have two effects. First, it will make the individual better off since new consumption possibilities will become open which were not available at lower wages (he can choose to work less but enjoy the same consumption, or work the same number of hours but enjoy more consumption). Secondly, it has altered the relative price of income and leisure. These two effects are the income and substitution effects.

To decompose the two effects it is usual to imagine raising the individual's wage rate but at the same time lowering his unearned income to such an extent that the new optimal solution is as before. This has the effect of increasing the price of leisure without increasing the individual's utility, so that he remains on indifference curve I_1, shown in *Figure 3.6*. The increase in w shifts the budget constraint from ABT to $A'BT$, but a reduction in real non-wage income from B to B' ensures that the individual remains on I_1. The movement along I_1 from E_1 to E_2 involves a reduction in leisure (an increase in work) hours from H_1 to H_2, which measures the substitution effect of the change in w. The (hypothetical) movement from E_2 to E_3, involving a movement to indifference curve I_2, is of course the income effect of the change. The net effect of the income and substitution effects is a reduction in leisure hours of $H_3 - H_1$. This is usually referred to as the 'price effect'.

Figure 3.6 has shown a negative income effect with regard to hours of work which does not outweigh the substitution effect. There are clearly two alternatives to this; the income effect may be positive or it may be negative but outweigh the substitution effect. The former would not affect the price effect and would tend to be associated with low wages and a small number of hours. However, when the second case holds, the familiar backward bending supply curve of labour is produced.

Having defined the income, substitution and price effects, their respective elasticities may easily be defined in terms of the

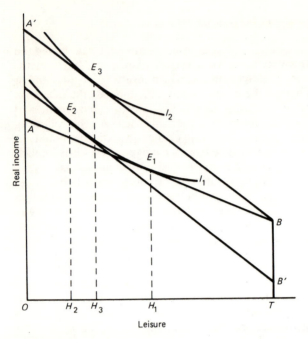

Figure 3.6 The substitution effect

relevant percentage changes[4]. The difficult problem of estimating the numerical values of these elasticities for particular groups of individuals is discussed at length in later sections of this chapter.

Household labour supply

The analysis has so far concentrated on the case of a single individual, but it is clearly also necessary to consider the labour supply behaviour of individuals within households or families. There have been two basic approaches to this subject. First, the earnings of other members of the family may be assumed to form part of the individual's non-market income. Although this approach has often been taken when examining the labour supply of married women, other earnings have often been ignored by those examining male labour supply (giving rise to what may be called a 'male chauvinist' approach)[5]. Secondly, the labour supply of a married couple may be regarded as the outcome of a joint decision. Here the family utility function is written as

$$U = U(C, L_h L_w) \tag{3.4}$$

where C is the aggregate consumption of the family and L_w and L_h are respectviely the amount of leisure of husband and wife[6]. This utility function will be maximized subject to the budget constraint

$$w_h (T - L_h) + w_w(T - L_w) + N = pC \qquad (3.5)$$

where w_h and w_w represent the hourly wage rates of husband and wife respectively.

In this model there are two relevant substitution effects for any given member. First, there is the single substitution effect on the member's labour supply of án increase in his or her own wage, called the own-substitution effect. In addition there is the cross-substitution effect on the individual's labour supply of an increase in the wage of the other family member[7].

The problems of estimating a family member's labour supply will be considered later in this chapter but there are further interdependences to consider arising from the activities of other people in the economy. Hamermesh (1971) has pointed out that increases in the wages of other members of the community will *ceteris paribus* produce two effects on labour supply.First, the falling relative wage of the individual will reduce the amount of hours offered. Secondly, because others are paid more, the individual's labour supply will increase in order to maintain relative levels of consumption. Whichever of these two opposing effects is the stronger will influence the supply of labour. It should be noted here that in the present model these effects ought to be only short-run, as mobility of labour would ensure that in the long run (under competitive conditions) all earnings grow at the same rate.

The basic analysis of this section has used a very simple budget constraint. However, it is necessary to examine more realistic and complex forms of the budget constraint.

3.3   The budget constraint and its problems

The previous section examined some comparative statics of labour supply using a very simple budget constraint in which the real wage per hour was assumed to be constant. In such a system, changes in the wage rate are equivalent to changes in the (constant) marginal tax rate. However, there are in practice a number of complications associated with the budget constraint, and these are considered in this section.

Overtime work

Suppose that there is a standard working week, within which the real wage rate is constant at w/p, as before. If there is an overtime premium of s (whereby the hourly wage increases to sw), then the gradient of the budget constraint will increase to sw/p for all working hours above the standard number. There is therefore an additional kink in the budget constraint, and although the latter is exogenous for each individual, the wage rate actually received is of course endogenous as it depends on the choice of the number of hours worked[8].

Figure 3.7 illustrates an interesting implication of the use of an overtime premium. Suppose that the individual initially faces the budget constraint ABT in *Figure 3.7*, and works TH_1 hours, reaching point E_1 on indifference curve I_1. If an overtime premium is then offered for hours in excess of TH_1 the budget constraint shifts to $A'E_1BT$, and the individual increases the number of hours worked to TH_2. This system can be seen to induce a larger supply

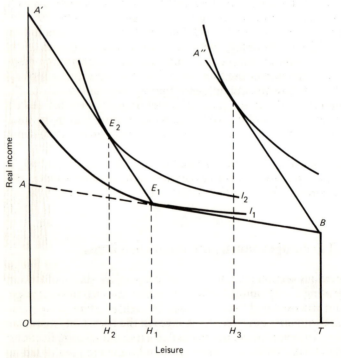

Figure 3.7 Overtime and the budget constraint

of labour than the simple offer of a higher wage of sw/p for all hours. The latter strategy would produce the constraint shown as $A''BT$ in *Figure 3.7*, with a labour supply of TH_3. It is clear that a form of price discrimination is in operation. The worker's real income is lower than if the higher rate had been paid for all hours. Indeed, it is true that an increase in weekly income via overtime premiums will always cause more hours to be supplied than an equivalent increase in the standard rate.

This is a clear prediction of the model, but in addition to the fact that more hours and wage rates are jointly determined (a problem for empirical analysis), there are theoretical difficulties associated with overtime. There may be problems raised by the use of different rates for different extra hours. For example, a premium of one and a half may be paid for overtime during week days, and a premium of two may be paid at weekends, so causing more than one kink. Even in the simplest case of a standard overtime rate there are problems. Previously when considering an increase in the wage rate it was possible for the price effect to be subdivided into income and substitution effects. This is unfortunately no longer possible with overtime.

Thus, further analysis of the overtime issue is worthwhile. Following Brown (1980), the problem is simplified by assuming that non-wage income is zero and the price (wage) elasticity of supply is zero, thus giving a vertical supply curve. In *Figure 3.8* the initial budget constraint is ABT and equilibrium at E_1, supplying TH_1 hours. The worker has a wage rate of w for the standard working week and ws for overtime. Thus the marginal wage rate at E_1 is ws. It can be seen that the worker would still be at the same equilibrium point if the same marginal rate had been paid for all hours worked and he had an initial non-wage income of TN_1, which is a hypothetical intercept introduced at zero hours. The hypothetical non-wage debt introduced by the overtime may be viewed as having been financed in the standard working week. This use of a hypothetical intercept, combined with the marginal overtime wage rate, is an important development which will again be considered in the context of estimation problems.

The effect of increasing the standard wage rate will be to shift the budget constraint to $A'B'T$ and make the negative 'intercept' larger at TN_2. The latter change may be viewed as an income effect which must be added to the price effect caused by the change in the slope of the budget constraint. Under the imposed restrictions of the model the intercept change may be viewed as causing movement down the income consumption curve (*ICC*) to point D and the price effect produces a movement up the

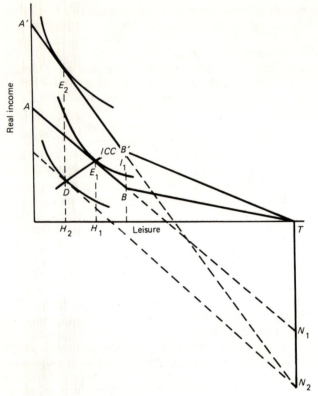

Figure 3.8 An increase in the wage rate with overtime

(assumed) vertical supply curve to E_2. It can be seen that E_2 involves a move to more work and less leisure. Obviously the model could incorporate a non-zero price elasticity, but the additional income effect will always be present.

Non-proportional taxes

It has already been seen that overtime introduces non-linearity into the model, and a similar problem is raised by the existence of a non-proportional tax system. The easiest way to illustrate this is to have a proportional tax combined with an exemption or tax threshold as in the United Kingdom. Here is is assumed for simplicity that there is only one tax rate.

Consider *Figure 3.9* where for simplicity it is assumed that non-wage income is zero. While the individual earns less than the

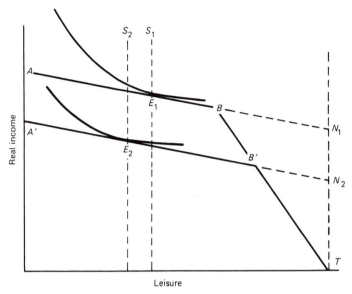

Figure 3.9 An increase in tax revenue by lowering the tax threshold

tax threshold the slope of the budget constraint is the real wage w/p. Suppose that the threshold is reached at point B in *Figure 3.9*. Beyond that point, for each extra hour worked the rate of exchange between work and leisure is reduced to $w(1-t)/p$, where t represents the constant marginal tax rate. Thus the budget constraint is given by ABT. A reduction in the tax rate would of course increase the slope of the section AB. A reduction in the exemption level shifts the kink to B' along BT in *Figure 3.9,* so that the new constraint is shown as $A'B'T$. The effect of such a change is shown as a movement from point E_1 to E_2, involving more work. It can be seen that, with the assumption of vertical supply curves, an increase in the tax rate would reduce labour supply. There is clearly an incentive for governments to increase tax revenue by lowering thresholds rather than by raising tax rates; but it should be noted that this result may not always hold for more complex models with non-zero income effects.

A general non-linear budget constraint

Clearly it is possible for many factors to occur together and so there will be a number of segments in the budget constraints. A fairly typical constraint for a British worker is shown in *Figure 3.10*. The gross wage w fixes the budget constraint until the tax exemption level, when tax is paid at rate t and the marginal wage rate become $(1-t)w$. Above the standard working week the overtime premium s is paid making the marginal wage rate $s(1-t)w$ up to the maximum number of hours that the firm requires the person. After this a second job may be taken for a number of hours at a different hourly wage rate, w_1[9].

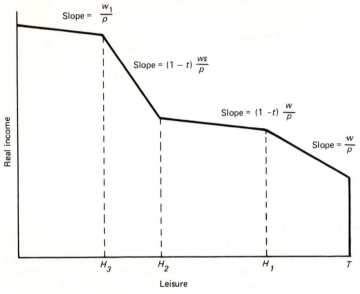

Figure 3.10 A general budget constraint

Budget constraints can naturally be more complicated than this, especially with many tax bands, and there is no reason why the segments need to be in the order stated. (For example, a person could have worked some overtime before he becomes liable for tax.) The position of the kink is interesting. Given that an individual has choice, and hence fits the assumptions of the model so far, it is possible for him to be at a kink, so that a change in the slope of the budget constraint may not affect him. However, a change in the kink itself probably would lead to a change in labour supply. This may be the case with someone, often the second income earner of a household, who earns less than the tax threshold. A change in the tax rate will have no effect, unless it is very large (in practice making t close to zero) but a change in the kink itself, that is a change in allowable income, will tend to move the individual. A similar point was noted earlier in the context of labour force participation.

3.4   Labour supply data

Sections 3.2 and 3.3 have examined the basic orthodox theory of labour supply and the problems associated with the construction of the appropriate budget constraint facing an individual. Before examining empirical work on labour supply it is first necessary to discuss the nature of the data which are available.

Cross-sectional data and sample selection

A fundamental problem in labour supply studies has been that of collecting and dealing appropriately with cross-sectional data. The advantage of cross-sectional data is that they enable the investigator to isolate and control for the influence of a range of factors, notably those of a qualitative or demographic nature. However, a group of individuals for whom the appropriate cross-sectional labour supply information is available will probably be drawn from a variety of industries, so that use of the data presupposes that workers in each industry face an elastic demand curve for their labour. A more disaggregated approach, industry by industry, clearly removes much of this difficulty but at a cost of reducing the range of variation in both income and wages, since it is likely that workers within an industry will display relatively more homogeneity than the aggregate.

The implication of using cross-sectional data is that all workers face similar prices for the market goods on which income is spent. In the UK regional discrepancies in prices are usually ignored while in the USA there is a strong case to be made for the incorporation of dummy variables to allow for the effect of particular locations, and their price differences on labour supply behaviour. Further, since standard tax rates and rates in the higher tax bands are identical across the whole of the cross-sectional sample, no effects of tax rate changes can be estimated.

It is useful to stress exactly what the use of cross-sectional data assumes about the reaction of an individual to a change in income, the wage rate or any other determinants of labour supply. It is presumed that the response of a particular worker to a change in conditions may be adequately approximated by the labour supply decision of another worker who already faces these conditions. Without doubt there are problems associated with this assumption underlying the use of cross-sectional data, but it may also be argued that similar problems apply to other areas of applied economic research.

The choice of which variables are to be included in any labour supply estimation is clearly constrained by the data available but in addition there is the problem of sample selection. In all statistical inference the aim is to construct a random sample of the population under study. With labour supply this has proved a very difficult goal. Many studies have confined themselves to the study of particular industries or weekly-paid workers, or special low-income groups, for example. Nevertheless, there will be a problem that the hours actually worked, for which data are usually available, are not synonymous with labour supplied. The recognition that time spent searching for a job is effectively time offered in the labour market raises the problem of the possible inclusion of the involuntarily unemployed in the analysis. However in general it is desirable to exclude individuals who are found to be in a disequilibrium position; indeed it is almost impossible to isolate the involuntarily unemployed and to measure the quantity of labour they are implicitly supplying. In most cases it is necessary to make the simplifying assumption that hours worked accurately measure labour supply, although more sophisticated studies discard data on individuals whose work hours appear to be constrained.

What is clear is that the findings of any study will be influenced by the way in which the sample is chosen. A particularly pertinent example of this would be an attempt to study the effect of a new tax programme aimed at helping the poor. There is no point in only examining those below the poverty line because a new programme could well affect the hours supplied of those who are currently above that line.

Even if it can be accepted that there has not been too much bias induced by the selection of the sample and by placing limits on the number of hours that people might be able to work, there is the further problem of the measurement of particular variables to be considered[10]. The major problem concerns the measurement of 'work effort', which may be associated with the payment of piece rates, bonuses or commissions in addition to standard wage rates. One resort would be to leave such people out of the sample but this is clearly very narrowing. An alternative is to leave them in the sample, but to appreciate that some bias may occur because of a simultaneous decision concerning both hours and effort, and hope that the sample will be sufficiently large.

Even allowing for this problem the measurement of the amount of time worked is not as simple as it may appear. The usual method of obtaining hours worked involves the use of a questionnaire where individuals are usually asked about their hours worked in the previous week (longer time periods raise difficulties because of faulty memory). However, this may not be a typical week in the person's yearly work pattern. To circumvent this problem a question is often phrased in terms of 'usual' hours, which will leave interpretational problems for the respondent. The third possibility is to assume that the employee has no voice in the number of hours he works, but of course this is rather against the spirit of the model the data will be testing. The additional problems of non-market work activities and time spent in a second job merely add to the difficulty of accurately measuring the number of hours worked[11].

The budget constraint

If some measure of hours can be ascertained there is still the problem of constructing each individual's budget constraint. In the case of wage rates the most important variable must be the money received for the last hour worked; that is, the net marginal wage rate. This is the measure of income after account has been taken of overtime premiums, taxation, wage rates on second jobs, national insurance contributions, and possibly benefits. The fact remains that the more information is available the closer is the researcher to being able to build the whole constraint.

The other element of the budget constraint is the measurement of any non-employment income. In practice the non-employment income is very wide, and tends to include all income which is not *directly* related to the employment of the individual. Into this category would fall transfer payments such as state means-tested benefits, which are to some extent dependent upon hours worked. As discussed in section 3.2, income of other household members may be counted as part of the non-employment income of an individual, affecting the labour supply decision[12].

All these data problems are exacerbated by the fact that individuals are often required to answer questions that they may not really understand, so that they may not actually answer the question posed. Brown (1980) gives excellent examples of the problems of gleaning technical information from broad questions. The question of whether people understand their budget constraint and so can be viewed as optimizing is another problem which faces the empirical economist. Brown and Jackson (1978) have illustrated that misconceptions abound, but the only work that attempts to measure the misconceptions is that of Rosen (1976), who nevertheless estimates a very small tax illusion.

There have been many econometric studies of labour supply functions using data obtained from questionnaires, and these are discussed in section 3.6 of this chapter. However, the following section examines some of the studies that have used interview data to examine responses without explicitly attempting to estimate supply functions.

3.5   Results using interview data

The surveys discussed in this section were all explicitly designed in order to examine the possible effects on labour supply of income taxation. The information required for studies of this kind is not of course available from data published by the Central Statistical Office, so that special sample surveys have been used when considering the findings, and those of the econometric studies, it is of course worth bearing in mind the difficulties associated with making inferences about the population as a whole from particular samples.

The major drawback of the straightforward interview technique is that the nature of the questions asked may well affect the results. Vague and general questions are unlikely to provide precise and useful information, while very detailed questions may tend to lead the interviewee and so influence his response. Some cross-checking of answers is clearly required[13].

Lower-paid workers

There have been two major surveys of lower-paid workers in the UK; those of a *Royal Commission on the Taxation of Profits and Income* (1954) and Brown and Levin (1974). The Royal Commission argued in their report that behaviour may be related to three factors. First, it depends on knowledge of the true facts about the tax system. Second, it may be influenced by incorrect beliefs about the tax system. Third, it is affected by general attitudes towards income tax not related to any specific facts[14]. The report was mainly interested in the first aspect, arguing that misconceptions can be altered, and concluded that 'whilst workers consider tax to be a deterrent and nearly all grumble about it . . . few carry the grumbling to the point of letting it affect their productive behaviour'.

Brown and Levin (1974) were primarily concerned with whether tax affected overtime. Respondents were asked if tax had made them work 'more overtime', 'less overtime', or 'doesn't apply/neither'. These questions were put after a large number of factual and attitudinal questions in which tax was not mentioned. The plausibility of the answers to the tax questions was then decided in terms of consistency with earlier statements, and consideration was given to the extent to which the overtime worked was constrained. (The most obvious constraint is that an employee may be required by his employer to work longer or shorter hours than he himself wishes.) The evidence suggested to Brown and Levin (1974, p. 847) that 'the aggregate effect of tax on overtime is small; it may perhaps add about 1% to the total hours worked'. They found that 74% of men claimed tax had no effect on overtime.

Higher-paid workers

Turning to the studies of higher-income groups, Break (1952) surveyed self-employed solicitors and accountants. These groups clearly possess certain characteristics which ought to assist the researcher in any investigation of incentive and disincentive effects. It is to be expected that accountants and solicitors will have considerable discretion in the amount of work they do, that they will be well-informed about the tax system, and that many will face higher marginal tax rates. Against this it ought to be noted that the labour supply of professional people may tend to be insensitive to normal financial variations, such as those brought about by changes in tax rates, and respond more to non-monetary factors[15]

Break was most careful not to 'lead' his subjects and placed internal checks to ascertain the consistency of replies. He found a significant proportion of the sample had a disincentive effect, which was almost offset by the proportion with a significant incentive effect. The disincentives seemed to be stronger amongst those who faced higher marginal tax rates while incentives were equally distributed across all income ranges. With respect to retirement (that is, long-run labour supply) Break found that 52% of his sample expected to postpone retirement when faced with higher tax rates[16].

The study by Fields and Stanbury (1971) is important because of its attempt to duplicate the work of Break (1952). Their study suggested that although there were individuals with significant incentives as well as others with disincentive effects, the net tax effect on labour supply is likely to be a disincentive effect. They also suggested that this effect is growing stronger over time. Criticisms have been raised concerning Fields and Stanbury's questionnaire, and its possible 'leading' of interviewees. Further, it should be mentioned that both Break (1952) and Fields and Stanbury (1971) considered the role of fixed commitments in labour supply, but with conflicting results[17]. One final result of these studies which is worth noting is that Fields and Stanbury (1971) found little difference between the number of hours worked by those experiencing a disincentive and those who claimed an incentive effect. Both suggested that the disincentives appear to hit the hard-working and ambitious, while incentives stimulate the unambitious and less hardworking. A summary of results is given in *Table 3.1*.

TABLE 3.1 Interview studies of labour supply

Author(s)	Proportion claiming tax disincentive	Proportion claiming tax incentive
Barlow *et al.*, (1966)	0.12	n.a.
Break (1952)	0.13	0.10
	(0.18)	(0.31)
Brown and Levin (1974)	0.11	0.15
Chatterjee and Robinson	(0.18) professional	(0.17)
(1969)	(0.24) non-professional	(0.32)
Fields and Stanbury	0.18	0.11
(1971)	(0.24)	(0.22)
Holland (1977)	0.15	not comparable

Note
Figures given are net of questionable influences. The gross figures are in parentheses.

The studies discussed briefly above only cover the United Kingdom but there are many similarities in the results for other countries. These include, for example, Barlow *et al.* (1965) and Holland (1977) for the US, and Chatterjee and Robinson (1969) for Canada. It would appear that there is no marked disincentive effect and there is evidence that there are both incentive and disincentive effects for small groups. Thus the net tax effect on the aggregate labour supply is small. It should be noted that there appears to be a higher proportion of those who claim that taxes have an incentive effect and a lower proportion with disincentives in the Brown and Levin study. This is not surprising, since these workers had relatively low marginal tax rates and the low incomes will provide more incentive. The move towards a disincentive effect over time is slight but may have gathered pace with higher inflation rates. How great an understanding of the tax system now exists among respondents is still unclear.

What should really be noted in survey work is that there is usually no way to unscramble the tax effects from the effects of other variables. Fields and Stanbury (1971) have pointed out that no interviewee can be expected to operate 'like a regression model measuring the partial effects of each of a host of variables'. In the above approaches it has been necessary for the researcher to weigh the merits of the variables considered. It ought to be possible to overcome this subjectivity by the use of appropriate econometric models, and such attempts are considered in the next section.

3.6   Econometric studies of labour supply

The econometric approach involves the specification of a relationship among the relevant economic variables, the collection of data that can be used in the estimation of the parameters of the relationships, and finally the application of an appropriate statistical technique in order to obtain numerical values of the parameters. There are far too many studies for them all to be discussed here. Hence consideration will be given to the general problems involved, and particular studies will be used to illustrate the points raised. Where possible UK studies will be examined, but it must be borne in mind that the determinants of labour supply may vary significantly among different countries, so that cross-country data cannot be used[18].

Before considering the specification of labour supply functions it is perhaps worth mentioning a general problem raised by what is called 'truncation bias'. This is in many ways a data collection problem which only really becomes important at the estimation stage. In a simple labour supply function the variation in labour supply will be related to a number of 'independent' variables, and the specification will include an 'error' term. Unfortunately, in cross-sectional studies a large proportion of the variation in hours worked often rests in the error term. This does not necessarily create a difficulty except, for example, where a constraint is placed on the dependent variable when the data are being collected. This may, for example, occur through the use of an income rule which restricts the amount of hours which will be available for each wage rate. Another possible truncation arises through the restriction of the sample to those who have worked a certain number of hours. Now if this occurs the error term will no longer be random, and bias will occur from the truncation. Clearly this should be borne in mind when the data are collected and, if it cannot be prevented, should be considered at the estimation stage of the analysis.

Simple labour supply functions

The model of labour supply presented in section 3.2 suggests that
the number of hours worked per week will be a function of the real
net wage (that is, the real wage after allowing for taxation and
other deductions), and the real value of non-employment income.
The supply of labour will of course also depend on the nature of
preferences, which affect the utility function.

Instead of beginning with a detailed specification of the utility
function, and deriving the implied form of the supply function,
many studies of labour supply have actually started from a simple
functional form which can be estimated using conventional regression techniques. An example is provided by the pioneering work
of Kosters (1966), who used a supply function of the form

$$H = \beta_0 + \beta_1(w/p) + \beta_2(N/p) + \sum_{r=3}^{k} \beta_r Z_r + u \tag{3.6}$$

where u is the error term and H, w and N are the number of hours
worked, the net wage and the non-wage income of the individual
respectively, and the variables denoted by the Zs measure those
factors that are thought to affect individuals' preferences. Many
such variables have been used, such as the value of family assets
that yield no pecuniary income, health, number of children, race
and education[19].

In equation (3.6) the coefficients β_1 and β_2 measure the uncom-
pensated wage and non-wage income effects, $\partial H/\partial w$ and $\partial H/\partial N$
respectively. These effects are assumed to be the same for all
individuals in the population. If the compensated wage effect (the
substitution effect of a change in the relative price of leisure) is
written as $\delta H/\delta w$, then the familiar Slutsky decomposition can be
written as

$$\partial H/\partial w = \delta H/\delta w + H (\partial H/\partial N) \tag{3.7}$$

Thus in terms of the coefficients in (3.6), the substitution effect
may be obtained as

$$\delta H/\delta w = \beta_1 - H\beta_2 \tag{3.8}$$

Since β_2 is expected to be negative, the substitution effect is larger,
the greater is the number of hours worked. It is usual when
presenting empirical results to give the value of the substitution
effect at the average number of hours worked.

It is worth examining the work of Ashenfelter and Heckman
(1973) which, instead of starting from a simple supply function, is

based directly on the Slutsky decomposition (3.7). For a cross-section in which all individuals face the same set of prices, the supply function (ignoring taste variables) can be written as

$$H = H(w,N) \tag{3.9}$$

with total differential

$$dH = (\partial H/\partial w)\, dw + (\partial H/\partial N)dN \tag{3.10}$$

Substitution of (3.7) into (3.10) gives

$$dH = (\delta H/\delta w)dw + (Hdw + dN)(\partial H/\partial N) \tag{3.11}$$

Ashenfelter and Heckman (1973) then assume that the substitution and income effects are constant at α_1 and α_2 respectively, so that the estimating equation based on (3.11) is given by (ignoring the stochastic term)

$$\Delta H = \alpha_1 \Delta w + \alpha_2 (H\Delta w + \Delta N) \tag{3.12}$$

where the Δs indicate discrete changes. Whereas in Kosters's (1966) model the slope of the supply function is assumed to remain constant, with the substitution effect varying with hours worked, the specification in (3.12) assumes that the latter effect is constant while the slope of the supply function varies. The slope is of course given by

$$\partial H/\partial w = \alpha_1 + H\alpha_2 \tag{3.13}$$

and is usually evaluated at the average value of hours worked[20].

Some empirical results

The above discussion has illustrated some of the general approaches taken by many of the early econometric studies of labour supply. A summary of the estimates that were found for this work is provided in the Appendix to this chapter. Results for males and females are given separately. It can be seen that there is broad agreement about the size of the substitution elasticity, which was found to be of the order of 0.2 or less (with the exception of Kalachek and Raines, 1970). Several of the studies, for example Cohen *et al.* (1970) and Greenberg and Kosters (1973), have considered the labour supply of participants only. It may therefore be expected that variations in the estimates of income and substitution effects may be partly explained by the fact that some studies ignored participation responses to changes in wages and income[21]. The estimates suggest that the substitution elasticity for total male work effort might reasonably be supposed to be between 0.20 and 0.25, with a corresponding income slope coefficient of -0.10 to -0.15.

Although the method appears to produce general agreement about the size of the parameters of labour supply functions, these empirical results are still very much open to question. The conventional analysis of labour supply contains several crucial assumptions and simplifications which ought to be discussed.

Some further problems

The wage rate employed in most of these studies is the gross average wage rate, and is obtained by dividing gross income by the number of hours worked. However, the analysis indicates that net income is the appropriate independent variable[22]. Further, the use of the wage rate is clearly missing all those who are not actually participating, a problem mentioned above. More seriously, the hourly wage rate will be too low for all those who worked more hours than normal in the survey week, and will be too high for all those who worked fewer than normal. This type of error will normally bias the wage rate coefficient downwards. When the number of hours worked during the survey week is the dependent variable, the wage rate will be negatively correlated with the error term and a downward bias will result. The belief, best iterated by Masters and Garfinkel (1977), is that the price elasticity estimate will be too large a negative number.

Even if it is accepted that these biases are probably quite small there is still one major problem remaining. This arises because the gross (or even the net) average wage and non-employment income do not uniquely define labour supply in the case of non-linear budget constraints. Brown *et al.* (1974a) have explained this point in detail and here it must suffice to say that it is simple to construct budget constraints with the same average wage rate but with many equilibrium positions consistent with this wage. Further, and in addition to the measurement problems, if the budget constraints are non-linear then the average wage depends upon the hours worked (this point has been discussed in section 3.3 above). But the supply functions are attempting to relate hours worked to the wage rate, with the latter as an independent variable. This difficulty is often referred to as the 'endogeneity' problem [23].

Linearized budget constraints

The main models which try to solve the 'endogeneity' problem return to the method used to examine substitution and income effects, which was discussed in section 3.3. The principle is to linearize the budget constraint and use the non-employment income which would exist were this budget constraint operative[24]. Examining *Figure 3.8* shows the advantage of this approach. The equilibrium position is the same under the non-linear budget constraint ABT, and under the linearized version ABN_1. The latter uses the hypothetical non-employment income which is effectively a 'debt' of TN_1. Thus labour supply is uniquely determined by the net marginal wage rate. Further, this approach must reduce the endogeneity bias, if the individual stays on the same segment of his budget constraint[25].

The British study which exemplifies the above approach is that of Brown *et al.* (1974b, 1976)[26]. Their estimating equation expressed hours worked as a linear function of the net marginal wage (and its square), the 'non-wage debt' associated with the net marginal wage, other income such as state transfer payments, and dummy variables used to capture 'need' and 'job satisfaction'. The marginal wage rates used allowed for income taxation, overtime and second jobs.

As can be seen from the table of results given in the Appendix to this chapter, theresults of this approach do have a significant advantage in that the substitution effect is as predicted by the theory[27]. It is clear that this approach circumvents some of the problems previously outlined but it still has the problem of the requirement that individuals do not change from one budget constraint segment to another.

An attempt to deal with several sections of the budget constraint has been made by Ashworth and Ulph (1981b), whose work evolved at much the same time as that of Wales and Woodland (1979) and Burtless and Hausman (1978). In all cases the broad approach is similar and should be applicable to any piece-wise linear budget constraint[28]. The procedure adopted is to use an indirect utility function and to find any possible points of equilibria on any segments. If there are two or more points then that yielding highest utility is chosen. Hence the utility function is used to predict the number of hours people wish to work and this is compared with the number of hours they actually work, in order to obtain the best fit.

Although in principle it ought to be possible to use any ordering of the budget constraint segments, Ashworth and Ulph (1981a) restricted their work to a particular specification, as shown in *Figure 3.10*. The segments have different slopes of the gross wage before the tax threshold is reached, the gross wage less the income tax, the net wage allowing for overtime, the net wage for the second job. The last segment is always less steeply sloped then than the third segment. The initial value of non-wage income is that used by Brown *et al.* (1974b), and all other intercepts are the hypothetical values of non-employment income associated with the given marginal wage rate in the relevant segment. The data were taken from the same study as Brown *et al.* (1974b, 1976) but the data requirements were such as to restrict further the size of the sample. What ought to be emphasized with this method is that the specification of the utility function chosen would appear to be crucial to the analysis.

The results from this type of study tend to support the idea that the previous studies have obtained biased estimates of the substitution elasticity by not allowing for the endogeneity problem[29]. It can be seen that with the preferred specification of the utility function, the Ashworth and Ulph (1981a) results give a price elasticity which is still a small negative number, but the change in the substitution elasticity is very marked[30]. This could be because of the limitation of the sample to those individuals with greater awareness of their position, so that the results may over-estimate the total labour response, especially as the sample includes only those who have decided to participate. The possible effect of using a different sample can be seen by applying the Brown, Levin and Ulph approach to the sample used by Ashworth and Ulph (1981a). It is found that the substitution elasticity increases, as compared with Brown, Levin and Ulph (1976).

An obvious omission from this study, and others of its kind, is the lack of variables to allow for differing 'tastes', because of the complexity of expressing the utility function. Clearly from the measures of fit which have been observed, variations in 'tastes' are responsible for a great deal of the variation in labour supply[31]. In Britain there is a further problem with the construction of the budget constraint which arises from the overlap between the many types of social security payments and income taxation.

3.7   The labour supply of married women

So far the discussion has been restricted to studies of males and especially married males. This is because the data sets for males are usually better in terms of the information they provide and are larger. However, it is worth considering the results which have become available for women to see if any consistent pattern is available. The labour supply of households will then be examined. The work on females has usually been restricted to married women, on the assumption that single females either mirror 'major wage earners' in their decisions, or are at too early a stage in their life to have a settled pattern.

Labour force participation

The major problem with most of the work already examined is the assumption that everyone is actually participating in work and so has a positive wage rate. Although this is a problem for studies of males it is clearly much more serious for the work on married women. This inevitably means that participation rates and the supply of hours should be examined together.

The labour force participation rate is the ratio of the economically active (employed or unemployed) to the population. It may be calculated for particular sub-sections of the population. Clearly, knowledge of this rate is useful for ascertaining the extent of labour reserves in the economy, and in order to examine the operation of the social security system. The analysis of female participation has been of two types. The first examines trends through time in conjunction with cross-sectional studies, and the second considers the relation between labour force participation and hours[32]. In terms of the present chapter the latter question is more pertinent, and so only a short summary will be given of the former.

The participation rate of married women has risen dramatically in this century. Early studies tended not to examine the role of the wife's wage on participation, focusing instead on the fact that the higher the earnings of males, the lower the labour force participation of married women. The participation rate of wives does, however, increase strongly with their own wage. In a cross-sectional study Mincer (1962) estimated that an increase in the income of husbands of $1000 reduced the labour force participation rate of wives by 0.62 percentage points while an increase in the income of wives by the same amount raised their participation rate by 1.33 percentage points. Similar results have been found in other studies such as Cain (1966), Bowen and Finegan (1969) and Cain and Dooley (1976) for the US, and Greenhalgh (1977) for the UK. The fact that the effect of the wage rate is larger than for males may be explained by the argument that housework is a more acceptable alternative to market work for females. However, the use of participation equations to predict changes in participation rates resulting from wage increases has been less successful. For example, in the UK Greenhalgh (1977) would have predicted a twelve percentage point rise in married women's participation over the period 1951–71, whereas it actually rose by 20 percentage points. There are clearly other factors at work besides those observed in cross-sectional data. It has become clear that the passage of time has had some effect and further that different socioeconomic groups have been differently affected. A large literature has emerged on the effects of schooling, race and fertility in the US[33]. However, from the viewpoint of this chapter it is the analysis in a cross-sectional manner which must be the primary concern.

Joint determination of participation and hours

So far hours of work and labour force participation have been treated as separate topics and although similar variables are used, this dichotomy is fairly common. However, it is possible to express a labour supply function as

$$Q(w,N) = H(w,N)R(w,N) \qquad (3.14)$$

where Q is labour supply, H is average hours for those with positive hours, and R is labour force participation for those with wage w and non-wage income N. The studies so far have been restricted to estimating H, and although this is probably not too different from Q for males, it is necessary to consider R when estimating the labour supply behaviour of women.

A general point to note is that R is always less than unity, so that H must always exceed Q. But more pertinently R is responsive to w and N and so a change in either of these variables will cause a different response in H from that of Q. The problem is how to integrate the participation and hours decision.

For primary workers, most of whom participate (the situation with men), the hours of work functions have often been estimated including non-participants with zero hours. For secondary workers a (0, 1) dependent variable has been used to estimate a participation function, and then an hours of work function has been estimated for participants. From these two functions an overall effect on labour supply has been calculated using a weighted average. Some criticisms of this method are given in the empirical studies but the major ones are in terms of the likely bias of estimates. Such bias may occur because of the limited variability of the participation dependent variable for secondary workers and because the selection of participants for the hours of work functions may still lead to truncation problems. Having made this general point, some of the empirical studies are examined below.

Some empirical results

Heckman (1974) has used a two-stage procedure which first estimates a predicted wage for non-working women, based on demographic characteristics of a sample of workers. It then assigns this wage (refered to as the offered wage) to non-workers. Secondly a function is used dealing with the value a woman places on her time (referred to as the asking wage), which depends on factors such as wife's hours of work, husband's wage, prices, non-emloyment income, and number of children. Now if the woman works the offered wage exceeds the asking wage and if she does not work, no offered wage matches her asking wage[34]. The model can be used to determine both the probability that a woman works and her actual hours of work.

Heckman's (1974) results for all women in his sample and for a sub-sample of those who are actually working suggest that there are noticeable differences in the make-up of the samples. The study gives high estimates for substitution elasticities[35] and has the expected results that the asking wage is positively related to net assets, children, husband's wage and labour supply. A further interesting point is that education appears to raise the offered wage more than the asking wage, implying that participation increases with education. Heckman's (1974) results suggest that there are benefits in this approach over using only working women.

The work for the UK has been concentrated in two main areas; the Stirling study[36] and work by Greenhalgh (1977, 1980). Greenhalgh's work has not examined the endogeneity problem described above (because of data deficiencies) but claims to have a method which makes the problem much less serious. Although the gross wage/non-employment income approach has been used this ought not to be too serious because few women work overtime, so they usually have only one kink in the budget constraint, at the tax threshold.

Although she feels that the possible bias in her results as a consequence of the 'wrong segment' problems will be slight, Brown (1980) has suggested that the random error will be very important as a large proportion of women work to the tax threshold. Brown (1980) is also worrried about Greenhalgh's use of a predicted wage rate. While it is clearly desirable to remove the measurement error bias from hours there is a problem that professional people are in the study. For professionals there is no reason to expect their average wage to explain their hours, as the preferences of professionals for work appear to be very different from those of other people. Killingsworth (1973) has posed further possible problems over using the predicted wage approach in that the goodness of fit of the equations that are used is often very poor, and many influences on wages are therefore omitted from the regressions. This causes fewer fluctuations in wages than would be otherwise expected. Even accepting these points, Greenhalgh's overall results, using a variety of functional forms, are interesting for their similarity to the study by Ruffell (1981) who used a supply function directly, and to the results of Ashworth and Ulph (1981b) who attempted to examine working women taking account of the movement between segments of the budget constraint. It should however be emphasized that these latter two studies did not consider the participation question. It would appear that for working women the wage elasticity (Greenhalgh has a gross wage elasticity) is positive and fairly large, the income effect is negative and larger than for men and the substitution elasticity is much larger than for men[37].

Although, there may be broad agreement about the relative sizes of the elasticities for working women there is clearly scope for more work on women. Naturally, this must involve the careful specification of preferences in the model. Further, it would appear that women ought to be examined in the household context and what work has been done on this will now be examined.

Household models

In the empirical work which has so far been examined, there has been no allowance made for an interaction between the labour supply decisions of household members. These models have often been referred to as 'male chauvinist models' as they make no allowance for the possibility that the wife's labour supply decision may influence the husband's decision, except possibly through effects on employment income. The main approaches to joint labour supply decisions have been outlined in section 3.2 of this chapter. They assume that there is a common budget constraint (which ideally would be treated for all the non-linear problems outlined above) but they differ in their approach to the utility function. On the one hand it is assumed that husband and wife (or in principle the two members of the household, though most studies deal with 'traditional' couples) maximize a joint utility function which depends on the consumption and leisure of the two members. This approach is described by Killingsworth (1976) as 'family budget constraint – family utility'. The main feature of this model is the equality of the cross-substitution effects but unfortunately few researchers in the area have found that this holds[38].

The alternative to the above is, using Killingsworth's description, 'the individual utility–family budget constraining model', explained by Leuthold (1968). While the budget constraint is still common (precluding any households who behave as if their budget constraint were separate) the requirement of the equality of cross-substitution effects is relaxed. In this approach the labour supply equations for the husband and wife are derived from a system of two equations, with the work efforts of the two members as endogenous variables. The reduced form of the model is used in the empirical work[39]. The model is such that there is no cross-substitution effect but an increase in the wage of the husband will have an income effect on the wife, plus an indirect income effect generated by the husband's substitution effect[40]. There is no requirement that this income effect should be equal for both parties.

Ashworth and Ulph (1981b) have attempted to compare the two models by using an extension of Leuthold's (1968) model. Instead of each member's utility being dependent on their own leisure and own consumption, each person's utility depends on joint consumption, their own leisure and the other person's leisure. If the two utility functions were identical then the family utility model is returned to. While the estimation prodecure did not take full account of all the problems previously mentioned (notably the change of segment problems) their results suggested that the models were different, with Leuthold's (1968) approach providing the better explanation of the data.

However, it should be emphasized that work on the household model is still not well developed. On the whole samples have been selected using the requirement that both members of the household are workers in order to avoid the problems associated with participation decisions (see Leuthold, 1968, 1979, and Ashworth and Ulph, 1981b). The problem of possible movements between segments of the budget constraint presents a minefield for the researcher hoping to deal simultaneously with both members of the household[41]. Having outlined some of the major weaknesses there are two results worth noting. All the work has suggested that the wage coefficient is positive for women and negative (or zero) for men, and Leuthold (1979) has found that the effect of children is to decrease the supply of labour of the woman and increase that of the man.

3.8　Conclusions

This chapter has examined a number of attempts to estimate labour supply functions. It has become apparent that although the basic theory of labour supply is fairly well established, major problems exist for the specification of the utility function and the complications of non-linear budget constraints.

Women appear to respond to changes in their budget constraints much more than men, although the changes of both would seem to be greater than was initially thought. The presumptions of the theory, that the substitution elasticity is positive and the income elasticity is negative (indicating that leisure is a normal good) are confirmed. The doubts clearly concern the size of these effects, and especially that of wage effect. For men the wage effect seems to be very small or just negative, but for women it seems to be positive (though there is a wider range of estimates).

The major concern is that although these results are interesting in themselves, it is difficult to incorporate them in wider models which can be used to help policy-makers; for example in considering tax changes. This has been the concern of the negative income tax experiments in the US (which cannot be discussed here), and for UK analyses of the move from income taxation to VAT (using a model incorporating labour supply and commodity demands)[42]. This seems to require simulation exercises, perhaps along the lines of that carried out by Glaister *et al.* (1981) using labour supply estimates and then recalculating the budget constraint for each individual after the change in tax[43]. Their tentative result for weekly-paid men and income tax (no transfer system is allowed for) is that a decrease of five percentage points in the tax rate will increase labour supply by over 3%.

It is clear that there is still a great deal of work to be done in the area of labour supply. It would appear that effort should be ultimately directed towards family models, incorporating the difficulties of the budget constraint, participation rates, and tastes. This incorporation of taste variables would appear to present the major problem as it will complicate already tortuous estimation procedures[44].

It may also be suggested that labour supply should be examined in a life-cycle context, as for example in the work of Heckman and McCurdy (1980), and in the more general context of the allocation of time (as in Becker, 1965), studies in part by Block (1973), Wales and Woodland (1977) and Bowen and Finegan (1969). Further, the role of commodities examined by Abbot and Ashenfelter (1976), and more recently by Atkinson and Stern (1979), is a major area of improvement to the model. For all this it is clear that data are going to be very expensive; information must be very detailed and for life-cycle studies may well take a long time to collect.

Notes

1. It should be noted that it will probably be impossible to separate w from N in practice. For example, high wages may lead to high saving leading to higher non-wage income.
2. An individual may require a minimum amount of income and leisure to exist.
3. Earlier retirement and greater access to full-time education depress participation rates. However, this may be offset by increases in female participation which reflect a decline in the amount of time it is economical for a wife to devote to the production of home goods.
4. The measurement of these effects is discussed in section 3.6, where the Slutsky equation is used, to show that it is not possible simply to add the income and substitution effects to yield the price effect.
5. On the 'male chauvinist' approach see Bowen and Finegan (1969) and Barth (1967).
6. The terms 'husband and wife' are used for convenience: they could refer to common law spouses. For the present, the Leuthold (1968) extension of two utility functions is ignored, but is discussed in section 3.7.
7. The structure of the model given is such that the cross-substitution effects are equal (see Ashenfelter and Heckman, 1974). The model implies that an income-compensated change in the husband's wage rate has the same effect on the wife's labour supply as a compensated change in the wife's rate has on the husband's supply. However, the cross-income effects are not equal so the total effects may differ.
8. It should be noted that in considering overtime, that with a single indifference curve and budget constraint, it is possible for two equilibrium points to occur. This is clearly not a problem in theory but when estimation is attempted a unique point is required. Ashworth and Ulph (1981a) have suggested that with choice this will never occur in practice.
9. The comparative statics now become much more complicated but it will often be the case that a person remains on the same segment. This eases the analysis considerably.

10. For example, it is not always clear whether 'normal hours' refers to arithmetic mean hours, or the modal number of hours.
11. Wales and Woodland (1976) have investigated housework and non-maket activities. For example, travelling to work falls into neither work not leisure and raises an additional problem.
12. Income from capital is being ignored here as a life-cycle model of accumulation would be required. Moreover, data for other members of the household are very difficult to obtain.
13. These problems are encountered in collecting data for all labour supply studies.
14. Brown and Dawson (1969) have many objections to the work of the Royal Commission.
15. Davidson (1953) in an earlier study of seven doctors reported this to be the case.
16. This is slightly dubious as retirement was a long way off for many of the sample. However, all of his sample stated they had already been forced by high taxes to delay retirement.
17. Break (1952) found a significant positive relationship which Fields and Stanbury (1971) could not replicate.
18. Given that the scope of this chapter is with the United Kingdom, the vast amount of fascinating work from the USA, in connection with various negative income tax 'experiments' has been omitted. An introduction to this work can be found in Godfrey (1975) and Brown (1980).
19. Kosters (1966) had two versions of his basic model, the one given and another using a non-employment income variable which was total family income less that income of the persons investigated. The substitution effect is still calculable but is not as straightforward.
20. In discussing the similarities between the Kosters (1966) and Mincer (1962) models, Ashenfelter and Heckman (1973) do not appear to distinguish clearly between full and whole income. They use whole income setting a limit of 2000 hours/year rather than 'potential permanent level of family income at zero leisure and home production' which would be full income. In a more recent analysis Ashenfelter and Heckman (1974) easily extend the model to husband and wife with the estimating equation.

$$\Delta L_i = \beta_1 \, \Delta w_m + \beta_2 \Delta w_f + \beta_3 \, \{L_m \Delta w_f + \Delta N\}$$

21. Even if a reasonable value of the participation substitution elasticity (0.1) is added to an elasticity of 0.2 for the hours component of labour supply, the resulting estimate of the

elasticity of total labour supply is still much smaller than the value obtained by Kalachek and Raines (1970).

22. This is not really serious because if there is a proportional tax in operation a given percentage increase in the gross income will be the same percentage increase in net income. If a logarithmic form is used (justified by Masters and Garfinkel, 1977) then a relatively small proportional tax will not bias the results. However, a progressive tax will make the wage rate coefficient smaller in absolute value than it ought to be. The income effect also is usually biased. It is too small in absolute value in the logarithmic form as the estimates are usually based on linear coefficients. For a fuller discussion see Masters and Garfinkel (1977).

23. The problem is the same for gross or net average wage rates.

24. Hall (1973) pioneered this approach using 'whole income after tax' at 2000 hours.

25. Greenhalgh and Mayhew (1981) have pointed out that the estimation method employed here may not be superior in certain respects. This is because tax rates are dependent on hours of work via the earnings limit (and because of the existence of various rates of full, part and overtime working) and so the marginal net wage is strongly endogenous. Hence studies which have been unable to construct the total budget constraint have used the gross wage approach; for example Greenhalgh (1979) and Hurd (1976).

26. Dickinson (1975) has employed this type of approach in the United States.

27. The adaptions by Greenhalgh (1979) have suggested this problem may be circumvented.

28. Ashworth and Ulph (1981a) are the only people really to attempt to deal with more than two segments of the budget constraint. The convex to the origin kink gives rise to possible estimating problems of two solutions where a unique maximum is required. They believe the problem of a discontinuous likelihood function is not crucial, as it is continuous at the places they are interested in.

29. Kalachek and Raines's (1970) results are still difficult to reconcile with other studies.

30. Wales and Woodland (1979) results bear out the Ashworth and Ulph (1981a) results but with their CES specification the change in the elasticity of substitution is not so marked. The price elasticity for Ashworth and Ulph's CES function is strange.

31. Greenhalgh (1979, 1980) and Hurd (1976) have proposed a different approach, using the gross wage, to circumvent the

endogeneity problem. It is conceptually simpler and enables tastes to be included. Zabalza *et al.* (1980) have a further technique which appears to be a compromise between the two approaches.

32. There is also a large literature on cyclical fluctuation in the participation rate but space precludes a lengthy discussion of this. Bowen and Finegan (1969) and Strand and Dernberg (1964) examine this area for the US.

33. See, for example, Bowen and Finegan (1969). A summary of the effects of fertility is given by Leibenstein (1974).

34. An alternative procedure (Boskin, 1973) is to estimate the probability of a potential worker being in the labour force and then estimate the expected hours conditional upon labour force participation. It should be noted that Heckman (1974) requires that the asking wage is a monotonically increasing function of hours and that the offered wage is the same for all hours, otherwise a unique equilibrium is in doubt.

35. This result is supported by Boskin (1973) who finds that income dominates for prime age men.

36. McGlone and Ruffell (1978, 1979) have considered women, but their main aim was to investigate preferences and how their inclusion above a strict dummy variable approach might affect the results found in the simpler model. They use a method like that of Brown *et al.* (1974b) and so their results are biased but the inclusion of preferences is of major import. Ashworth and Ulph (1981a) use so many data restrictions that their sample is very small. See Layard *et al.* (1980) for a further study of female labour supply.

37. Ashworth and Ulph (1981a) and Ruffell (1981) have shown by using an econometrically more sound method, the possible extent of the bias. Thus Greenhalgh's claim that she has circumvented much of the problem may be justified given her results.

38. See Rosen (1978) and Wales and Woodland (1976, 1977).

39. Leuthold's (1968) results are discussed by Green and Tella (1969).

40. The substitution effect will cause the husband to work harder, generating more income. This may have a further effect on the labour supply of the wife.

41. The problem of the error terms of the husband and wife being related and so causing bias can be partially circumvented using the method of seemingly unrelated least squares, as Leuthold (1979) has done.

42. Brown (1980) has pointed out that the labour supply data used by Atkinson and Stern (1979) are poor.

43. Glaister *et al.* (1981) have emphasized the problem of people near kinks; in the tax case this is the exemption level. Although changes in the rate of tax may have little effect, a change in the exemption level upwards could cause those below it to work harder and those above the kink to work less hard. What Glaister and his colleagues suggest is that for people near this kink the price effect may not be the relevant indicator but that the substitution elasticity should be used.

44. Taste variables include education, health and children. It has been shown that children appear to increase the utility of money in men.

References

Abbott, M. and Ashenfelter, O. (1976). Labour supply, commodity demand and the allocation of time. *Review of Economic Studies* **43,** 389–411

Ashenfelter, O. and Heckman, J. J. (1973). Estimating labour supply functions. In *Income Maintenance and Labour Supply* (ed. by G. Cain and H. Watts), pp. 265–278. Chicago; Markham

Ashenfelter, O. and Heckman, J. J. (1974). The estimation of income and substitution effects in a model of family labour supply. *Econometrica* **42,** 73–86

Ashworth, J. S. and Ulph, D. T. (1981a). Estimating labour supply with piecewise linear budget constraints. In *Taxation and Labour Supply* (ed. by C. V. Brown), pp. 53–68. London; George Allen and Unwin

Ashworth J. S. and Ulph, D. T. (1981b). On the structure of family labour supply decisions. In *Taxation and Labour Supply* (ed. by C. V. Brown), pp. 117–133. London; George Allen and Unwin

Atkinson, A. B. and Stern, N. H. (1979). On labour supply and commodity demands. In *Essays in the Theory and Measurement of Consumer Behaviour* (ed. by A. S. Deaton), pp. 265–296. Cambridge; Cambridge University Press

Barlow, R., Brayer, H. E. and Morgan, J. N. (1966). A survey of investment management and work behaviour among high-income individuals. *American Economic Review, Papers and Proceedings* **55,** 252–264

Barth, P. S. (1967). A cross-sectional analysis of labour force participation in Michigan. *Industrial and Labor Relations Review* **20,** 244–249

Becker, G. (1965). A theory of the allocation of time. *Economic Journal* **75,** 493–517

Block, F. (1973). The allocation of time to market and non-market work within a family unit. *Technical Report No. 114, Institute for Mathematical Studies in Social Science. Stanford*

Boskin, M. J. (1973). The economies of labour supply. In *Income Maintenance and Labour Supply* (ed. by G. Cain and H. Watts), pp. 163–181. Chicago; Markham

Bowen, W. G. and Finegan, T. A. (1969). *The Economics of Labour Force Participation.* Princeton; University Press

Break, G. F. (1952). Income taxes and incentives to work: an empirical study. *American Economic Review* **47,** 529–549

Brown, C. V. (1980). *Taxation and the Incentive to Work.* Oxford; Oxford University Press

Brown, C. V. and Dawson, D. A. (1969). *Personal Taxation Incentives and Tax Reform.* PEP Broadsheet **56**

Brown, C. V. and Jackson, P. M. (1978). *Public Sector Economics.* London; Martin Robertson

Brown, C. V. and Levin, E. (1974). The effects of income taxation on overtime: the results of a national survey. *Economic Journal* **84,** 833–848

Brown, C. V., Levin, E. and Ulph, D. T. (1974a). On taxation and labour supply. *University of Stirling Discussion Paper in Economics* No. 30

Brown, C. V., Levin, E. and Ulph, D. T. (1974b). On estimating labour supply. *University of Stirling Discussion Paper in Economics* No. 31

Brown, C. V., Levin, E. and Ulph, D. T. (1976). Estimates of labour hours supplied by married male workers in Great Britain. *Scottish Journal of Political Economy* **23,** 261–277

Burtless, G. and Hausman, J. (1978). The effect of taxation on labour supply – evaluating the Gary negative income experiment. *Journal of Political Economy* **86,** 1103–1130

Cain, G. G. (1966). *Married Women in the Labour Force.* Chicago; University of Chicago Press

Cain, G. G. and Dooley, M. D. (1976). Estimation of a model of labour supply, fertility and wages of married women. *Journal of Political Economy* **84,** S179–S199

Cain, G. G. and Watts, H. W. (eds.) (1973). *Income Maintenance and Labour Supply.* Chicago; Markham

Chatterjee, A. and Robinson, J. (1969). Effect of personal income tax on work effort: a sample survey. *Canadian Tax Journal* **17,** 211–220

Cohen, M. S., Rea, S. A. and Lerman, R. J. (1970). A micro-model of labour supply: US Bureau of Labour Statistics. *Staff Paper 4.* Washington; US Government Printing Office

Davidson, R. (1953). Income and incentive: the Doctor's viewpoint, *National Tax Journal* **6**, 293–297

Dickinson, J. G. (1975). The estimation of income–leisure structures for prime age males. *Ph.D. Dissertation.* University of Michigan

Fields, D. B. and W. T. Stanbury (1971). Income taxes and incentives to work: some additional empirical evidence. *American Economic Review* **61**, 435–443

Godfrey, L. (1975). *Theoretical and Empirical Aspects of the Effects of Taxation on the Supply of Labour.* Paris; OECD

Glaister, K. E., McGlone, A. and Ulph, D. T. (1981). Labour supply responses to tax changes – a simulation exercise for the UK. In *Taxation and Labour Supply* (ed. by C. V. Brown), pp. 163–188. London; George Allen and Unwin

Green, C. and Tella, A. (1969). Effects of nonemployment income and wage rates on the work incentives of the poor. *Review of Economics and Statistics* **51**, 399–418

Greenberg, D. H. and Kosters, M. (1973). Income guarantees and the working poor: the effect of income maintenance programs on the hours of work of male family heads. In *Income Maintenance and Labour Supply* (ed. by G. Cain and H. Watts), pp. 14–101. Chicago; Markham

Greenhalgh, C. (1977). A labour supply function for married women in Great Britain. *Economica* **44**, 249–267

Greenhalgh, C. A. (1979). Male labour force participation in Great Britain. *Scottish Journal of Political Economy* **26**, 275–286

Greenhalgh, C. A. (1980). Participation and hours of work of married women in Great Britain. *Oxford Economic Papers* **32**, 296–318

Greenhalgh, C. A. and Mayhew, K. (1981). Labour supply in Great Britain: theory and evidence. In *The Economics of the Labour Market* (ed. by Z. Hornstein, J. Grice and A. Webb), pp. 41–66. London; HMSO

Hall, R. E. (1973). Wages, income and hours of work in the US labour force. In *Income Maintenance and Labour Supply* (ed. by G. Cain and H. Watts), pp. 102–162. Chicago; Markham

Hamermesh, D. S. (1971). Interdependence in the labour market. *Princeton University Working Paper in Industrial Relations*

Heckman, J. J. (1974). Shadow prices, market wages and labour supply. *Econometrica* **42**, 679–694

Heckman, J. J. and McCurdy, T. (1980). A life-cycle model of female labour supply. *Review of Economic Studies* **47**, 47–74

Holland, D. H. (1977). The effect of taxation on incentives in higher income groups. In *Fiscal Policy and Labour Supply*, Institute for Fiscal Studies, pp. 41–54

Hurd, M. (1976). The estimation of non-linear labour supply functions with taxes from a truncated sample. *Research Memorandum* No. 36, Centre for the Study of Welfare Policy, Stanford Research Institute

Kalachek, E. D. and Raines, F. Q. (1970). Labour supply of lower income workers in President's commission on income maintenance programs. *Technical Studies*. Washington; US Government Printing Office

Killingsworth, M. R. (1973). Neo-classical labor supply models: a survey of recent literature on determinants of labour supply at the micro level. (mimeo). Fisk University Nashville

Killingsworth, M. R. (1976). Must a negative income tax reduce labour supply? A study of the family's allocation of time. *Journal of Human Resources* **11**, 354–365

Kosters, M. (1968). Income and substitution effects in a family labor supply model. *Report P3339*. Santa Monica; Rand Corporation

Layard, P. R. G., Barton, M. and Zabalza, A. (1980). Married women's participation and hours. *Economica* **47**, 51–72

Leibenstein, H. (1974). An interpretation of the economic theory of fertility. *Journal of Economic Literature* **12**, 457–479

Leuthold, J. H. (1968). An empirical study of family income transfers and the work decision of the poor. *Journal of Human Resources* **3**, 312–323

Leuthold, J. H. (1979). Taxes and the two-earner family: impact on the work decision. *Public Finance Quarterly* **17**, 147–161

Masters, S. and Garfinkel, I. (1977). *Estimating the Labour in Supply Effects of Income-Maintenance Alternatives*. London: Academic Press

McGlone, A. and Ruffell, R. J. (1978). Preferences and the labour supply of married women. *University of Stirling Discussion Paper in Economics,* No. 62

McGlone, A. and Ruffell, R. J. (1979). On preferences and labour supply of married women. *Economic Letters* **1**, 167–168

Mincer, J. (1962). Labor force participation of married women. In National Bureau of Economic Research *Aspects of Labor Economics,* pp. 63–105. Princeton; University Press

Rosen, H. (1976). Tax illusion and the labour supply of married women. *Review of Economics and Statistics* **58**, 167–172

Rosen, H. S. (1978). The measurement of excess burden with explicit utility functions. *Journal of Political Economy* **86**, 121–135

Royal Commission on the Taxation of Profits and Income (1954), Second Report. Cmnd 9105. London; HMSO

Ruffell, R. J. (1981). Direct estimation of labour supply functions with piecewise linear budget constraints. In *Taxation and Labour Supply* (ed. by C. V. Brown), pp. 101–116. London; George Allen and Unwin

Strand, K. T. and Dernberg, T. F. (1964). Cyclical variations in civilian labour force participation. *Review of Economics and Statistics* **46**, 378–391

Wales, T. J. and Woodland, A. D. (1976). Estimation of household utility functions and labour supply responses. *International Economic Review* **17**, 397–410

Wales, T. J. and Woodland, A. D. (1977). Estimation of the allocation of time for work, leisure and housework. *Econometrica* **45**, 115–132

Wales, T. J. and Woodland, A. D. (1979). Labour supply and progressive taxes. *Review of Economic Studies* **46**, 83–96

Zabalza, A., Pissarides, C. A. and Piachaud, D. (1980). Social security, life-cycle saving and retirement. In *Income Distribution: The Limits to Redistribution* (ed. by D. Collard, R. Lecomber and M. Slater), pp. 83–99. Colston Papers No. 31. Bristol; Scientechnica

Appendix: Econometric studies of labour supply

TABLE 3.2 Labour supply elasticities for men

Author	Data source	Demographic group	Estimation method[e]	Own price elasticity[b]	Spouse's price elasticity	Income elasticity	Substitution elasticity
Ashenfelter and Heckman (1973)	Survey of Economic Opportunity 1967	American married men, wives not working	1			−0.27[a]	0.12
Ashenfelter and Heckman (1974)	US Census 1960	American male labour force participation rates for standard metropolitan statistical areas (SMSAs)	1			−0.10[a]	0.06
Ashworth and Ulph (1981)	Stirling SSRC 1971	British married men below 65, weekly-paid, working at least 8 hours	2 with separate other income	−0.001		−0.02	0.31
			2 with other income in intercept	0.06		−0.02	0.15
			3	−0.07		−0.101	0.50

Study	Data	Sample	Model				
			5 Leuthold model	−1.413	1.261	−0.03	
			5 neoclassical model with preference variables	−0.03	−0.16	−0.03	2.17 / 0.75[g]
			5 Leuthold-type model with preference variables	−1.00	0.87	−0.03	0.47 / 1.48[g]
Boskin (1973)	Survey of Economic Opportunity 1967	American married men 20–59	1			−0.17[a](white) / −0.06[a](black)	0.10 (white) / 0.00 (black)
Brown, Levin and Ulph (1974b)	Stirling SSRC 1971	British married men below 65, weekly-paid, working at least 8 hours	1	−28.5[c]		−0.22[c]	−18.1[c]
			2 using actual hours intercept	−25.4[c]		−0.56[c]	0.54[c]
			2 using intercept from kink hours	−16.1[c]		−0.37[c]	1.3[c]

Notes: see p.90

TABLE 3.2 – *continued*

Author	Data source	Demographic group	Estimation method[e]	Own price elasticity[b]	Spouse's price elasticity	Income elasticity[a]	Substitution elasticity
Brown Levin and Ulph (1976)	Stirling SSRC 1971	British married men below 65, weekly-paid, working at least 8 hours	2	−16.4[c]		−0.68[c]	16.4[c]
				−0.18		−0.01	0.18
Cohen, Rea and Lerman (1970)	Consumer Price Survey 1965	American males 22–54	1			−0.08 to 0.03	negative
Dickinson (1975)		American married men, 25–60 (white – wage $3.25–4.30)	2	−50.5[c]		−0.101[c]	170.0[c]
				−0.10		negative	0.133
Greenberg and Kosters (1973)	Survey of Economic Opportunity 1967	American married men less than 62 Income less than $15000	1			−0.15 to −0.34 (author's preference −0.29)	0.02 to 0.20 (author's preference 0.20)
Greenhalgh (1979)	Census 1971	British married men (participation rates)	4	0.09	−0.08	−0.07	

Hall (1973)	Survey of Economic Opportunity 1967	American married men 20–59 with predicted wage per hour $3.00	2		white -0.24 to -0.51^a black -0.12 to -0.28^a	white -0.20 to 0.39 (weighted on 0.06) black -0.68 to 0.25 (weighted on -0.1)
Kalacheck and Raines (1970)	Consumer Price Survey 1966	American males 24–61 with income $8500	1		-0.31 to -0.33^a	0.86 (white) 0.96 (black)
Masters and Garfinkel (1977)	Survey of Economic Opportunity 1967	American prime age males	1	-0.16	0.10	-0.08
Ruffell (1981)	Stirling SSRC 1971	British married men below 65, weekly-paid, working at least 8 hours	2	-0.07	-0.05	0.09
			3	-0.07	-0.03	0.04
			3^d minimum distance approach	-0.05	-0.02	0.03
Zabalza, Pissarides and Piachaud (1980)	OPCS Survey 1977	Older British men	4	0.06	-0.26	

Notes: see p.90

TABLE 3.3 Labour supply elasticities for women

Author	Data source	Demographic group	Estimation method[e]	Own price elasticity[b]	Spouse's price elasticity	Income elasticity[a]	Substitution elasticity
Ashenfelter and Heckman (1974)	US Census 1960	American married women; labour force participation rates for SMSA	1			−0.28[a]	1.2
Ashworth and Ulph (1981)	Stirling SSRC 1971	British married women below 60, working at least 8 hours	2 with separate other income	−0.21		0.004	−0.23
			2 with other income in intercept	−0.09		−0.10	−0.04
			3	0.63		−0.35	0.84
			5 Leuthold model	−3.37	3.91	0.0001	
			5 neoclassical model with preference variables	−1.18	1.73	−0.001	−1.14
							1.81[g]

	Data source	Sample	5 Leuthold type model with preference variables				
			−4.46	5.05	0.02	−5.02 6.41[g]
Greenhalgh (1977)	New Earnings Survey 1971	British married women, 16–59	4	1.10 to 1.35[f]	−0.88	−0.26 to 0.32	1.36 to 1.67
Greenhalgh (1980)	General House-hold Survey 1971	British married women, 16–59 (participation rates)	4	0.36[f]	−0.45		0.43
		British married women workers, 16–59	4	0.72[f]	−0.22		0.80
		Total supply		1.08[f]	−0.67		1.19
Hall (1973)	Survey of Economic Opportunity 1967	American married women, 21–59	2			2.1[a] (white) 1.4[a] (black)	white 1.6 to 2.7 weighted over 2.5 black −0.59 to 3.7 weighted over 0.26
Kalacheck and Raines (1970)	Consumer Price Survey 1965	American women, 21–64 from low income families	1			−0.41 to −0.75	white 0.76 to 0.84 black 0.14 to 0.58

Notes: see p.90

TABLE 3.3 – *continued*

Author	Data source	Demographic group	Estimation method[e]	Own price elasticity[b]	Spouse's price elasticity	Income elasticity[a]	Substitution elasticity
Ruffell (1981)	Stirling SSRC 1971	British married women under 60, working at least 8 hours	2	0.00		−0.11	0.04
			3	0.43		−0.25	0.51
			3[d] minimum distance approach	0.72		−0.16	0.77
Zabalza, Pissarides and Piachaud (1980)	OPCS Survey 1977	Older British women	4	0.42		−0.44	

Notes to tables

a The income elasticity is in these cases the total income elasticity, which is the conventionally measured income elasticity weighted by the proportion of earnings to income.
b The price elasticity is given only where relevant to the text.
c There are 'effects', not elasticities.
d Ruffell gives three sets of results; this is the central value.
e Estimation approaches are
  1 – average wage/true non-employment income;
  2 – marginal wage/'as if' intercept;
  3 – construction of total budget constraint;
  4 – adapted versions of 1;
  5 – family model of 'non-chauvinistic' type.
f Gross wage elasticity
g Gross substitution elasticity

Chapter 4

Occupational choice and investment in human capital

4.1 Introduction

In the mid-1970s about 11.5 million men and 7.5 million women in the working population had received some training since entering the labour force. This represented over 60% of the working population; three-quarters of the men and half of the women. All had received some formal education before entering the labour force but, as with training, the pattern of education over the life cycle, its overall duration and the methods of study varied greatly among individuals.

This chapter deals with the economics of decisions about education, training and mobility, with particular reference to occupational choice. Such decisions directly affect labour force participation in both the short and long run. The rise in educational participation rates during the 1950s and 1960s had important consequences for the age distribution and qualifications of young entrants to the labour force. This had both quantitative and qualitative implications for employers. It affected their ability to recruit from young age groups and required changes in training schemes. The supply of training opportunities is still dominated by employers, notwithstanding the increasing involvement of the state during the 1970s. Since training is provided to ensure an adequate supply of skilled people to the organizations concerned, variations in the number of training opportunities are intimately related, through recruitment and lay-off activities, to changes in the demand for different skills. So from the point of view of young people the training opportunities available to them were much affected by employers' reactions to the state of the economy, rather than some notion of equity in access to training, as was the case in education. In addition, the ability of employers to adjust to new conditions in the labour market for young people influences the quality as well as the quantity of training opportunities available. Disappointment with the allegedly selfish and short-sighted attitudes of some firms gave rise to government intervention, initially in the form of the Industrial Training Act of 1964. However, there was also criticism of the education system, by employers especially. This criticism partly concerned the level of basic attainment in literacy and numeracy achieved by young people, and partly the effects of schools in the socialization of young people. It was argued that schools and colleges were tending to reinforce, or even implant, attitudes and occupational preferences which made young people unsympathetic towards industry and particularly the more technical occupations.

These points raise two of the main themes that recur throughout the debate on manpower and educational policy. One relates to the supply of training opportunities and draws attention to the so-called 'poaching' of skilled-labour by employers who refuse to do their 'fair share'. The other relates to the demand for training opportunities and charges educational institutions with having distorted the process of educational and occupational choice by young people and having paved the way to rejection of 'real jobs' in the wealth-creating sector of the economy.

During the 1970s the labour market situation changed dramatically from the one envisaged when the Employment and Training Act of 1973 was passed. Reports of labour shortages persisted but the preoccupation with skill bottlenecks, which had so characterized the boom of 1972–1973 and influenced the Act, gave way gradually to a wider concern with labour market problems and a complex mix of policies designed to deal with them. The primacy given by policy-makers to satisfying the demands for skilled manpower as expressed by employers was replaced by a somewhat more critical appreciation of labour market processes; one which belatedly began to look at the variety of factors determining the supply of skills.

The focus of this chapter is therefore upon those aspects of research and policy connected with investment in human capital which have tended to be neglected but are now becoming increasingly important as the education and training systems face prospects of high levels of unemployment well into the medium term. The two subjects which receive most attention in what follows are the educational and occupational choices leading up to first entry to the labour market. These are the main determinants of the demand for education and training. Reference is also made to the determinants of the supply of training and the factors that influence changes of occupation during working life. The notion of occupational choice is introduced in section 4.2, followed by three illustrations of certain problems of analysis and policy. Section 4.3 then examines explanations of investment in education and training that arise out of human capital theory, summarizing the evidence available for Britain. Section 4.4 briefly introduces some theoretical and empirical matters which relate more closely to job search strategies and occupational mobility but have implications for initial occupational choice. Finally, section 4.5 returns to questions of educational and training policy. The rationale for government intervention and its effectiveness in practice are considered in terms of equity and efficiency in the labour market and the general state of the economy.

4.2 Occupational choice and entry to the labour market

There is an extensive sociological literature on occupational choice and much of it has been influenced by three early American studies[1]. The multi-disciplinary research strategy adopted by Blau *et al.* (1956) has most affinity with the treatments of occupational choice provided by economists. These authors distinguish between the formation of occupational preferences by the individual and actual entry into a particular occupation. Occupational choice is then a *process* influenced by the individual's hierarchy of preferences and his expectations of success. Economic and sociological as well as psychological variables are expected to determine the outcome of this process and Blau *et al.* (1956) believe that, having used their framework to guide the selection of relevant variables, it is an empirical question as to which turn out to be most important in different circumstances. In contrast Ginsberg *et al.* (1951) concentrate upon occupational choice as the formation of preferences whilst Super (1953) includes the whole process of entry into an occupation during which the development and modification of preferences cannot be distinguished from the compromises made by the individual when faced with limited opportunities.

There has been surprisingly little economic analysis of occupational choice in Britain, especially when considering the substantial research activity concerned first with investment in human capital and then with labour supply[2]. Changes in the labour force participation of young people, though significant, have been treated as a subsidiary area of labour supply modelling, since their effects on aggregate supply have been dwarfed by the dramatic rise in the participation of married women. There has perhaps been a tendency to regard the main determinants of these changes for young people as self-evident; but the explanation of falling labour force participation rates among young people is no more straight-forward than that of the rise observed for married women.

To some extent the small amount of econometric modelling of occupational choice is a consequence of the lack of data. But for Britain it also reflects a tendency for economists interested in empirical labour market research to work either at the disaggregate level (for example with particular local labour markets or occupational or industrial groups) stressing the interplay of market forces and institutional factors, or to work at high levels of aggregation (for example, modelling wage inflation or the employment–output relationship). No strong tradition of modelling quite specific, though still large, sectors of the labour market has been established in which the insights of microeconomic studies and the techniques of more aggregate analysis are combined.

During the 1970s progress has however been made in the direction of modelling labour markets (estimating demand, supply and wage relationships) with the aim of examining the effects of alternative economic policies. The availability of national survey data has also made possible the econometric analysis of cross-sectional data containing individual information on personal, social and economic characteristics. The results add new insights which should help the model-building process, though there has perhaps been some exaggeration of its potential usefulness for time-series forecasting. Regrettably the emergence of the New Earnings Survey, the General Household Survey and the EEC Labour Force Survey, all providing individual as well as group data, has been accompanied by a reduction in reliable time-series data on the occupational and age structure of employment. This has hampered the development of formal models of specific occupational–industrial labour markets incorporating explicit treatments of supply and demand.

Problems of analysis and policy

There has been a great deal of government policy concerned with education and training, and much of it has embodied quite strong implicit assumptions about the nature of occupational choice. In policy discussion there has been a tendency to blur the distinction between the labour market and the market for educational and training opportunities. Indeed the notion of the latter market has hardly been discernible in debates about the provision of post-compulsory education and industrial training. The sector of the market for educational and training opportunities which is dominated by non-profit-making suppliers whose main activity is education and/or training is simply regarded as part of education. The sector dominated by profit-making suppliers whose main activity is not in fact the provision of education and training but the production of goods or other services is regarded as part of the labour market. Concern is then expressed over the failure of the education system to 'serve the needs' of the labour market and over the failure of the labour market to ensure an adequate supply of those skills for which it is responsible. In order to illustrate the types of problem that arise, and the importance of understanding the process of educational and occupational choice in the formation of policies, three examples are discussed below.

The labour market for young people

Faced with falling labour force participation among young people, rising unemployment and rising relative pay it may be argued that participation has dropped because young people are discouraged by high unemployment, and that the latter is caused by excessive increases in the relative price of young labour. But such a simple model of labour supply does not provide a convincing explanation of these phenomena. It would require an unrealistic combination of substitution and income effects plus substantial changes in tastes, raising the disutility of work. A more satisfactory account of developments in the labour market for young people would give the role of pacemaker not to a sequence of excessive pay awards for the younger age groups but a perception of the benefits of post-compulsory education and increasing opportunities to participate in it. If tastes have changed it is not so much through an increasing distaste for work on the part of young people but through an increasing desire for education.

The question remains of the degree to which the rise in unemployment among young people may be attributable to excessive increases in their pay. Numerous institutional factors can be advanced to explain the marked increases in relative pay in the 1970s. However Makeham (1980) shows that, for both males and females, changes in relative pay make no significant contribution to explanations of the post-war rise in unemployment of young people (which is strongly correlated with the rise in adult unemployment).

Prior to the dramatic rise in unemployment at the beginning of the 1980s there was a considerable reduction in the growth of educational participation. The increase in unemployment led to the development of a host of special employment measures. These, particularly the Youth Opportunities Programme (YOP), provided a new light by which to judge traditional modes of education and training for working life. The mixture of further education, vocational training and work experience provoked questions not only of the value of YOP itself but also of the way general education, skill acquisition and occupational choice are handled in Britain. If unemployment remains high, as it has done and will probably continue to do so during the 1980s should more young people be induced to stay on in full-time education? Is the levelling of educational participation rates an indication that some students are better served by new institutional arrangements for providing education and training? Would these amount to a partial 'by-passing' of the labour market for young people by replacing a large number of present employment contracts with what would amount to training contracts heavily influenced by state assistance to both employees and employers? However ingenious are the attempts to devise new programmes, will the process of skill acquisition and occupational choice for many young people be undermined by lack of sense of purpose as high levels of unemployment continue?

Skilled craftsmen

Central to the development of training policy in Britain has been a concern to avoid skill constraints on economic growth (as reviewed by Briscoe *et al.*, 1980). Much attention has been devoted to skilled trades in the engineering and construction sectors which are particularly faced with uncertainties about future product demand and long training periods. These problems combine to form the classic case with which manpower policy is expected to cope. Policy intervention through the Industrial Training Boards has been conceived primarily in terms of judgements not about the desired level of supply of training opportunities but the desired level of demand for employees to undergo training. The manpower agencies have been at their most confident in trying to influence the recruitment decisions of employers rather than promote the supply of high quality training opportunities independently of employment decisions. Despite the efforts of the manpower agencies, industry has been slow to modernize its craft training and to provide adequate incentives by way of pay and other conditions of employment, including the removal of differences in status which act to the disadvantage of manual workers. Difficulties of attracting suitable apprentice recruits reflected the difficulties of retaining trained craftsmen, a situation which was exacerbated by large fluctuations in the recruitment of apprentices in the absence of good manpower planning.

On the other hand the demand for skilled manual workers probably fell for a decade before the severe unemployment situation of the late 1970s and early 1980s. The skill shortages in the boom of 1972–1973 and their persistence to some degree even during subsequent years of rising unemployment have drawn attention to the lack of flexibility in the training system and the need for policy to support schemes providing for the training and re-training of adults as well as the initial training of young people. Changes in technology and industrial structure over the long term suggest that prospects for skilled manual employment are much less promising than they were three decades ago. The evidence indicates that the main constraint on the supply of newly trained craftsmen was not the supply of willing recruits four years or so previously, but the demand for recruits by employers.

Scientists and technologists

One of the most controversial aspects of educational and occupational choice is that concerned with the education and training of scientists and technologists. As in the case of engineering craftsmen there was some evidence suggesting that the approach to science and industry in schools made life difficult for employers seeking to attract able young people into the more technical occupations. Yet the labour market strategies of employers seemed to be equally at fault.

The basic criticism of the education system derived from the assumption of a dynamic excess demand for people in technical occupations together with a belief, not that the education system had failed to *bias* children sufficiently in favour of relevant subjects and occupations, but that it was not giving science and technology a *fair chance* in the general educational process. Thus a particular view of the state of the post-war labour market is combined with an objection in principle to unbalanced education and its influence on occupational choice. The latter becomes especially important when, as has been argued by some sociologists, attainment is a more important determinant of subject choice than is interest (Butler, 1968). If subjects are chosen with a view to 'batting from strength' then the information on which strength is judged needs to correct for differences in the effectiveness and intensity of teaching given.

If this diagnosis is accepted it suggests that distortions to the perceptions of aspiring students should be removed as a matter of priority and, in case this proves a difficult task, the higher education system should be prevented from legitimizing the undesirable pattern of student demand through supplying courses intended to satisfy it. However, from higher education's point of view this involves the risk of reducing demand even further by adjusting the pattern of subject provision to meet some notion of economic need only to find that the new opportunities are not sufficiently attractive to students. This is all the more important when, with stable age participation rates, demographic changes will reduce the number of full-time students to about 70% of the 1981 level by 1995[3].

There are however strong grounds for doubting the efficacy of this kind of policy as a means of boosting the supply of the *more able* scientists and technologists. Scepticism about the thesis was strengthened not so much by a rebuttal of the 'unbalanced education' argument but by the accumulation of evidence against the notion that it was impossible to produce more scientists and technologists than the economy actually demanded. When it became clear that the relative pay of qualified scientists and technologists had deteriorated, it was recognized that if employers were not sufficiently convinced of the value of these skills to raise their pay and status, then there was probably little the higher education system could do to alter the supply position very much. So what began as a case of biased occupational choice became a case of deficient labour market operation against a background of industrial failure which held down the demand for highly qualified technological manpower.

4.3 Human capital: investment in education and training

Although the general ideas behind the notion of human capital emerged early in the history of economic thought, they began to be developed much more formally in the late 1950s. Until then there had been a tendency to treat the demand for post-compulsory education as the demand for a consumption good[4]. This was so even though it was recognized that skill acquisition involved an investment in human capital, that the extent of the investment by the individual was measured by the earnings forgone during training, and that the benefit obtained was the additional lifetime income derived from using the human capital created.

Thus despite the fact that the elements of an economic theory of educational and occupational choice had existed for some time, the corresponding field of empirical analysis was left to other social scientists. Since the variables that most interested them were more likely to change substantially only over the long term, convincing explanations of variations in educational participation and occupational choice on a shorter time-scale were not likely to emerge and the methodological approach was in any case not geared to estimating empirical models.

Human capital theory not only introduced a more rigorous approach to education and training but emerged in a methodological climate which stressed its predictive aspirations. However these have been somewhat tempered because of the difficulties of testing theories of educational demand when in many countries observed enrolments are partly supply constrained because governments are so heavily involved in providing as well as financing education.

The other aspect of human capital theory with which this section is concerned is the light it sheds on decisions about training: more precisely that form of investment in human capital which is undertaken, *usually* when the individual is in employment, with a view to enhancing the productivity of the individual through the acquisition of particular skills. The spectrum of education and training is very broad and the elements of it merge together rather than have sharply defined boundaries. The force of the seminal contribution by Becker (1964) came through his introduction of a distinction between 'general' and 'specific' investments.

> Completely general training increases the marginal productivity of trainees by exactly the same amount in the firms providing the training as in other firms . . . . Completely specific training can be defined as training that has no effect on the productivity of trainees that would be useful in other firms. Much on-the-job training is neither completely specific nor completely general but increases productivity more in the firms providing it and falls within the definition of specific training. (p. 18).

Since firms do not have property rights in the skills of their employees, completely general training would not then be financed by employers except as an activity profitable in itself. The costs of specific training could be shared between employer and employee in several ways. The lack of empirical work on the demand for and supply of training opportunities stems partly from the difficulty of establishing the costs and circumstances of training in these respects. It also reflects the strongly neoclassical perspective adopted which tends to ignore market imperfections, encouraging the estimation of reduced form equations for wages on the assumption of a competitive labour market and distracting attention away from estimating demand and supply functions.

If Becker's approach is determinedly neoclassical, it is also rather lop-sided. References to the determinants of the demand for training by employees (or the supply of recruits to jobs with training involved) are in fact confined largely to places where the reactions of workers must be taken into account in explaining the strategic positions of firms[5].

Finally, in both education and training, the *private* and *social* returns will usually differ. Empirical evidence for the UK and its policy implications are discussed in section 4.5.

Educational and occupational choice

The standard approach to the econometric study of educational or occupational choice involves ordinary least squares regression analysis in which a dependent variable such as the number of young people entering a course of education or training (or the proportion of the age group doing so) is related to a set of independent variables. Usually the variables are transformed by taking logarithms so that the estimated coefficients in the log –linear regression are direct measures of the relevant elasticities. Logarithmic transformation is not often a crucial determinant of overall explanatory power in this field but is used for convenience.

Human capital theory asserts that a major determinant of the personal demand for opportunities to invest in education and training is the private rate of return to such investment. The empirical analysis of occupational choice then requires some measure (or combination of measures) of the rate of return to different occupations. In behavioural terms the measure used should reflect the state of affairs perceived by the decision-maker. It is usual to suppose that in reviewing the information available individuals base their expectations of future earnings particularly on the observed earnings of older people already in the occupation concerned. Similarly, estimates of forgone earnings and other costs of training are based on current information. Thus it may be assumed that occupational and educational choices are influenced by cross-sectional information about the earnings of individuals in different age groups. Individuals' decisions will of course also depend on their optimism (or pessimism) concerning their ability to succeed in any occupation, which affects their expected *relative* position in the distribution of each age group. It is however usual to ignore this aspect and to attempt to measure expected average private rates of return (the discount rate at which the present values of expected costs and returns are equalized)[6]. Because of the great difficulties involved, the estimation of rates of return has become a substantial research area in itself. Time series of rates of return are not easily obtainable for many occupations, so it is often necessary to make extremely simplistic assumptions about the profile of average earnings with age[7].

Apart from some measure of the return to making the particular educational or occupational choice under investigation, account must be taken of the relative probability of finding and keeping a job. Normally a relative unemployment term is included for this purpose, assuming that recent unemployment rates are indicative of relative future prospects. Other variables which may be regarded a priori as influencing the decision will depend on the study concerned but indices of structural change affecting the jobs to which an educational choice might lead are an obvious example. The preamble to empirical analysis sometimes employs a degree of theorizing in probabilistic terms followed by the specification of demand functions for education and training (or occupational supply functions) which have a distinctly familiar look and intuitive appeal. Thus relative wage and unemployment variables appear and, where the dependent variable is specified as a *level* rather than the *proportion* of the population 'at risk' of making the decision in question, these are joined by a measure of the relevant population variable.

Educational participation

The range of estimates of private average rates of return obtained for years during the 1960s is 7–13% for 'A' levels or equivalent and 11–15% for first degrees or equivalent. Rates of return to undertaking degree level courses in (at least) science and engineering appear to have declined slightly in the last half of the 1960s, and more rapidly in the early 1970s. The private average rates of return to becoming an engineer and to becoming a scientist had both fallen to about 9% by 1976/77 from about 14% a decade earlier[8]. Such information has clear implications, according to human capital theory, about what should have happened to educational participation rates[9].

Prior to the 1970s any attempt to model the demand for post-compulsory education in Britain would have been undermined by concern over whether the observed data reflected changes in demand at all and, even if they did, the difficulty of producing reliable estimates when the educational participation rate exhibited minor counter-cyclical variations about a strong time trend. However the 1970s witnessed a marked reduction in the growth of the participation rate. It may therefore be suggested that, in rough and ready terms at least, 'demand' for education (rather than the supply of places) was being observed. Pissarides (1981a) takes advantage of this to estimate a model of the proportion of the 16-year-old age group in full-time education. Notwithstanding some theoretical and econometric difficulties, the results provide a striking explanation of changes in the 18-year-old staying-on rate for both boys and girls.

Pissarides's model links the staying-on rate to starting salaries and their rates of growth (which together are intended to capture 'lifetime earnings'), measures of unemployment, a variable to represent permanent income, and an index of structural change affecting opportunities for educated manpower. The coefficients on the first two variables are statistically significant and have the expected signs. The staying-on rate was also shown to be strongly and positively related to the general level of unemployment in the economy but not significantly related to other unemployment variables tested[10].

The potential value of such analysis is illustrated by Pissarides in his examination of the main factors determining the slow-down in participation rates for males in the two periods 1969–1972 and 1975–1978. For boys the actual staying-on rates rose by 1% in 1969–1972 and fell by 1% in 1975–1978 after rising at a trend rate of 5% per annum during 1955–1969. During the first period the fall in the average starting salary of more educated people relative to that of school-leavers, who enter the labour force directly, is the main explanatory factor. During the second period it is the fall in real per capita consumption (the proxy for permanent income) which most affects educational participation, followed by a continuing fall in relative earnings; but the latter is more than offset by the effect of the rise in general unemployment. In both periods the relative growth rate of the earnings of educated people rises and hence helps to support the staying-on rate while starting salary changes bring it down.

The decision to stay in full-time education beyond the school-leaving age may of course be reviewed by the individual on an almost continuous basis. The decision to remain long enough to obtain qualifications for entry to higher education (universities, polytechnics and other institutions providing degree-level courses) and then to seek entry is the next aspect considered here. Strictly speaking the 'decision' involves two stages but there has been a close correlation since the mid-1960s between changes in the qualified leaver rate (the number of students obtaining two or more 'A' levels as a percentage of the relevant age group) and changes in the higher education entry rate (entrants to higher education as a percentage of the same age group as for the qualified leaver rate). Both have remained virtually constant during the 1970s at about 15 and 10% respectively, after increasing substantially during the 1960s. Whilst changes in the labour market for young people relative to that for new graduates, or changes in educational policy, could break the close connection between the two rates in future, the past lack of variation provides little scope for estimating models of the higher education entry rate which incorporate variables in addition to the qualified leaver rate.

An analysis of changes in the qualified leaver rate has been made by Pissarides (1981b). As might be expected, a major influence is the staying-on rate two years before (the elasticity is 0.67). However two other variables are also important – per capita consumption and the ratio of the (estimated) present value of earnings of new graduates to that of pupils leaving school at age 16. The general rate of unemployment does not exert any signifi-cant separate effect upon the qualified leaver rate. Pissarides shows that the levelling off of the qualified leaver rate during the 1970s was a consequence of the slower growth of the staying-on rate plus the independent effect of two factors which, together with rising unemployment, were themselves largely responsible for the change in staying-on rate: the fall in graduate earnings relative to the earnings of those who leave full-time education earlier and the slower growth of 'permanent income'.

Some further comments are in order. First, the qualified leaver rate is assumed to be demand determined (conditional on passing two 'A' levels). Secondly, the independent variables in the regres-sion analysis are highly correlated. Thirdly, the staying-on rate is assumed not to be a function of *expectations* about the ultimate chances of entrance to higher education (where the entry rate is itself implicitly regarded as demand determined). Fourthly, it is not clear how much better the relative present value measure performs than would other simpler measures of the returns to education. The results are certainly indicative of economic respon-siveness but, because of this last point, do not support human capital theory as strongly as do the results for the staying-on rate.

One element of the present value calculation is the student maintenance grant, and it would be of particular policy interest to know whether changes in its real value have a significant effect on entrance to higher education. Unfortunately the lack of variation between the qualified leaver rate and the higher education entrance rate makes empirical analysis of this issue very difficult[11].

Subject choice and economic incentives

There is a small number of British studies of the responsiveness to economic incentives of the pattern of subject choice in post-compulsory education. For example Klinov–Malul (1971) provides an early attempt to link enrolments to relative earnings. She examined university entrants by subject of first preference in order to get closer to an indicator of the demand for places than is provided by total actual enrolments by subject. The study was confined to a pooled cross-sectional time-series regression analysis using the percentages of students entering each of 10 science and engineering subject groups over a four-year period as dependent variables. This transformation of the dependent variable is not justified a priori and the results show no significant relationship between changes in the distribution of students amongst these subject groups and the measure used to estimate changes in relative present values of future income.

An analysis of what may be termed 'successful' student choice has been conducted by Bosworth and Wilson (1980) who examine the flow of newly qualified scientists and engineers[12]. They also assume that this is determined by the demand for related higher education rather than its supply. Bosworth and Wilson (1980) report regression results relating the flow of new scientists or engineers to the number of people qualifying for entry to higher education and the average earnings of professional scientists or engineers relative to average male manual earnings. The elasticity with respect to the number of qualifiers is not significantly different from unity, indicating that without changes in relative earnings new scientists and engineers would constitute constant proportions of qualified leavers. The relative earnings elasticities for scientists and engineers were 0.6 and 1.3 respectively, suggesting that the latter are more responsive to market conditions than the former[13]. It is argued that the reductions in relative earnings for both groups during 1960–1977 are mainly responsible for large reductions in the proportion of total qualifiers who eventually gain science and engineering qualifications (from about 19% in the early 1960s to 15% in 1976/77 in the case of scientists, and from 23 to 10% in the case of engineers).

Specific occupational choice

A further aspect of educational and occupational choice is the choice of specific occupation following an education which could be exploited in different ways. Zabalza (1979b) explains changes in the proportion of graduates seeking entry to teaching in terms of parameters of the relative age–earnings profiles and a measure of unemployment amongst new graduates. It is assumed that during the period of analysis (1963–1971) there was a general shortage of teachers in all five subject groups into which they are classified, so all observations are on the supply curve. Zabalza then conducts a pooled time-series/cross-sectional regression, splitting the sample according to sex, and experimenting with three treatments of relative earnings: relative average wages alone, relative starting salaries alone and relative starting salaries plus the estimated relative slope differential. The results show the usefulness of the third method of incorporating relative earnings, particularly in the comparison of elasticities for males and females. These were 2.5 and 0.3, respectively, for relative average wages; 3.6 and 2.2 for relative starting salaries alone and 3.2 and 3.4 for relative starting salaries together with 1.7 and 0.6 for the relative slope differentials. Thus the responsiveness of male and female graduates to relative starting salaries does not differ significantly but the shorter average working life envisaged by women makes them less responsive to changes in prospective salaries. The overall explanatory power of the equations is not much affected by the choice of earnings variables but the behavioural interpretation is improved. Unemployment among new graduates has a significant positive elasticity of roughly 0.3 for males and females.

The supply of young people to an industry

The engineering industry attracts substantial numbers of young people for employment, with various commitments to provide training. One of the major industrial investments in human capital is the training of young people as engineering craftsmen. The models specified by Lindley (1974) to explain the total supply of young people to engineering and the supply of apprentice recruits are similar to those used to deal with educational participation. The level of apprentice recruitment was related in a log–linear regression to the total number of young people under 18 entering employment in Britain (the population at risk of recruitment), proxies for the average earnings of apprentices and qualified craftsmen in engineering relative to those of youths and adult manual workers not entering skilled engineering trades, and unemployment of engineering craftsmen relative to total unemployment in the economy. The elasticity of recruitment with respect to relative adult earnings was found to be about 2, and with respect to relative unemployment about -0.3. Neither the variable representing the aggregate supply of young people to the labour market nor the variable representing the relative earnings of apprentices contributed significantly to the explanation of variations in recruitment. This lack of a significant relationship between the total number of young people entering the labour force and the recruitment to apprenticeships in engineering is somewhat surprising. Had there really been supply problems during most of the 1951–1971 period to such an extent that changes in earnings could not have been expected to increase the supply of suitable recruits very effectively, then the large increases in school-leavers in the early 1960s would be expected to have had an effect on recruitment[14]. The absence of medium-term planning of manpower resources in order to anticipate short-run supply inelasticities would seem to be a major cause of difficulty, suggesting that a demand-determined explanation of apprentice recruitment could be more acceptable. This is considered below.

Investment by employers

The formal empirical analysis of investment in training by employers is beset by difficulties which relate to the sheer complexity of training arrangements, their intimate links with production activity (making the attribution of costs very difficult), and the lack of basic data[15]. Woodhall (1974) suggests that for some industries it is possible to estimate roughly that the costs of training were perhaps 3 to 4% of total wages and salaries in the early 1970s. Applying this range to the economy as a whole would imply that the combined expenditure of government and employers on in-service training could amount to about 25–40% of total expenditure on formal education. But the method of calculation, as Woodhall stresses, is extremely crude and underestimates the real resource costs of training by omitting such important opportunity costs as output forgone during training. Faced with this problem it is then necessary to rely on certain physical indicators of training such as the number of trainees, together with price indicators such as the wages of trainees, to obtain some impression of changes in expenditure on investment in training over a given period. These indicators are available on a time-service basis for a minority of sectors of the economy even during the 1970s.

Further, it is extremely difficult to measure the financial benefit obtained by employers. Empirical analysis of costs and benefits of training by employers in Britain have been conducted by Thomas *et al.* (1969), Woodward and Anderson (1975) and the Engineering Industry Training Board (1972). The first of these deals with operative training in a clothing establishment, the second with apprentice training in a shipbuilding company and the third with the estimation of net costs of training craftsmen, technicians and technologists under different schemes, including benefits only as far as they offset the costs of training during the training period[16].

In this context it is very difficult to test human capital theory. A British study to examine econometrically the determinants of employers' investment in human capital was carried out by Lindley (1975). This was designed to complement the analysis of the supply of apprentice recruits described above and examined two models of the demand for apprentice recruits during 1951–1971. First, a 'current production hypothesis' is advanced to explain changes in demand. This amounts to assuming that recruitment policy is sensitive to the current state of the labour market (rather than to the results of manpower forecasting exercises by companies which imply an investment view of recruitment). The demand model assumes a constrained-output, cost-minimizing objective function, and allows short-run substitution possibilities between trained craftsmen and apprentices and hence, at the margin, apprentice recruits. Regression analysis is again used and elasticities of recruitment with respect to output, the wages of apprentices relative to those of craftsmen, and unemployment of craftsmen are all significant and take values of about 1.9, -3.3 and -0.5 respectively. However, if these current variables strongly influence firms' expectations about the future, the estimated equation is not incompatible with an investment interpretation. The second model therefore introduced gross fixed capital formation as a proxy for the combined view of desired production now and in the future. With this additional variable the regression results improved markedly[17].

4.4 Job search and labour mobility

The process of occupational choice can be divided into three stages. First, there is the formation of general occupational preferences. Secondly, there is the making of more specific occupational choices which guide the individual in planning investments in human capital. Thirdly, the process involves short-run job search in which no major change in the individual's human capital takes place. The second stage therefore involves the specification of occupational areas in which job search is eventually planned and executed. This stage develops from the first by virtue of the need to take decisions about education and training not directly connected with a particular job. These decisions require the individual to stipulate the strategic position to be adopted from which to launch job search. Economists during the 1970s have concentrated upon job search in the context of the short-run dynamics of the labour market, and have largely ignored its connection with occupational choice[18]. Job search activity is not confined to initial entry or re-entry to the labour force but punctuates the working life of the individual. Its relationship to occupational mobility and investment in human capital made at a later stage in life is a complex one. Neoclassical models of mobility (see Gallaway, 1967) can be extended to incorporate human capital considerations but empirical analysis of occupational mobility has been severely constrained by a lack of longitudinal data, or even time series of occupational flow statistics. The National Training Survey of 1975 has provided new opportunities for analysis of occupational choice and mobility and their relationship with factors such as education, training, qualifications, employment and unemployment experience, and a large number of personal characteristics.

Metcalf and Nickell (1981) use regression analysis to examine the occupational mobility of males as captured in the New Training Survey. As usual the dependent variable relates to *actual* mobility, not to desired moves, so will embody demand as well as supply effects. Metcalf and Nickell transform the flows among a set of mutually exclusive occupations into flows among different earnings categories. The latter are obtained by re-classifying each of 396 occupations to one of 20 ranges of average hourly earnings according to where the mean earnings for the occupation fell in 1975. The 20 ranges are the 'occupational groups' used in subsequent analysis. The use of pay as the criterion of classification may be seen in the human capital context, but it leads to a collapsing of two separate phenomena into one; change of occupation and change in pay. Thus it is not possible to examine the effect of mobility upon earnings and vice versa, though the extent of movement can be related to the frequency of job change. Their treatment, as they acknowledge, ignores three aspects which obviously affect the measure of mobility: changes over time in the *ranking* of occupations according to earnings, the narrowing of earnings differentials between high and low status occupations, and the presence of substantial intra-occupational mobility. In addition, the analysis of occupational mobility data needs to distinguish between changes in opportunities for mobility assuming occupational structure had remained stable and the extent to which the occupational structure of the economy has changed.

Metcalf and Nickell confirm several features of occupational mobility also identified in other studies, such as the relationship between mobility and age and the more upward than downward mobility observed. The latter reflects both the upward shifts in occupational structure and the fact that the sample movements are made by people who are gaining work experience during the period. Turning to the educational and training characteristics with which mobility is associated, straightforward tabulation of the survey data suggest three in particular.

(1) About 70% (a figure insensitive to broad type of qualification) of movers with educational qualifications occupied higher occupations in 1975 compared with 60% of those without.

(2) For those aged 45–64, only slight differences exist in mobility according to extent of vocational training, whereas those aged 25–39 with 1–52 weeks of training were more mobile than those without training and those with more than one year: they were also most likely to move upwards.

(3) Those with the highest educational qualifications and the longest vocational training tend to be least mobile and also least likely, on moving, to go upwards.

For those seeking reassuring evidence of social mobility, particularly a certain fluidity in opportunities for advantageous occupational moves from low paying occupations, the results of most *ad hoc* surveys are usually something of a mixed bag. It is with a view to sorting out the relative effects of many factors upon occupational mobility that resort is made to the cross-sectional regression analysis, using as dependent variable the logarithm of the ratio of average hourly earnings classification in 1975 to that recorded in 1965 (an earnings measure of the occupational distance travelled by each of almost 18 000 individuals). The analysis is not concerned with the ultimate occupational attainment of a given cohort of the population but with the factors that explain the direction and extent of occupational mobility during a decade amongst a closed sample of the population: that is, those who were in employment in 1965 and 1975. The very broad cross-section used, the fact that it covers all those aged 25–64 in 1975 (so the average age rises during the period of mobility) and the ignoring of within-period mobility mean that great care is required in the interpretation of the results.

The explanatory power of this kind of regression is likely to be poor and, indeed the multiple correlation coefficient (R^2) is 0.05. The results relating to education and training suggest that advantageous occupational moves are highly associated with attendance at grammar school (there is no control for ability, however); educational qualifications held in 1965 or acquired by 1975; and participation in a *short* course of vocational training during 1965–1975 (four weeks or less). Loss of occupational position is associated with an extra year of schooling when the individual has no qualification, and spells of unemployment and sickness over three months during 1965–1975. No significant gain appears to result from pre-1965 training or longer periods of training during 1965–1975 than four weeks.

The above show the potential significance of the results and indicate the difficulties of interpretation in the analysis of 'retrospective' longitudinal surveys[19]. For example, the findings with respect of vocational training seem to suggest a more limited and immediate association between it and advantageous occupational change than is the case for educational qualifications. But it would be a mistake also to see evidence of diminishing returns to extended training, for the analysis deals with mobility not ultimate attainment.

Mayhew and Rosewell (1981) pursue a similar study of occupational mobility using data for 10000 men aged betwen 18 and 64 in 1972 from the Oxford Mobility Study. Adopting as their measure of occupational distance, movement along the Hope–Goldthorpe scale, based on survey respondents ranking occupations according to general prestige, they looked at both achievement at several stages and movement along the scale between different stages. The cross-sectional regression analysis for different entry cohorts showed considerable explanation of the Hope–Goldthorpe rating of first job and job in 1972 by variables representing education and parental background. In addition there is some suggestion that the effects of lower levels of educational attainment and vocational training are more inclined to weaken over time as determinants of occupational attainment, perhaps reflecting greater vulnerability to becoming outdated[20].

British research on occupational mobility has taken a step forward recently. There is however still a need for further information relating to education and training policy. The lack of time-series data showing movements between broad occupations deprives the more elaborate cross-sectional studies of a much-needed framework within which to interpret their more specific findings.

4.5   Policy: its rationale and effectiveness

The economic analysis of educational and occupational choice clearly requires much development. Yet there does seem to be evidence of economically responsive behaviour. It has been seen that occupational mobility is rather more problematical, partly because there are no basic time-series or longitudal data akin to the various educational participation series. For example if there were an annual mobility survey of movement between very broad occupational groups, a start could be made by trying to explain the gross flows between manual and non-manual jobs in terms of demand and supply factors. Such aggregate time-series analysis would provide a valuable anchor for the various cross-sectional studies beginning to emerge for the UK.

No attempt has been made in this chapter to summarize the findings of the many *ad hoc* surveys of occupational choice and mobility. The focus has been upon regression studies. This is not to deny the importance of general surveys in assisting discussion of policy, but theories of labour market intervention point to the need for estimates of relevant elasticities from which to derive the effect of alternative policies. This final section deals first with the more technical issues of policy evaluation and then with policy developments which seem to embody most strikingly the dilemmas of trying to influence the level and pattern of investment in human capital.

Models of market intervention

Though complex theories of labour market intervention have been evolved to deal with policy questions against a background of structural imperfections in the labour market (see Johnson, 1979). Layard (1972) provides a simpler treatment which is particularly helpful here.

Attempts to move away from naive variants of cost-benefit analysis and manpower forecasting have initially aimed at using the techniques as *complementary* aids to planning, if not as synthesis of the methods themselves. Layard (1972) examines the relationship between the two methods and the relative roles they might play in educational planning. He suggests (1972, p. 128) that, 'rate of return analysis is a method of evaluating the base from which a forecast is made and adjusting it to eliminate the effect of current imbalance'. The relative importance of correcting for current imbalances as opposed to anticipating future shifts in demand depends on the supply lead times and demand elasticities.

The higher the former and the lower the latter, the greater is the need for forecasting. Layard is referring to what may be called 'naive' rate of reurn analysis which is based on cross-sectional data only, and where no attempt is made to calculate expected future cost and income streams. Thus 'current imbalance' refers to the perpetuation of the same sub-optimal equilibrium position, A, with supply and demand schedules fixed, as shown in *Figure 4.1*.

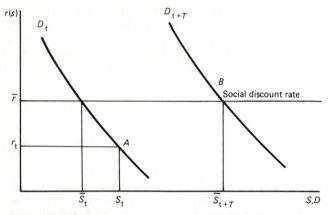

Figure 4.1 Imbalances in the supply and demand for skilled manpower

At point A the supply of skilled manpower S_t has been expanded beyond the point at which further training would be socially profitable. If demand were static then S_t would be allowed to decline (for example, through retirement) until reaching $\bar{S}_t$, the point of indifference between a marginal investment yielding $\bar{r}$ and no investment. When demand shifts to D_{t+T} during a period T the target level of supply will be $\bar{S}_{t+T}$. If $T > L$ where L is the supply lead time some decline in S_t will probably be desirable prior to the eventual increase to $\bar{S}_{t+T}$. This will depend on the costs involved in making downward adjustments to supply. However, the demand schedule may not simply be moving to a new position of stability, D_{t+T}. A whole set of demand shifts may be envisaged up to and beyond the planning horizon.

When applying the above analysis to industrial training the assumption of an administered supply which is highly inelastic in the short run without government intervention is even less appropriate than in the case of education, where at least government controls the capacity of the system, if not its utilization beyond the school-leaving age. Moreover the supply of skills in the future comprises not simply those people currently employed in relevant occupations together with the skilled unemployed plus new entrants less retirements. A complex of flows, including occupational mobility within the labour force, gives rise to changes in the occupational distribution of the employed labour force. Whether or not planners rely more upon calculations of rates of return than upon manpower forecasts to indicate the optimal stock of skilled manpower, they need a model of the pattern of supply. From the point of view of active manpower planning or 'supply management' the shape and determinants of the supply schedule S_t in *Figure 4.1* should be explored. This first involves investigating the changes in manpower flows which give rise to changes in stocks of employment and unemployment in order to move closer to the supply phenomenon itself (though each flow will to some degree result from the joint effects of demand and supply). Secondly, the most important flows then need to be analysed econometrically. Flows into post-compulsory education, from the education system to employment and/or training, and between occupations, industries and regions are all potentially relevant.

The estimation of social rates of return

In estimating the social rates of return to education or training a number of changes must be made to the private accounts from which private rates of return are calculated. The most important are (i) costs are no longer the post-tax income forgone plus the financial contributions made by the participants but the value of the output forgone plus the resource costs of education; (ii) benefits are no longer the additional post-tax income of participants attributed to the investment but the additional output produced over their lifetimes.

All transfer payments are excluded from the social rate of return calculation whereas they play a significant role in obtaining private rates of return. The standard measure adopted for output forgone in calculating the social rate of return is the gross average earnings of the unqualified group of which it is assumed the student or trainee would otherwise have been a number during the period of education or training. The measure of net output produced is similarly equated to the gross average lifetime earnings differential of the qualified group it is presumed the individual will join relative to the unqualified group. This chapter does not pursue the familiar arguments over whether or not the value of the marginal product is adequately represented by earnings paid in the occupation concerned, nor the significance of economic externalities and non-economic costs and benefits. However there are two aspects of the calculation of private and social rates of return which arise in investment analysis of both education and training but have, rather curiously, been recognized in one but not the other. First, the relevant earnings will only reflect income forgone and earned as a result of undergoing instruction if the person would have been or is employed respectively: some adjustment for the probability of being employed must be made. In addition, in the case of estimating social returns this adjustment needs to accommodate the extent to which the vacancy left behind whilst the person is under instruction is filled by someone else (the replacement effect) and the job entered after qualifying is obtained, once qualified, at the expense of some other worker (the displacement effect). Only when both effects are zero is national output forgone measured by the wage forgone by the individual and national output gained, the wage differential obtained as a result of the investment.

The second aspect relates to the effect of education or training *per se* upon the individual's productivity and earning power. Other factors likely to be correlated with the education and training received will also have their effects possibly in an additive fashion but at least through interaction with education and training: innate ability and social background will influence potential productivity and motivation which together will affect realized productivity in any given job. So some of the earnings differential may be a consequence of these factors rather than investment in human capital, depending on how well the unqualified control group provides an appropriate benchmark. Dennison's much used rule of thumb by which two-thirds of the differential is attributed to the effects of such investment has now become something of a lower bound.

It is noteworthy that none of the British cost-benefit studies of government training has made the adjustment for social background and innate ability whereas much effort has been devoted to taking into account the 'replacement' and 'displacement' probabilities. In contrast, the reverse is the case for cost-benefit studies of education, though (as mentioned in section 4.3) for private rates of return the probability of being employed has sometimes been taken into account.

Finally, beyond the problem of deciding what proportion of the earnings differential can be regarded as a return to the investment, there is a further issue. What investment activity is being undertaken: the provision of productivity-enhancing education/training or the screening for qualities identified rather than developed by the education/training process? Thus the relatively high productivity of those with higher qualifications may be attributed more to their underlying personal characteristics which make them capable of obtaining qualifications rather than the procession of the skills and knowledge imparted in the educational process (with important and obvious exceptions). For example, because length of schooling is highly correlated with IQ, employers seeking the most able people may screen for those with higher qualifications. Individuals would still be well advised to obtain such qualifications if they can, though they might resent the absence of a less time-consuming way of proving themselves.

Screening theory does not therefore offer an alternative to the human capital theory's view of the personal demand for education and training opportunities, nor does it sensibly compete with the latter's treatment of *investment* by employers. But it does challenge the application of human capital theory to the explanation of the inter-personal distribution of earnings and productivity and the *recruitment* strategies of employers. Screening theory also demands that the usual economic rationale for government expenditure on education and training should be tested against the reality of its effects upon labour markets characterized by imperfect information[21].

The two main areas of British social cost-benefit analysis have concerned higher education and formal off-the-job training in government training centres (GTCs, now called Skillcentres). In the first, a number of single year estimates have been made for various levels of education. Recently Adamson and Reid (1980) and Wilson (1981) have attempted the estimation of comparable social rates of return for several years together. In the second, Ziderman (1969, 1975a, 1975b) has produced the first estimates of social rates of return relating to the mid-1960s and early 1970s. The training activity conducted in GTCs falls somewhat between conventional education and traditional industrial training in that it is more closely related to the labour market than the former but its organizational structure means that the evaluation of social costs and benefits is not quite as fraught with difficulty as is the case with the latter.

The social rates of return calculated by Adamson and Reid, Wilson, and Ziderman all exceed the Treasury test discount rate of 5%, with those for industrial training achieving values in excess of 20% depending on the assumptions made about replacement and displacement effects. Estimates for education during the 1970s suggest a marked fall in rates of return to 'A' levels and HNC in the early part of the decade followed by a little recovery after 1975. For first degrees in aggregate there appears to have been a slight rise initially followed by a decline in the middle of the decade and some evidence of a pick-up towards the end. For science and engineering degrees, there is a substantial drop in the early 1970s followed by a rough levelling. The relative significance of changes in earnings differentials, educational costs, and other factors is explored by Adamson and Reid (1980) and Wilson (1981). By 1978/79, social rates of return to all the above mentioned areas of post-compulsory education are at most 1 or 2% in excess of the test discount rate. Rate of return analysis is intended to give indications of the appropriate direction of *marginal* changes in policy. The above results suggest that there is little case for either expansion or contraction and the appropriate response would be to mark time whilst continuing to monitor rates of return. Nor do the results support any marked shift in the distribution of higher educational expenditure in favour of science or engineering.

Taken in conjunction with the estimates of private rates of return to education produced by Adamson and Reid (1980) and Wilson (1980) the most striking feature is that during the 1970s private rates were generally at least three times the social rates for first degrees in aggregate but little more than 50% higher in the case of science and engineering degrees. There does appear to be some discrepancy in the two sources for 1971 for which Adamson and Reid provide a subject breakdown of their aggregate results, showing that not only were science and engineering social rates of return roughly on a par with the subject average but so was the case for private rates of return. Taking Wilson's findings for science and engineering in conjunction with the aggregate findings of Adamson and Reid it could be concluded that not only would it be unwise to attempt an expansion of science and engineering on social grounds but that any attempt to do so could be frustrated by a poor student response because the pattern of private rates is distinctly unfavourable towards scientists and engineers. The policy would need to involve reducing opportunities elsewhere, which flies in the face of the (implicit) social rates of return to arts and social science. If it is assumed that the subject differentials found by Adamson and Reid for 1971 applied also to the present, then although the social rates of return do not provide strong grounds for expanding science and engineering, at least the private rates would not indicate that the additional supply of students might be slow to materialize.

Thus here is a case in which not only is the *rationale* of policy inconsistent with the cost-benefit analysis but the *effectiveness* of policy may be undermined by a mistaken impression of the conditions governing the demand for the type of education in question. Too much should not be made of the particular case given but it does show how important it is to monitor rates of return carefully and systematically if they are to be used to guide government attempts to influence the occupational structure of labour supply. Isolated measures of rates of return are not much more help than *ad hoc* surveys of occupational mobility.

Ziderman's (1975a) methodology for the social cost-benefit analysis of industrial training stresses another aspect of rate of return analysis in which the treatment of labour supply has considerable implications for policy. Here the issue is not so much the manner in which rate of return estimates are deployed but the method of estimation itself. In the present context the main interest is in two aspects: the modelling of the effect of training upon the trainee group's work experience and the effect upon the work experience of the rest of the labour force.

Ziderman tackles the first problem of representing what would have happened to people had they not entered training by means of a stochastic model of work experience. He explores the second through the choice of a range of parameter values for the replacement and displacement effects. It is enough here to stress two particular difficulties. First, the definitions of the states of employment and unemployment activity used in the model are not well-related to the characteristics affected by training and the structure of the labour markets affected. Secondly, the selection of alternative sets of parameters of the model (transition probabilities) does not help very much to specify the range of labour market conditions for which the evaluation is being conducted. This means that the treatment of these labour market flow effects comes close to the very kind of mechanistic approach which supporters of rate of return analysis have criticized in manpower forecasting. The degree of judgement required in assessing the rates of return is such as to involve a large arbitrary element, some of which could probably by reduced by giving more attention to the manpower flow system.

The general conclusion reached is that in order to apply cost-benefit analysis to training it is necessary to have a model of those sections of the labour market involved. Hedging the simple calculation of rates of return on the basis of direct costs and benefits with adjustments for replacement and displacement effects leaves too much room for rather arbitrary guesswork in judging the simulation results.

The use of the terms 'naïve manpower forecasting' or 'manpower requirements approach' have come to imply a very mechanistic or at best a behaviourally very simple model of labour demand. However the epithet 'naïve' applies to both sides of the 'rate of return analysis versus manpower forecasting' debate. In practice both rate of return and manpower forecasting studies bear the marks of an inadequate model being forced upon inadequate data. In particular, both pay little attention to the determinants of the supply of labour, despite the fact that policy is often especially concerned with its control. Manpower policies are mainly executed by operating upon *flows* of manpower and too much research has tended to treat the system of flows as a black box.

Whether or not naïve rate of return analysis or naïve manpower forecasting is the lesser of the two evils is thus of little relevance given the options open to researchers. Improvements to both methods may be sought through the study of demand and supply responses to developments in labour markets. The construction of forecasting models and the development of the rate of return methodology are both necessary conditions for improving the economic analysis of alternative investments in education and training. The first is required in order to anticipate the impact of different policies in terms of their effects upon future resources and prices, and the second is required in order to evaluate these outcomes for the purposes of comparison with each other and with opportunities for other types of social investment

Policy initiatives and dilemmas

The lack of coherence in government policy towards the labour market affects the development of educational and training policies as much as the experiments with employment subsidies, controls on incomes and the treatment of the public sector (Lindley, 1980; 1981a). In the case of training policy the central strategic problem which policy-makers have to face is to ensure adequate skill acquisition in an economy engaged in painfully slow recovery from deep recession and likely to be in substantial labour surplus for a long time. Conditions of excess supply persisting for five years or more can dramatically alter any calculations of social rates of return. Whether or not governments will follow employers in reacting to falling rates of return to education and training by reducing investment in human capital is a crucial question. In fact government and the manpower agencies have to some extent resisted doing this but the strain in maintaining the traditional economic rationale for investment in education and training is beginning to tell. That rationale was basically orientated towards the manipulation of labour supply to meet labour demand by influencing the supply of educational and training opportunities on the presumption that the demand for those opportunities would materialize. However the demand by young people for education and training in craft skills, science and technology proved to be disappointing to employers. In the case of science and technology the higher education system was blamed for failing to supply courses which attracted good students and satisfied industrial requirements as regards course content. In the case of craft skills, criticism had to be closer to home and employers who trained their labour force complained of those who 'poached'. It is probably fair to say that the labour market for scientists and technologists, where training capacity is governed by the education system, has worked no worse than has that for skilled manual workers, where training capacity is controlled mainly by industry. In both cases criticism of earlier stages in the educaton system has been voiced, arguing that it has made young people (through ignorance or prejudice) less favourably inclined towards the occupations concerned. However the evidence suggests that young people are not so badly informed as some have argued and that the provision of more information, though desirable, is alone unlikely to alter substantially the educational and occupational choices of pupils and students in the direction favoured by industry (Lindley, 1981b).

As regards higher education there have been proposals for student loans or graduate taxes as a method of influencing student choice sufficiently to bring about a closer relationship to the pattern of demand for highly qualified manpower. As regards industrial training there has been discussion of the effect upon training costs of the rise in relative pay of trainees, increases in off-the-job training and proposals to reduce the period of training. Such developments would, however, probably help to attract more recruits. But in both higher education and industrial training, realization was slow that problems with the supply of students and trainees were related also to the relative pay and status obtained by the qualified person.

Two further ingredients of the policy debate during the late 1970s and early 1980s are worth stressing. First, the responsiveness of the higher education system seemed to leave something to be desired, suggesting that if students were to be more exposed to economic pressures then the fortunes of institutions should be related more to student demand. In addition, to bring education and industry closer together in the planning and design of a wide range of courses, the question of selective joint finance of higher education institutions and groups of employers took on more significance. Secondly, as industrial training policy once again came under scrutiny, the distinction betwen 'general' and 'specific' skills, which previous legislaton had failed to take into account, at last began to have a significant influence in the form of proposals for dealing with so-called 'transferable' skills. This introduced more directly than before the possibility of changing the balance of financial contributions towards training obtained from employers, the state and trainees.

The discussion of post-compulsory education and training has taken place against a rapidly worsening economic situation. Policy initiatives in these fields have been caught up in the major arguments ranging over the management of the economy and the role of market forces. However, after a period of much development both in higher education and in industrial training, some fundamental reappraisal was in any event likely to be required. The emergence of the Youth Opportunities Programme in response to labour market difficulties has on the other hand added a particular edge to debate. It invites comparison with the treatment of young people within the conventional full-time education system and raises major questions of policy about the content of education, the institutional framework within which it is offered, the methods of financial support to those receiving it, the relevance of industrial experience to the educational process itself, and the most appropriate way of absorbing 16–19-year-olds into the labour force.

Thus three major issues, all concerning investment in human capital, have been under consideration: how best to provide for the further education and training of young people, how to revitalize higher education in the interests of national economic welfare and how to promote efficiency and equity in the acquisition and deployment of skills by the labour force as a whole, after initial entry and occupational choice. In grappling with these issues the institutional framework of education and training together with the habits of past policy debate have conspired to blur the distinction between the labour market and the market for educational and training opportunities. Decisions in the latter relate in varying degrees to the situation in the former but the two should be allowed a separate identity. This point has been argued in the case of higher education but applies also to industrial training. The importance of recognizing the distinction between the two markets is that it provides an 'intellectual umbrella' beneath which constructive proposals for long-term reform of the education and training systems can be considered in spite of the extremely hostile economic and labour market environment likely to exist in the medium term. Otherwise any attempt to plan for adequate skill acquisition for the long term is in danger of appearing to be a glorified social welfare programme as the economy remains in substantial labour surplus well into the 1980s.

Both sides of the market for post-compulsory education face costs and prices which are largely disconnected from the true resource costs, and the pattern of supply which institutions can provide is subject to quantitative constraints. The market for training opportunities is characterized by a *joint* transaction involving a training opportunity and a job and tends to be dominated by the conditions governing the market for jobs (though subject to government intervention to influence the amount of training undertaken).

Thus discussion of education and training within a market framework specific to those activities is discouraged not only by the very powerful institutional forces at work in the supply of and demand for education and training and also by great imperfections in the labour market to which the market for educational and training opportunities should relate. It can be argued that education policy has failed to consider adequately the role which the system might play in promoting economic development, despite the fact that a very large proportion of it is concerned with vocational education. Industry has tended to react to the difficulties by associating the training process as closely as possible with the process of recruitment and employment, even though a substantial part of training is general to (or transferable within) an industry or occupation rather than specific to a firm. Yet the main tax-subsidy schemes for training have been orientated towards the firm as supplier of training rather than the individual seeking to be trained. The alternative notion of industry supplying the service but government subsidizing the consumer has not been the basis of the system.

During the late 1970s there have been significant advances in the way training policy is discussed in the UK and numerous, if sometimes experimental, programmes for tackling training have been undertaken. The translation of good sense into practical arrangements for training is however falling foul of the serious economic situation which has developed. Both government and industry appear to be more than usually convinced that they cannot afford to do much, at the same time as being more than usually convinced that much deserves to be done. It remains to be seen whether major reform will eventually result, but a first step would be to recast the discussion of vocational education and training in terms of creating a much more developed market for educational and training opportunities. This would involve giving far more attention to the position of the individual, the determinants of educational and occupational choice, and the conditions under which the demand for educational and training opportunities should be met. The sovereignty of labour demand for certain types of training has dominated policy thinking for a long time; it is sad to reflect that it may have gone on doing so had the present massive waste of human resources not occurred.

Notes

1. Butler (1968) and the collection of articles edited by Williams (1974, especially the introductory essay by Sofer) cover most of the work relevant to the British situation plus the major American studies, of which those by Ginsberg *et al.* (1951, 1964), Super (1953) and Blau *et al.* (1956) have strongly influenced the theoretical approaches of British studies. Gordon (1981) provides a very useful supplement to these two sources, concentrating on the determinants of educational rather than occupational choices but dealing with some of the recent literature relevant to the latter as well as to the former.
2. Greenhalgh and Mayhew (1981) survey studies of labour supply in Britain and discuss 'the composition and quality of the labour force'. The lack of any mention of human capital theory and its implications for the supply of different skills and of empirical analysis dealing with occupational choice or the supply of skills is partly indicative of the dearth of material.
3. The problematical state of the demand for higher education is discussed in Lindley (1981b).
4. No attempt will be made to offer a full exposition of human capital theory. The reader is referred to Blaug (1972) for an introductory treatment of many issues connected with education and training. Blaug (1976) reviews substantial areas of the enormous literature that the human capital research programme has produced.
5. Becker has been criticized for failing to stress that the distinction between 'general' and 'specific' training needs to take into account not only the effects of training upon relative productivity in different firms but also the factors determining the risk of employees leaving the firm during or after training. To the extent that workers are immobile, general training will amount to specific training and firms may find it economic to

finance it. See Oatey (1970) for a discussion of this and other aspects of training from the firm's point of view.

6. The rates of return calculated by economists are sometimes described as 'marginal' but this relates to their being estimates of the return conditional upon undertaking an extra stage of education, not the return to the marginal entrant to that stage. Such estimates would be better described as 'incremental average' rather than 'marginal' rates of return. The individual should be concerned about the true marginal return but ignoring such distinctions is only one amongst many compromises which have to be made in obtaining empirical results. See Blaug (1972, Chapter 6) and section 4.5 below.

7. Three main devices have been used: (i) relative starting salaries; (ii) relative average or median earnings; and (iii) a combination of (i) and (ii) to represent the age–earnings distribution by means of two parameters rather than one. The third alternative assumes a simple linear infinite form for the age–earnings profile: in practice, at the rates of return implied, discounting makes the extension to infinity unimportant and the linear restriction a reasonable first approximation. The slope and intercept parameters of the assumed profile can then be determined from starting and average salaries over the lifetime. Moreover, by entering the starting wage and rate of growth as separate variables, the supply elasticities with respect to each characteristic of the expected earnings profile can be derived. See Zabalza (1979a).

8. See Wilson (1980) for a review of British studies of private rates of return to education and both Wilson (1980) and Adamson and Reid (1980) for estimates of private rates of return for several years.

9. Marked changes also took place in rates of return in the United States but some authors, notably Freeman (1981), were quick to explain the fall in enrolments in terms of market responsiveness, and to predict developments for the last half of the 1970s.

10. The permanent income variable plays a significant part for boys, but not girls, whereas the reverse is true for the index of structural change. Real per capita consumption is used as a proxy for permanent income and its high significance for males, with an implied elasticity of 2.5, is attributed by Pissarides (1981a, p. 5) to the presence of the 'consumption-good side of education'. This interpretation does not seem to take enough account of either the crudity of the chosen proxy for permanent income or the extent to which rising permanent

income provides opportunities for current consumption and investment to increase future consumption. Education may be viewed as current consumption or as an investment in a durable consumer good or as an investment in a net-income generating asset. If rising family income is used to finance education as an investment good there is more to the observed 'consumption effect' than is implied by Pissarides. Rationalization of the results for girls relative to those for boys is somewhat difficult especially in view of the high correlation between the consumption variable and the demand index.

11. This raises methodological questions suggesting that survey research based on investigating responses to hypothetical circumstances would generate new insights. Fulton and Gordon (1979) use this approach to investigate the potential impact upon staying on in full-time education of a maintenance grant to those aged 16–19 years. They conclude that an £8 per week grant (1977 prices) would increase the number of both sexes staying on by about 5%.

12. They do not however allow for significant responsiveness of the science and engineering groups taken as a whole relative to other broad subject groups.

13. Additional work using a priori more satisfactory measures of relative earnings on the lines mentioned earlier has been accompanied by relatively unreliable parameter estimates. (I am grateful to Robert Wilson for this preliminary judgement on research still in progress.) This problem was also evidently experienced by Freeman, the person most associated with this sort of analysis. His findings for the United States also indicate significant supply responses to relative earnings and substantial variation between fields of study. Taking his results (summarized in Freeman, 1981) for enrolments not graduates, the short-run elasticities range from 1 to 2 and the long-run elasticities range from 3 to 4 (calculated from a partial adjustment specification).

14. Such an effect is observed in the case of all young people entering the engineering industry: the elasticity is 0.7.

15. Ziderman (1978) describes the human capital approach to training and reviews the theoretical and empirical literature.

16. See Ryan (1980) for a recent case-study where particular care is exercised to establish the costs of on-the-job training in a US company.

17. Despite institutional developments in the late 1960s and 1970s which suggest that at least a limited investment view is taken because of the extent of initial off-the-job training, Ryrie

(1976) reports evidence from the mid-1970s which he believes provides some support for Lindley's 'current production hypothesis'. This points to the still very considerable scope for employers to exercise a substitution option between apprentice recruits and craftsmen in the short run. Clearly there will be a mix of the two influences. A fuller discussion of the two competing hypotheses is given in Lindley (1975) together with comments on empirical and econometric questions in support of adopting a demand rather than supply explanation of changes in apprentice recruitment.

18. Exceptions to this are the long-run departures from an essentially short-run theoretical treatment of labour market adjustment by Pissárides (1976) and the generalized theory of job search developed by Whipple (1973).

19. See Psacharopoulos (1981) for a review of related analysis of earnings and employment using a variety of surveys including longitudinal sources.

20. The cross-sectional analysis of occupational mobility over selected periods was reportedly unsuccessful and, whilst acknowledging that of Metcalf and Nickell using a different survey and dependent and independent variables, Mayhew and Rosewell consider the possibility that regression analysis based on a continuous transformation for the mobility variable is in fact inappropriate. Their experiment with discriminant analysis, identifying three groups – upward movers, downward movers and stayers – indicates that education and parental background variables do help to allocate people in the sample to the correct group. However they make very modest claims for their results which point to methodological difficulties with the use of continuous occupational achievement scales rather than methodological solutions through discriminant analysis.

21. See Blaug (1976, pp. 845–850) and Peston (1981, pp. 129–133) for further discussion of problems of measuring social rates of return.

References

Adamson, A. B. and Reid, T. M. (1980). The rate of return to post-compulsory education during the 1970s: an empirical study for Great Britain. Department of Educaton and Science (mimeo)

Becker, G. S. (1964). *Human Capital*. New York; National Bureau of Economic Research

Becker, G. S. (1965). A theory of the allocation of time. *Economic Journal* **75**, 493–517

Blau, P. M. (ed.) (1956). Occupational choice: a conceptual framework. *Industrial and Labor Relations Review* **9**, 531–543

Blaug, M. (1972). *An Introduction to the Economics of Education*. Harmondsworth; Penguin Books

Blaug, M. (1976). The empirical status of human capital theory: a slightly jaundiced survey. *Journal of Economic Literature* **14**, 827–855

Bosworth, D. L. and Wilson, R. A. (1980). The labour market for scientists and technologists. In *Economic Change and Employment Policy* (ed. by R. M. Lindley), pp. 297–329. London; Macmillan

Briscoe, G., Dutton, P. A. and Lindley, R. M. (1980). Skilled labour in engineering and construction. In *Economic Change and Employment Policy* (ed. by R. M. Lindley) pp. 240–296. London; Macmillan

Butler, J. R. (1968). *Occupational Choice*. Department of Education and Science, Science Policy Studies No. 2. London ; HMSO

Engineering Industry Training Board (1972). *The Costs of Training: A Preliminary Report*. Occasional Paper No. 2

Freeman, R. B. (1981). Response to change in the United States. In *Higher Education and the Labour Market* (ed. by R. M. Lindley), pp. 86–119. Leverhulme Programmes of Study into the Future of Higher Education, Monograph No. 1. Guildford; Society for Research into Higher Education

Fulton, O. and Gordon, A. (1979). The British pool of ability: how deep, and will cash reduce it? *Educational Studies* **5**, 157–169

Gallaway, L. E. (1967). *Interindustry Labour Mobility in the US 1957 to 1960*. US Department of Health, Education and Welfare. Office of Social Security Administration, Research and Statistics. Research Report No. 18. Washington

Ginsberg, E. (ed.) (1951). *Occupational Choice: An Approach to General Theory*. New York; Columbia University Press

Ginsberg, E. *et al.* (1964). *Talent and Performance*. New York; Columbia University Press

Gordon, A. (1981). An examination of the factors affecting the educational choices of young people. University of Bristol; Department of Social Administration (mimeo)

Greenhalgh, C. and Mayhew, K. (1981). Labour supply in Great Britain: theory and evidence. In *The Economics of the Labour*

Market (ed. by Z. Hornstein, J. Grice and A. Webb). London; HMSO

Johnson, G. E. (1979). The theory of labour market intervention. Paper presented to US Department of Labour/Manpower Services Commission Conference on Unemployment and Unemployment Policy.

Klinov-Malul, R. (1971). Enrolments in higher education as related to earnings. *British Journal of Industrial Relations* **9**, 82–91

Layard, P. R. G. (1972). Economic theories of educational planning. In *Essays in Honour of Lord Robbins*. (ed. by M. H. Peston and B. A. Corry), pp. 118–149. London; Weidenfeld and Nicolson

Lindley, R. M. (1974). Manpower movements and the supply of labour. In *Problems in Manpower Forecasting* (ed. by J. S. Wabe), pp. 239–281. Farnborough; Saxon House

Lindley, R. M. (1975). The demand for apprentice recruits by the engineering industry, 1951–71. *Scottish Journal of Political Economy* **XXII**, 1–24

Lindley, R. M. (1980). Employment policy in transition. In *Economic Change and Employment Policy* (ed. by R. M. Lindley), pp. 330–382. London; Macmillan

Lindley, R. M. (1981a). Education, training and the labour market in Britain. *European Journal of Education* **16**, 7–27

Lindley, R. M. (1981b). The challenge of market imperatives. In *Higher Education and the Labour Market* (ed. by R. M. Lindley), pp. 120–147. Leverhulme Programme of Study into the Future of Higher Education, Monograph No. 1. Guildford; Society for Research into Higher Education

Makeham, P. (1980). Youth unemployment. *Department of Employment Research Paper* No. 10

Mayhew, K. and Rosewell, B. (1981). Occupational mobility in Britain. *Oxford Bulletin of Economics and Statistics* **43**, 225–255

Metcalf, D. and Nickell, S. (1981). Occupational mobility in Great Britain. In *Research in Labor Economics* IV (ed. by R. Ehrenberg) (forthcoming). Greenwich, Connecticut; JAI Press

Oatey, M. (1970). The economics of training with respect to the firm. *British Journal of Industrial Relations* **8**, 1–21

Peston, M. (1981). Higher education policy. In *Higher Education and the Labour Market* (ed. by R. M. Lindley), pp. 120–147. Leverhulme Programme of Study into the Future of Higher Education, Monograph No. 1. Guildford; Society for Research into Higher Education

Pissarides, C. A. (1976). *Labour Market Adjustment*. Cambridge; Cambridge University Press

Pissarides, C. A. (1981a). Staying-on at school in England and Wales. *Centre for Labour Economics, London School of Economics, Discussion Paper* No. 63 (revised)

Pissarides, C. A. (1981b). From school to university: the demand for post-compulsory education in Britain. *Centre for Labour Economics, London School of Economics, Discussion Paper* No. 70 (revised)

Psacharopoulos, G. (1981). Lifetime profiles of earnings and employment: a Survey. *Social Science Information* (forthcoming)

Ryan, P. (1980). The costs of job training for a transferable skill. *British Journal of Industrial Relations* **18,** 334–352

Ryrie, A. C. (1976). Employers and apprenticeship. *British Journal of Industrial Relations* **14,** 89–91

Sofer, C. (1974). Introduction. In *Occupational Choice* (ed. by W. M. Williams), pp. 13–57. London; George Allen and Unwin

Super, D. E. (1953). A theory of vocational development. *American Psychologist* **8,** 185–190

Thomas, B., Moxam, J. and Jones, J. (1969). A cost-benefit analysis of industrial training. *British Journal of Industrial Relations* **7,** 231–264

Whipple, D. (1973). A generalised theory of job search. *Journal of Political Economy* **81,** 1170–1188

Williams, W. M. (ed.) (1974). *Occupational Choice*. London; George Allen and Unwin

Wilson, R. A. (1980). The rate of return to becoming a qualified scientist or engineer in Great Britain, 1966–1976. *Scottish Journal of Political Economy* **27,** 41–62

Wilson, R. A. (1981). Rates of return. *Institute for Employment Research University of Warwick* (mimeo)

Woodhall, M. (1974). Investment in industrial training: an assessment of the effects of the Industrial Training Act on the value and costs of training. *British Journal of Industrial Relations* **12,** 71–90

Woodward, N. and Anderson, T. (1975). A profitability appraisal of apprenticeships. *British Journal of Industrial Relations* **13,** 245–256

Zabalza, A. (1979a). A note on the estimation of subjective rates of discount from labour supply functions. *Economica* **46,** 197–202

Zabalza, A. (1979b). The determinants of teacher supply. *Review of Economic Studies* **46,** 131–147

Ziderman, A. (1969). Costs and benefits of adult retraining in the United Kingdom. *Economica* **36,** 363–376

Ziderman, A. (1975a). Cost-benefit analysis of government training centres in Scotland: a simulation approach. In *Contemporary Issues in Economics* (ed. by M. Parkin and A. R. Nobay), pp. 271–287. Manchester; Manchester University Press

Ziderman, A. (1975b). Costs and benefits of manpower training programmes in Great Britain. *British Journal of Industrial Relations* **13,** 223–243

Ziderman, A. (1978). *Manpower Training: Theory and Policy.* London; Macmillan

Chapter 5

The structure of pay

5.1 Introduction

Some types of pay inequality

Pay inequality has many dimensions. In April 1980, average gross weekly earnings for a male professional manager aged 21 or over in Britain were £167.70[1]. The average for a man aged 21 or over working in catering or cleaning full time was £93.80. One in eight of full-time men working in catering or cleaning would be defined as low paid under the generally accepted definition in 1980 of gross earnings less than £60 per week, whereas only 1% of male professional managers fell into that category. More strikingly, nearly half the women aged 18 and over working full time in catering or cleaning fell into the low paid category, and on average earned less than 70% of earnings of men in that occupational group.

Full-time manual women received hourly earnings averaging 70% of those paid to manual men in April 1980, whereas non-manual women averaged only 61% of male non-manual hourly earnings. Only 2% of men were recorded as part-time in the *New Earnings Survey* although 34% of women were so recorded. Part-timers on average received *hourly* earnings only 80% of those received by their full-time counterparts, and nearly half of part-time women earned less than £1.50 an hour.

Average gross weekly earnings for men in catering or cleaning in the best-paid region, Greater London, were over 22% higher than in the worst-paid region, Wales. Professional managers in Greater London, however, received on average 30% more than their counterparts in the worst-paid region which was, somewhat surprisingly, the West Midlands. Finally, mean weekly earnings of men working in catering or cleaning aged between 50 and 59 were just over 10% greater than for those aged 21 to 24, whereas professional managers aged 50 to 59 averaged over 80% greater earnings than their counterparts aged 21 to 24.

Some alternative explanations

The purpose of this chapter is to examine these types of inequality, through a number of competing theories of the pay structure which are outlined in the following sections. The flavour of these diverse explanations may be obtained from a brief commentary on the illustrative statistics just quoted. Thus an intuitively plausible explanation of the disparity in average earnings between professional managers on the one hand and catering and cleaning workers on the other is that the former are better educated and more adept at taking the difficult decisions necessary in their occupation. Thus earnings are related to the particular characteristics of individuals and of occupations. Nevertheless, level of educational attainment provides at best a partial explanation of differences in individual earnings: American studies, for example, found that in the case of college educated white adult males, 30% had incomes which were below the median incomes for those educated only up to high school (Phelps Brown, 1977, p. 242). The inherent riskiness of business decisions, as perhaps illustrated by the greater variance of earnings in higher-paid occupations, might explain their higher average earnings assuming the population is generally risk-averse (Phelps Brown, 1977, section 8.1). However, it may be questioned whether many higher-paid occupations are inherently risky, and the evidence suggests that less-skilled individuals bear greater risks in the form of variability of employment rather than variability in rates of pay[2].

An alternative explanation is that rates of pay are not attached to individuals or occupations but to job structures. Certain kinds of job, especially in higher-paid occupations, are organized into hierarchical structures with fairly well-defined levels of pay related to, for instance, age[3]. Thus from the earlier illustration, older managers earn a good deal more than younger managers, unlike workers in catering and cleaning. In higher paid occupations, individual qualifications, such as a higher education, are treated as surrogates for or indirect measures of personal competence. Consequently, average earnings for different levels of education are determined by the supply of different qualifications relative to the given structure of jobs. The ability, or productivity, of the individual is not a major consideration in determining his or her pay.

If personal and occupational characteristics were the major cause of pay differences, it might be inferred that women earn less than men by virtue of lower inherent productivity, education and so on. However, while some dimensions of productivity, such as physical strength, may differ between men and women, it is difficult to believe that this is of significance in the majority of occupations. Moreover, educational qualifications are roughly similar between the sexes up to the level of higher education[4] and the significant difference between the sexes is the flatness of the age–earnings profile of women relative to men in the same education–occupational category (Phelps Brown, 1977, section 5.2.1). Possible reasons for this difference are numerous, including differential lifetime work experience, differential type of job, and overt discrimination whether by employer or male employees.

Differential regional disparities among occupations raises the important question of labour mobility. In the example, regional disparities are higher among professional managers than among workers in catering and cleaning, which might be attributed to the homogeneity of less skilled labour relative to managerial occupations. Nevertheless it can be argued that unskilled labour should be less mobile geographically than higher income occupations as a result of differences in housing type and differential access to labour market information (Evans and Richardson, 1981, pp. 113–115). If mobility plays a part in equalizing rates of pay within occupations, differential geographical mobility among occupations should explain divergences in the regional dispersion of pay among occupations. But whether in practice the labour market embodies sufficient flexibility to promote such equalization is a central issue in judging the validity of alternative theories of the pay structure since orthodox neoclassical theorists argue that flexibility of the pay structure plays a central role in the allocation of labour whereas alternative theories emphasize institutional constraints on mobility which generate stable pay inequalities and segmented labour markets.

Outline of the chapter

The questions raised by this preliminary discussion, concerning the impact of education on earnings, the explanation of differences in age–earnings profiles, the structure of jobs and the mobility of the labour force, will be central concerns of the discussion that follows. In section 5.2, the pay distribution in Britain is examined in more detail and the distinction between cross-sectional and lifetime pay distributions is emphasized. In section 5.3 the neoclassical explanation of wage structure is briefly described and set against the evidence. In section 5.4 alternative explanations of pay structure are discussed, in particular the notions of the job queue, segmented labour markets and discrimination. The empirical evidence and the problems of testing alternative theories are then examined in section 5.5. Section 5.6 briefly presents the conclusions, and some policy implications.

5.2   The distribution of individual earnings

Weekly earnings

The distribution of individual weekly earnings exhibits very similar statistical properties in many countries. This regularity among quite disparate economies and years has been regarded as sufficiently noteworthy to require explanation, and a large number of studies have attempted to explain this distribution as a statistical phenomenon[5]. However, the primary concern of the present chapter is to examine the economic forces that operate on the pay distribution.

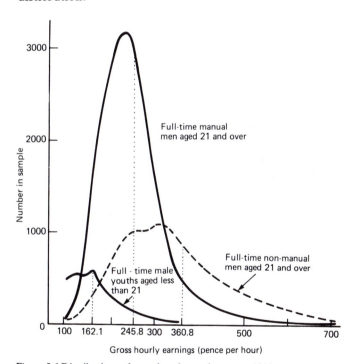

Figure 5.1 Distributions of gross hourly earnings, men 1980

Source: Department of Employment *New Earnings Survey* 1980, Part A, 1980, Table 20

It is first useful to disaggregate the pay distribution into broad occupational categories. *Figures 5.1* and *5.2* provide disaggregations for the hourly earnings of men and women respectively. *Table 5.1* provides the relevant summary statistics of the distributions. It should be noted that these figures are derived from the *New Earnings Survey* which is an annual 1% sample of employees

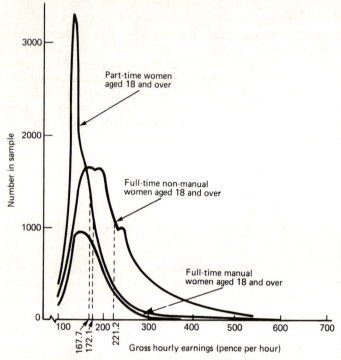

Figure 5.2 Distributions of gross hourly earnings, women 1980

Source: Department of Employment *New Earnings Survey* 1980, Part A, 1980, Table 20

who are recorded as members of the PAYE income tax scheme. The survey therefore excludes some workers, especially those in part-time employment, who fall below the lower earnings limit for national insurance contributions. It obviously also excludes those who are not paying tax through PAYE, such as the self-employed.

Among full-time men, 59% are in manual occupations compared with 27% of full-time women. The dispersion of non-manual hourly earnings for both men and women is greater than for the corresponding manual distributions as indicated by *Figures 5.1* and

TABLE 5.1 Summary statistics of alternative hourly earnings distributions

Category	Mean (pence per hour)	Median (pence per hour)	Quartiles as % of median	
			Upper	Lower
Full-time manual men aged 21 and over	245.8	234.8	118.7	84.5
Full-time non-manual men aged 21 and over	360.8	330.2	130.9	77.8
Full-time male youth aged under 21	162.1	154.2	125.9	77.6
Full-time manual women aged 18 and over	172.1	165.1	118.0	84.9
Full-time non-manual women aged 18 and over	221.2	201.2	128.4	80.7
Part-time women aged 18 and over	167.7	154.8	120.9	89.1

Source: Department of Employment, *New Earnings Survey*, 1980

5.2 and the quartiles in *Table 5.1*. More striking is the low dispersion in hourly earnings for part-time women with almost all individuals bunched around the median. This is despite the fact that part-time women are almost equally divided between manual and non-manual occupations. This contrasts to part-time men, who comprise a much smaller proportion of the labour force (and are not shown in *Figure 5.1*) for whom the dispersion of earnings is far greater with an upper quartile 155.8% of median earnings.

An obvious conclusion to be drawn from these distributions is that the aggregate distribution of earnings is comprised of quite dissimilar distributions. A major reason why these distributions differ is the variation in age–earnings profiles between the sexes and also between broad occupational categories. *Figure 5.3* shows that full-time, non-manual earnings profiles for both sexes rise over a longer part of the working life than the corresponding profiles for manual workers. The profile for part-time women is almost identical, other than in the level of earnings, to that of full-time manual women despite the number of part-time workers in non-manual occupations. The explanation of the shape of non-manual age–earnings profiles is that such occupations tend to be organized in hierarchies with incremental salary structures related to length of service. For example, non-manual men aged 50 to 59 with 10 or more years of service earned 23% more than men with less than 10 years, whereas the difference was only 11%

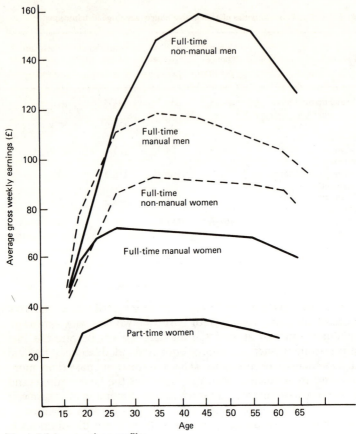

Figure 5.3 Age-earnings profiles

Source: Department of Employment *New Earnings Survey* 1980, Part E, Table 124

for manual men (see *New Earnings Survey*, Part F, 1979, Table 169). Thus women, and part-time women in particular, who have or are perceived by employers in general to have interrupted working lives have flatter age–earnings profiles. In general the flatter the age–earnings profile the less the dispersion of the earnings distribution observed in *Figures 5.1* and *5.2* and *Table 5.1*.

Lifetime earnings

This discussion of age–earnings profiles raises the important question of lifetime earnings. There is a case for arguing that the distribution which alternative theories should attempt to explain is that of lifetime earnings rather than the distribution of earnings at a point in time, since measures of the inequality of earnings at a point in time are obtained by aggregating over individuals with different lifetime earnings profiles. Inequalities among individuals of particular ages reflect the fact that different occupations have peak earnings at different points in the life cycle. Now according to human capital theory, which is examined in more detail in section 5.3, individuals are able to choose among different lifetime earnings profiles and thus under certain competitive assumptions individual lifetime earnings, discounted and adjusted for costs of training, may be equalized. Moreover, individual earnings at a point in time may embody transitory or stochastic components which might be expected to cancel out over longer periods. These arguments have led the Royal Commission on the Distribution of Income and Wealth to suggest that distribution of lifetime earnings should show more equality than distributions of individual earnings at a point in time (1975, Report No. 1, p. 147).

This proposition has important welfare implications, not least concerning the value attached to reducing inequalities, but it is unfortunately not easy to test without detailed data on individual earnings histories. Creedy (1977) estimated the dispersion of lifetime earnings within various occupations on the basis of the observed dispersions of earnings for each age group, and using indirect estimates of the pattern of year-to-year changes in individual earnings. He showed that the dispersion of lifetime earnings, while lower than in the age group which has the highest dispersion, is not lower than the dispersion of every age group. Further, there was a low rank correlation between the dispersion of lifetime earnings and average discounted lifetime earnings.

A second important point concerns the age–earnings profiles depicted in *Figure 5.3*. These compare the earnings of different individuals of various ages in the same occupation. They are not earnings histories, or longitudinal profiles, for particular individuals. Use of these age–earnings profiles, in order for example to estimate the rate of return to education, may be misleading as cross-sectional age–earnings profiles are not identical to longitudinal profiles. Creedy and Hart (1979) use longitudinal data to show that the earnings profiles of successive cohorts of individuals 'overtake' preceding older cohorts so that the longitudinal profiles are much steeper than cross-sectional profiles. In their sample, the cross-sectional earnings profile reaches a maximum at age 45, although when the longitudinal profile is considered, the maximum is at age 54 (p. 282; see also Phelps Brown, 1977, p. 265).

Contrast this with *Figure 5.3*. The implication of these results is that each successive cohort embodies trend productivity growth in the economy, as do successive vintages of capital goods. Whatever the distribution of lifetime earnings and the explanations for it, however, it is essential to remember that the major issues concerning pay inequality, such as policies towards low earnings, should refer to pay inequality over the lifetime and not at a point in time.

5.3   The orthodox theory of pay inequality

Occupational and inter-industry wage differentials

Neoclassical theory attempts to explain both the determination of the pay structure and mechanisms by which the actual pay structure converges to a new equilibrium in the face of shifts in the underlying relationships. Such an account is easiest to understand when the labour market is assumed to be competitive, with real wages adjusting in the short run while supplies and demands adjust in the long run, and it is with such an account that this section begins. However, modern neoclassical economics has evolved more sophisticated theories in order to explain why adjustments are sluggish in the labour market, and therefore why earnings differentials persist which appear to be incompatible with competitive theory. Such theories incorporate search under uncertainty, non-price adjustment mechanisms and explanatory equations which reconcile the evidence with the theory by postulating quality differences among workers, and non-wage job attributes. These developments are considered later in this section. The danger with these more sophisticated versions is that the greater realism and predictive power of econometric equations is only obtained by sacrificing what would appear to be key elements of the underlying theoretical framework, such as price flexibility. The result is an account of the pay structure which is rather catholic in its implicit assumptions.

Consider therefore the simplest case, where the labour market is competitive in the sense that there are no elements or monopoly or monopsony in the contractual process and where labour is perfectly mobile geographically with full information. Then an equilibrium wage structure will exist giving a set of relative wage levels for different occupations or skills. Where labour is homogeneous, then in the long run labour supply is perfectly elastic to any occupation or skill and relative wage levels are determined by the net non-pecuniary advantages of particular jobs, such as working conditions and status.

If labour is not homogeneous, the analysis must be modified. In the short run, certain kinds of labour, a particular skill for example, may not be in perfectly elastic supply. The demand for that skill will therefore enter into the determination of its wage relative to other skills. An exogenous increase in its demand will lead to an increase in its employment which will induce a rise in its relative wage until the wage is just equal to the marginal revenue product of the last man employed (note that the wage is the dependent variable). On the other hand, unless there are monopolistic elements on the supply side, shifts in the supply function should not be observed in the short run since net advantages can be taken as given in all but the long run. Therefore there should be a positive correlation between changes in employment and changes in wages for particular skills in the short run.

In the long run, even if labour is not homogeneous, net advantages should dominate and there should be no correlation between employment changes and wage changes. For if a particular skill is in excess demand, employers will be encouraged to substitute other skills or machinery for that particular skill asuming some technological substitutability in the production function. Further, workers will be encouraged to invest in acquiring that particular skill and the increased supply of labour will drive down the relative wage. Therefore in long-run equilibrium, in the absence of imperfections, discounted lifetime earnings net of non-pecuniary advantages will be equalized.

The approach to inter-industry wage differentials in competitive markets is similar to that used to explain occupational differentials. If non-pecuniary differences between industries are ignored, then under competition all industries will pay the same wage for a particular grade of skilled labour. Since skill mix differs among industries, inter-industry wage differentials will be determined by differences in the skill mix. As Reder (1962) points out, in equilibrium there should be no correlation between the quantity of labour and capital employed, or changes in them, and relative wage levels, since in the long run factor supplies and demands should adjust so that inter-industry wage differentials solely reflect non-pecuniary net advantages (which may be industry-specific as well as skill-specific). In the short run changes in inter-industry wage differentials may stem from differential industrial growth in combination with relatively inelastic supply functions for particular skills. However, skills should not generally be industry-specific and labour of the same skill ought to be mobile among industries. Thus Sawyer (1973) argues from cross-sectional data that there is no evidence for a rising supply curve of labour to either the plant or the industry, as opposed to skill or occupation.

One important consequence of this argument is that over long periods the pay structure, whether inter-occupational or inter-industry, should be relatively stable. Routh (1980) argues that the stability of the ranking of average earnings by industry over periods of ten or twenty years, for example, constitutes a fundamental criticism of 'the doctrine that supply and demand determine price'. However, Routh is not correct on this particular point, because stability in the long run is quite consistent with the definition of equilibrium outlined previously, although of course it is also consistent with other interpretations. Such a criticism of competitive theory would be justified if it were found that in the short run, prices were not adjusting to eliminate excess supplies and demands. Instead, the difficulty with the long run in competitive theory is that the pay structure is then determined by non-pecuniary factors to which it is difficult to apply the tools of conventional analysis.

The correct test of neoclassical theory as offered by Crossley (1966) and Reder (1962) is therefore that a positive correlation between employment and earnings changes should only exist in the short term, and both quote evidence to this effect. It is therefore a little worrying to find that in contrast, using data from Wragg and Robertson (1978), it appears that the relation between employment growth and the growth of earnings per head is stronger in the longer term. Using their data for 82 industries, it is possible to calculate the correlation between the growth of employment and the growth of earnings per operative for periods of different length. For the period 1954 to 1973, the correlation coefficient is +0.315 whereas it is only +0.124 for the shorter period 1963 to 1973, largely because the dispersion of earnings growth in the shorter period is greater and apparently unrelated to employment growth. Periods of 10 years cannot of course be considered as the short term. Studies for much shorter periods do show a significant positive correlation between employment changes and changes in earnings per head, although sometimes the estimated coefficients imply an extremely elastic short-term labour supply function which, as Crossley (1966) points out, may be implausible.

Wragg and Robertson (1978) do, however, test other relationships and generate results which accord with neoclassical theory. Under competitive conditions, earnings per head should be related to the marginal revenue product of labour and not its average productivity as measured by, for example, the capital –labour ratio. Therefore over time the growth of productivity per head in different industries as a consequence of the use of more or better machines should not be reflected in the differential growth of earnings per head. Rather, differential productivity growth among industries is reflected in a changing structure of relative prices of output and therefore in the differential growth of output and employment. Wragg and Robertson (1978) find that this is broadly correct, although other 'demand-side' interpretations of these results have been suggested in which differential productivity growth is not the cause but the effect of movements in output, employment and relative prices.

Underlying neoclassical theory is the presumption that labour markets are sufficiently competitive to incorporate the predicted adjustment mechanisms of prices in the short run and quantities in the long run. Non neoclassical theory, as will be seen in the next section, emphasizes the uncompetitive nature of product and labour markets and especially the existence of oligopolistic firms and trade unions. Studies of inter-industry wage differentials have therefore often attempted to introduce both competitive and monopolistic market structures into their econometric explanations. The result in some cases is a tendency to *ad hoc* theorizing. Sawyer (1973) finds that manual earnings across manufacturing industries are positively correlated with skill proportion but not the semi-skilled proportion, and that plant size is an important determinant of earnings. He attributes this to higher labour quality or non-pecuniary disadvantages of larger plants. Hood and Rees (1974) explicitly argue that wage differentials result from 'imperfections' such as concentration and trade unions, and include other variables such as the capital–labour ratio which should have no effect in a competitive model. Both studies find that a measure of industrial concentration, which is an obvious imperfection, is not significant when plant size is introduced into the regression. Neither author tries to isolate supply and demand functions, although this criticism cannot be applied to Metcalf *et al.* (1978) who attempted to explain simultaneously hours and earnings, the latter being the dependent variable on the demand side.

Education and the distribution of earnings

The theory of investment in education is described in Chapter 4 and is not examined in full detail here. This section is concerned with the relation between educational attainment and the distribution of earnings. Competitive theory predicts that the returns offered by different occupations, adjusted for different costs of education and non-pecuniary advantages, ought to be equal. If adjusted returns are not equal, a greater supply of entrants should be attracted to those occupations with an above-average return. However, American estimates quoted by Phelps Brown (1977, pp. 239–240) suggest that net discounted lifetime earnings for different occupations adjusted for training costs differ quite sharply. This suggests that higher returns to an occupation do not always induce a greater supply of entrants, either because of barriers to entry or imperfections, whether of information or in capital markets. In particular, a plausible hypothesis suggests that individuals from lower socioeconomic groups face social barriers to entry and are more uncertain about expected returns in various occupations (given the observed dispersion in age–earnings profiles in all occupations) which leads them to apply higher discount rates to future earnings, and face constraints in the capital market.

Competitive theory seems to be on stronger ground when examining returns on education averaged across occupations. Here the average rate of return seems to be fairly uniform for different average levels of educational attainment, and close to returns on other types of investment. Nevertheless, differences in educational attainment, as measured by years of schooling, do not explain the greater part of differences in earnings. Mincer (1976), for example, finds that differences in educational attainment explain only 7% of the inequality of earnings among urban white males in the 1960 US Census. Differences in educational quality are a possible explanation for this finding, but it is difficult to measure quality differences without being involved in circular reasoning; that is, measuring higher quality by higher returns.

In general the long-term growth of educational attainment resulting from greater public provision has been seen as an important explanatory variable for the gradual decline in the differential between skilled and unskilled labour and between white-collar and manual workers. In Britain, for example, whereas male skilled workers earned 131% and male clerks 122% of average earnings in 1913–1914, by 1978 these percentages had fallen to 110% and 93% respectively (Routh, 1980, Table 2.29). Nevertheless, disaggregated studies for individual occupations and industries suggest that this process by which differentials have been compressed over time is erratic and has largely taken place in times of major upheaval such as war and drastic inflation. Routh (1980, Chapters 3 and 4) goes so far as to argue that the evidence therefore provides little proof for neoclassical theory and suggests that custom, or notions of 'fairness', explain the stability of the pay structure except in periods of rapid social change when concepts of justice themselves alter. Certainly the overall distribution of individual earnings has remained remarkably constant, as Routh (1980, p. 214) shows for British manual workers from 1886 to 1974, which is perhaps a paradox if differentials are predicted to narrow in the long term .

Non-price adjustments in labour markets

In the first part of this section, it was argued that in neoclassical theory, under competitive conditions, market convergence to equilibrium implied short-term adjustments of earnings differentials to reflect excess supplies or demands for particular skills. Modern macroeconomic theory argues that markets, particularly the labour market, do not operate in this fashion. Labour is not hired on a day-to-day basis in most occupations and the contract between firms and workers often contains provisions for relative security of tenure and future earnings. This may be a rational response to uncertainty and suggests that firms may use adjustment mechanisms other than prices, such as hiring standards, hours worked and inventories, especially where fixed costs are substantial and employers are bargaining with trade unions[6].

If the firm wishes to minimize turnover costs and to offer price stability as a form of insurance for workers, certain consequences follow, as outlined by Casson (1981). First, turnover costs are lowest for the least skilled groups as a result of low specific training by the firm. Secondly, in order to maintain the goodwill of workers, employers may be prepared to guarantee employment and wage and salary structures even when falls in product demand generate temporary excess employment in the firm. Because firms find it easier to discriminate in employment conditions in labour markets than among customers in product markets, privileges can be offered to selected groups of workers, usually the more skilled among manual and non-manual employees. This generates a 'dual labour market' in which some workers obtain wage stability and job security while others do not (see section 5.4 for further discussion of this point). Of course, in periods of generalized demand deficiency of regional labour markets with heavy unemployment, hiring and firing practices may differ considerably from this model (Cheshire, 1981). Even so, it is rare for firms to implement wage cuts for selective groups of workers, as indicated in the famous argument of Keynes (1936, Chapter 2) concerning the efficacy of general real wage cuts as opposed to selective money wage cuts.

In general the theory implies that there is a trade-off between wage rate adjustments and turnover costs. Some firms in a labour market may pay lower wage rates than the average and incur higher turnover costs, while others offer higher wages and minimize turnover costs (such as costs of specific training). This might explain the dispersion of occupational earnings levels in local labour markets observed by many authors, such as Addison (1975). Moreover, adjustments in hiring standards by employers lead to higher-paying firms employing higher quality labour so that part of the earnings dispersion can be explained by quality differences.

Nevertheless, in a competitive situation, it is surprising that firms with similar skill mix facing the same local labour market are able to pursue differing strategies in relation to wage levels and turnover costs, unless these happen to be equiprofitable. In addition, while quality differences are sometimes measureable[7], they are sometimes introduced to the argument *ex post* to explain outcomes such as pay dispersion for given measured characteristics which are incompatible with the underlying theory. Neoclassical theorists often criticize theories of the type described in the next section for lacking rigour in hypothesis testing and for *ex post* rationalization of phenomena in the labour market. Nevertheless, no set of theories seem immune from these types of methodological error[8]. The question to be considered next is whether alternative accounts of the pay structure offer a superior explanation of observed inequalities.

5.4   Alternative theories of pay inequality

Although neoclassical models of the labour market presently dominate the discussion of pay structure, alternative theories of the pay distribution have a long history and have often been influential. One strand stems from the observation that different groups of workers coexist in relatively distinct labour markets and form what have been called 'non-competing groups'. In some of these markets, it has been argued, wages are fixed by institutional procedures which bear little relation to 'the forces of supply and demand'.

The idea of non-competing groups has a long history, going back to Mill (1848) and Cairnes (1874) in the nineteenth century and, more recently, institutional economists such as Dunlop (1957) and Clark Kerr (1954) in the United States. Its modern equivalent, which is considered below, is the theory of segmented labour markets. The argument that wage structures are established by reference to institutional bargaining procedures rather than market forces also has a long history in both the United States and

Britain; in the latter case respresented by authors such as Wootton (1955), Routh (1980), to some extent in the work of Phelps Brown (1977), and recently Wood (1978). Most of these writers suggest that because the existence of monopoly and monopsony in large parts of the labour market leads to collective bargaining, wage structures are determined within a 'range of indeterminacy' (which is presumably rather wide) and a crucial role is played by established wage relativities and notions of 'justice' and 'fairness'. Again, conventional theoretical explanations play little part.

A second, more recent, strand in alternative theories stems from the empirical work carried out in urban areas in the United States in the late 1960s in which it was argued that investments in education and training failed to raise significantly the earnings of minority groups in the labour market, such as blacks and women. Differential wages and patterns of employment experience seemed to persist and these could not be easily explained by orthodox theories, namely through differences in individual productivity (Gordon, 1972, Chapter 1). Of course, orthodox theories have analysed issues such as the existence of racial discrimination, but in general they believe that in the long run wage differentials that are not related to differences in individual productivity would disappear.

A third strand in alternative theories is the recent resurgence of Marxist economics. Unlike some institutional theorists, 'classical' Marxist analysis operates with a model of competitive capitalism which is similar in certain respects to neoclassical theory. Thus competition among firms maximizes the growth of the economy (the accumulation of capital) and excess supplies of labour, created by labour-saving innovation in both industry and agriculture, drives down real wages. Modern capitalism is of course more complex and contains both a competitive sector as well as oligopolistic firms and partially unionized labour markets. Such an analysis argues that one of the key elements in interpreting movements in the pay structure and the operation of various labour markets is the structure of control by managers and owners over workers in the work-process. Thus Edwards (1979) describes the complex historical process in the United States by which differing strategies of management control, changes in the pay structure and types of behaviour in the labour market are linked together. Such a macroanalysis yields interesting empirical insights, but it is clear that it is not easily amenable to orthodox hypothesis testing.

Although the genesis of these three strands is dissimilar, they overlap sufficiently to generate predictions concerning labour market structure, the inadequacy of human capital theory, and the existence of discrimination, to merit a combined account. These predictions are now considered, and subjected to empirical investigation in section 5.5. It should be noted, however, that many of these insights can be incorporated into orthodox analysis. The essential difference between orthodox accounts rests in the degree of importance attached to them. For example, Hicks (1932, p. 80) writes, in a well-known phrase: 'rules of fairness and justice are simply rough-and-ready guides whereby the working of supply and demand is anticipated'.

A central question, therefore, concerns whether unorthodox accounts can indeed generate a consistent theoretical but testable account of the pay structure which is alternative to the orthodox theory. This is precisely where some sceptics, such as Cain (1976), have had their doubts.

Segmented labour markets

The theory of labour market segmentation has been described and criticized by a number of authors. Good recent surveys from various perspectives are those of Gordon (1972), Wachter (1974) and Cain (1976). Because orthodox economic theory might accept certain kinds of immobility among sectors of the labour market, the present discussion is narrowed down to consider only a bipartite division of the labour market, the so-called dual labour market theory, and a variant of this, the tripartite division.

Dual labour market models argue that there are two sectors of the economy; a primary sector and a secondary sector. The primary sector is composed of 'good' jobs which on average pay high wages wih fringe benefits, higher levels of job satisfaction, less coercive methods of control, strong unions or staff associations and predominantly male, white labour forces. A consequence of these characteristics is that job stability is high and turnover of employees low. Within firms operating in the primary sector, internal labour markets exist through which individuals are shifted between jobs or promoted to superior ones. Entry to the firm from the outside market is limited to certain 'ports of entry', usually at the bottom of the hierarchy when the entrant is relatively youthful. The wage structure of the firm is determined by the formal or informal rules governing the operation of the internal labour market; the simplest view of it is as a hierarchical structure in which wage and salary grades are institutionalized and personal performance is related to his or her position in the hierarchy (by such criteria as length of service) rather than to individual productivity. Considerations such as the relative excess supplies or demands for any particular skill are largely irrelevant to the relative pay of that skill. Individual qualifications may determine where the individual enters the hierarchy, but plays little part in the determination of earnings thereafter although specific training may play a part. Further discussion of internal labour markets may also be found in Chapter 7 of the present book.

The secondary labour market, however, operates more closely along the lines of an orthodox market. In this market are 'bad' jobs with less skilled types of work, lower wages, routine and coercive methods of control, weak trade unions and the 'marginal' sections of the workforce such as immigrants, racial minorities and women. Turnover is high and job stability low. High turnover, coupled with the barriers to entry to the primary sector imposed by limited ports of entry, means that once in the secondary sector, workers tend to remain there throughout their working lives. Finally, even if workers in the secondary sector have qualifications, they do not gain enough experience and specific training in any one job to obtain the age–earnings profile usually associated with better education and training. Since all workers who are denied access to the primary market, as well as 'marginal' workers who leave and enter the labour force according to economic conditions, enter the secondary market, there is a roughly uniform ruling wage in the secondary sector irrespective of individual characteristics, such as age and education, of workers in that sector.

The overall wage structure depends not on the individual characteristics of the labour force but on the supply of 'good' jobs in an hierarchical wage structure relative to the supply of 'bad' jobs with a homogeneous ruling wage. The relative supply of these kinds of job depends not on the supply of different skills but on the size of employment in the primary sector relative to the secondary sector. By analogous reasoning, inter-industrty and inter-regional wage structures are also determined by the relative supplies of different types of jobs.

A variant of the labour market segmentation approach is offered by Edwards (1979). In his analysis, there are three kinds of labour market. The secondary labour market is identical to that described in the dual approach, but the primary labour market is divided into a subordinate primary and an independent primary segment. The subordinate segment corresponds to what he calls the 'traditional proletariat', namely most blue-collar jobs, whereas the latter comprises what he calls 'the middle layers', or white

collar and some skilled manual jobs. The subordinate primary
market shares some of the characteristics of the secondary labour
market but differs in other respects, most notably in the unionization of its workforce. Thus while this sector is more 'open', since a
fully-fledged internal labour market does not exist, the presence of
unions ensures that wages and employment conditions are better
than in the secondary labour market. The latter therefore contains
what Edwards (1979) calls the 'working poor'. Finally, he quotes
estimates suggesting that in the United States the proportion of the
workforce in the secondary market is approximately 17%, in the
subordinate primary 47% and in the independent primary 36% (p.
236).

In the context of the pay distribution, this further subdivision
has some merits, not least because if an hierarchical model of pay,
along the lines suggested perhaps by Lydall (1968), characterizes
part of the labour market, the evidence suggests that such a model
can only be applied to the upper tail of the earnings distribution.
Therefore the segmentation theory has greater merit if an hierarchical model of earnings is only applied to the upper part of the
primary segment – Edwards's (1979) independent primary sector.
Whether the segmented labour approach as a whole offers a
satisfactory explanation of the overall pay distribution is a more
general question, which is postponed to section 5.5.

The final question which might be posed at this stage concerns
why the labour market should be organized in this manner. Some
of the advocates of a dual approach, such as Doeringer and Piore
(1971), argue that specific training and fixed costs explain the
existence of internal labour markets, and it may be presumed that
these are in turn linked to the technological structure of different
industries. This fits in with the argument advanced in the last
sub-section of 5.3. Imperfect information may also play a role
(although discussion of this is postponed until various theories of
discrimination are analysed below)[9]. In the secondary labour
market, on the other hand, specific training and other fixed costs
are low and there is no incentive for employers to discourage
turnover by paying higher wages. This in turn reinforces the
preferences of individuals employed in the secondary sector and
these revealed preferences in the form of unreliability, absenteeism and so on are used by employers as indicators of the low
productivity of those workers.

An important distinction between orthodox and segmented
labour market theories in the light of the last point is that whereas
technology and tastes are largely exogenous in the orthodox
theories, they are endogenous in many versions of the theories of

segmentation. Thus, on the question of tastes an orthodox theory might use the propensity to quit of an individual as a variable 'explaining' his or her low wages whereas the two are interdependent acording to segmentation theorists. Similarly, technology measured by, say, plant size or capital–labour ratio, are typical exogenous variables in orthodox theories, but endogenous in other theories. Edwards (1979), for example, sees particular methods of production (technologies) as introduced by management in conjunction with a variety of wage regimes as alternative strategies for controlling labour. Unfortunately, the more parameters become variables in models of labour markets, the more difficult it is to find a test which offers a satisfactory method of assessing the explanatory power of the various models.

Screening and job competition
In the model of segmented labour markets, the determinants of pay structure differ in the two segments. In the primary sector, wage differentials are determined in hierarchically organized job structures, while unskilled workers and those with weak attachment to the labour market are crowded into a secondary segment characterized by bad job conditions and a largely homogeneous ruling wage rate irrespective of personal characteristics. It is not a particularly unorthodox observation to argue that personal characteristics are of less importance in some jobs than others; rather the question is who fills particular jobs. The job competition theory of Thurow (1976) offers a slightly different interpretation of the labour market to that offered by segmentation theorists. Nevertheless his account also provides an alternative to the orthodox account of the role of individual qualifications such as education in determining the position of the individual in the pay structure.

A neoclassical economist would argue that even if wages are attached to jobs not individuals, higher paid jobs are in general filled by more qualified individuals because such individuals embody more human capital. Thus if the supply of individuals of a particular quality is increased, the greater number of individuals competing for jobs utilizing that qualification will force wages down for those jobs relative to others. This reduces the return to that qualification (Addison and Siebert, 1979, pp. 120–121).

Thurow starts from the observation that different jobs embody different skills, but that these skills are not obtained from training outside the firm but from on-the-job-training within the firm. Jobs are in effect training slots and individual wages are in part related to the extent of on-the-job-training rather than to prior qualifications. For the employer, such training offers a relatively cheap way of obtaining higher productivity, since most on-the-job-training is informal. The employer will select individuals for employment who are thought able to learn quickly, so that the immediate advantages of high productivity compensate for the fixed wage for that job. The advantage for the employee is that because most on-the-job-training is informal and related to experience, the employer is likely to guarantee security of tenure and stable or rising real wages to the workforce in order to induce existing workers to pass on their acquired knowlege. An important consequence, in the context of government retraining programmes for example, is that outside training poses a threat to this informal relationship because informal training is the basis of security of tenure and measures to circumvent it will thus be resisted by workers. The overall consequence of this model for the distribution of pay is that this pay distribution is determined by the distribution of skill requirements (technology) and the subjective preferences of employees as to what is 'fair', since this alone guarantees the reproduction of informal training (Thurow, 1976, Chapter 5).

What determines which workers are offered these training slots? Employers screen applicants according to their 'trainability' and the relevant background characteristics in the screening process include education. In effect, applicants are ranked in a queue by employers and where background characteristics are roughly similar, subjective elements such as sex and race may come into play. This is the basis of the statistical theory of discrimination discussed below. Nevertheless the crucial point here is that more qualified individuals are not hired by employers becaue they are thought to embody more human capital, but because on average they will be more trainable. Increasing the supply of qualified individuals will not reduce the return on training by lowering the wage for that particular qualification, but by forcing some unlucky qualified individuals to accept jobs which offer less training. Thus the average return to the qualification declines although not by the orthodox mechanism outlined previously. This is not simply a pedantic point because the screening theory implies that increasing educational attainment, as a way of raising low incomes, will not work unless the number of training slots is increased (just as labour market segmentation theorists argue that the supply of 'good' jobs needs to be expanded). Similarly, such a theory explains why individuals 'overinvest' in education even when the return is declining for fear of losing their place in the queue. This phenomenon is also emphasized, for different purposes, by Hirsch (1977).

While the process by which job and wage structures are generated according to Thurow (1976) seems plausible, some of his ideas, most notably that education does not embody human capital and is solely a screening device, have received substantial criticism from orthodox theorists. The criticisms are again examined in section 5.5.

Labour market discrimination

A third central issue in the debate between orthodox and unorthodox theories concerns the explanation of discrimination, which may be defined as paying a distinct group of workers less than their marginal product. Discrimination may be revealed either by differential wages for equally productive workers or, when wages are attached to jobs, by segregation of groups of workers as the discriminated group are unable to obtain employment in some sectors of the labour market.

In principle, competitive labour markets offer no scope for discrimination. A theory of discrimination in such circumstances, of the kind offered by Becker (1971), therefore postulates that employers have a 'taste' or preference for discrimination which leads them to sacrifice profits willingly either by paying the non-discriminated group more or by offering less employment to the group discriminated against than would be warranted by their collective marginal productivity. However, unless every actual or potentially competing employer has identical 'tastes' for discrimination, competition ensures that in the long run discriminating firms will be forced out of business. This theory would therefore be implausible as a long-run theory of discrimination irrespective of its doubtful assumption of an exogenously given 'taste' for discrimination.

On the other hand, monopoly in product markets might explain discrimination, since long-run competitive constraints are ruled out in the product market, even if not the financial market. But as Cain (1976, p. 1233) points out, neoclassical economists generally minimize the extent of monopoly. This is not surprising, because if discrimination is pervasive in the economy, so too must be monopoly, and this is not conducive to other parts of the neoclassical framework.

However, there is no evidence for the proposition that it is monopoly in factor markets which *directly* increases discrimination (Ashenfelter, 1972; Nickell, 1977) although segregation of women and racial minorities may have taken place as a result of trade union activities[10].

The main difference between neoclassical and unorthodox theories of labour markets concerning discrimination is in the treatment of what is normally taken as exogenous, the preferences or tastes of individuals. As with the behaviour of workers in the secondary sector, unorthodox theories make some attempt to endogenize discriminatory preferences. In its simplest form, this attempt may rely on the assertion that wage structures are institutionally given, and that women and racial minorities, particularly if these groups are relatively new to the labour market, are fitted into the existing wage structure in accordance with social prejudices. If this is correct, then whether or not such groups receive their marginal products is largely irrelevant because other workers are also not paid by that criterion. Such social factors also explain pre-entry discrimination. For example, the fact that women choose to work part-time or leave the labour force for prolonged periods can be used as a reflection of individual or household preferences in the neoclassical model, or as a manifestation of wider social inequalities in alternative theories.

Furthermore, unorthodox theories argue that discrimination may represent collusive strategies rather than individual preferences for discriminatory behaviour. Collusion among emloyers (outside the market) may be a means of keeping down the wages of a significant group of workers, such as blacks in South Africa and the American South, in order to raise profitability. Similarly, workers may collude to exclude women in order to reduce the labour supply offered to employers and thereby to raise their own and family wages (Humphries, 1977). Nevertheless collusive strategies are always likely to be under pressure in competitive labour markets.

Finally, it is useful to note a theory of discrimination which, although stemming from orthodox economists, fits in well with the view of qualifications taken by Thurow (1976). If qualifications are used as a screening device and wages are fixed, in other words costs of obtaining information concerning individual productivities are too high to merit search for perfect knowledge, then employers will use overt factors such as race or sex to discriminate among workers. For example, women will be discriminated against because they are perceived as *on average* being less productive, prone to quitting or unreliable. This perception is certain to be false for particular individuals in the group discriminated against, and may indeed be so for the whole group. In the latter case, the same problem emerges as with competitive theories of discrimination; it is in the interests of some to hire the group discriminated against in order to raise profitability. It is easy therefore to explain discriminaton against individuals but, strictly speaking, a statistical theory of discrimination against groups has to postulate that information concerning the discriminated group is less reliable and that employers are risk averse. Even then, the model would seem to work best for small minorities or immigrants, groups for which there is little reliable information, rather than for long-term discrimination against substantial groups such as women.

Competitive theory can posit the existence of discrimination but suggests that there are tendencies that undermine it in the long run. Unorthodox theories imply that competition is less pervasive, that markets may not signal correct informaton, and that social perceptions may permit and reinforce collusive strategies among employers. A test of the merits of the alternative theories might therefore be as to whether there are long-run differences in earnings among distinct groups which cannot be explained by differences in personal and job characteristics.

Poverty and unemployment

According to Cain (1976, p. 1217) the most important social problem motivating alternative accounts of labour market structure is the persistence of poverty in the United States despite the political commitment to full employment and various anti-poverty programmes. Side by side with the existence of poverty, they argue, is the existence of what can effectively be termed 'structural' unemployment. This is defined in this context as high unemployment among specific groups of workers, such as racial minorities, which does not appear amenable to traditional reflationary policies.

There are several strands in the explanation of this persistence in the unorthodox literature. The first is that 'good' jobs are in short supply and specific groups such as racial minorities are crowded into low-paying jobs in the secondary sector. These are the 'working poor' as categorized by Edwards. Job instability, coupled with high rates of entry to and exit from the labour market, lead to high unemployment rates for workers in this sector. Further, since there are no opportunities for advancement in the secondary sector and limited ports of entry to the primary sector, a 'cycle of poverty' develops. This group of workers experiences low wages at work, prolonged work interruption, and frequent exit from and re-entry to the labour force. An expansion of aggregate demand may induce a 'trickling down' effect by which 'good' jobs are created, some of which are filled by workers who are, or would otherwise have been, locked into the secondary sector. However the inference of alternative theories is that these opportunities are very limited, and an expansion of aggregate demand will probably lead to an increased rate of wage inflation in the primary sector because of barriers to entry rather than the creation of substantial extra primary sector employment.

In so far as this account has realism, it is clearest in its application to 'ghetto' unemployment in the United States (Gordon, 1972). Nevertheless a similar argument has been advanced concerning unemployment and poverty in the inner city areas of Britain. A similar policy inference is also drawn, namely that even if increased employment opportunities are provided in inner city areas, the labour force within these areas will not necessarily benefit, since applicants may be drawn from outside that spatial labour market to fill these jobs (Cheshire, 1979).

A neoclassical theorist might respond with some justificaton that there is nothing in the orthodox account of pay structure to predict that poverty or unemployment would be eliminated, even in a relatively prosperous economy. Nevertheless there is a difference of emphasis because orthodox theorists would emphasize the importance of supply side characteristics, for instance increased education and training, in reducing pay inequality and the concentration of the incidence of unemployment among relatively well defined groups. In the absence of such policies, low-wage earners are in poverty by virtue of their lower productivity. Thus direct labour market intervention to eliminate low wages, such as minimum wage legislation, will simply exacerbate unemployment. Such workers are not 'structurally' unemployed, but simply the most vulnerable in recessions because of their lack of specific training.

Moreover, modern orthodox theories typify the process by which jobs are found and lost in a different manner from theorists in the alternative framework. The former argue that the unemployed engage in a process of job search, by which individuals set a 'reservation wage' which should reflect reasonable expectations of the wage offer distribution which they are likely to face. Theory would predict that a lack of education and training would reduce the probability of job offers to disadvantaged groups, while the higher ratio of unemployment insurance benefits to net expected wages for such groups would reduce the intensity of search. Thus they would predict an inequality of unemployment experience among various groups in the labour market. Nevertheless an unanticipated expansion of aggregate demand (technically, an unanticipated expansion), by creating new employment opportunities, should induce a fall in unemployment rates among all types of worker, irrespective of personal characteristics.

5.5   Testing the alternative theories

This section considers empirical tests of the alternative theories and, in so far as it is possible, it concentrates on the British evidence. The American literature is now so extensive that a concise summary is impossible.

Segmented labour markets

The dual labour market hypothesis has been held to imply that because 'good' and 'bad' jobs are distinct, this polarization should be reflected in a bimodality of some kind, whether of job characteristics, incomes or whatever. As Wachter (1974) points out, however, there is no agreed empirical dichotomization. Thus, firms principally operating in the primary sector may also hire workers for some of its grades of employment from the secondary market (the sectors here being defined as distinct labour markets). Psacharopoulos (1978), for example, argues that in the British context there is little evidence for a bimodal distribution of earnings, or of 'good' and 'bad' jobs, where jobs are defined along the Hope–Goldthorpe scale according to their desirability (see Goldthorpe and Hope, 1974). In fact, the distribution of 'good' jobs along this scale is multi-modal but it is difficult to attach too much importance to this result when the scale in question was subjectively designed for other purposes.

Most critics of the dual labour market theory therefore point to the uni-modal distribution of earnings to cast doubt on the predictions of dual labour market theory. However, such critics rarely consider the consequences of aggregating dissimilar distributions and what predictions would stem from such a procedure. Suppose, for example, that all part-time workers were assigned to the secondary sector and all full-time, non-manual workers to the primary sector. Aggregating these two distributions might produce a uni-modal distribution with a long upper tail. Nevertheless, a glance at those particular distributions for Britain, in *Figures 5.1* and *5.2*, suggest that the two distributions are quite distinctive, with the part-time distribution concentrated around median earnings irrespective of occupational status, much as the dual labour market theory might suggest. The difficulty in inferring the existence of a dual labour market from such a disaggregation of the overall distribution is that the implied bimodality of the pay structure is derived *ex post*, when what is needed is a prior classification of jobs before earnings bimodality can be proven.

There are two further difficulties in utilizing pay distributions as a measure of duality. The first is that even if a distinct structure of earnings exists in the two sectors, the evidence is open to alternative interpretations. Suppose that some kind of hierarchical model explains the distribution of earnings in the primary sector but not in the secondary sector. Such a distinction could be compatible with a number of theories. Wachter (1974, pp. 644 –648), for example, accepts that an hierarchical structure of earnings exists in the primary labour market but argues that it has efficiency consequences; in particular that the internal labour market screens workers and places the good ones in good jobs. Although this is not incompatible with some of the arguments of dual labour market theorists, paralleling for example the purpose and functioning of what Edwards (1979) calls 'bureaucratic control', it also implies that entering the primary labour market does not necessarily guarantee secure advancement and that marginal productivity considerations are still implicitly determining the pay structure within the primary sector. If this is correct, then individual characteristics should still play a leading role in determining individual earnings, just as orthodox theorists predict.

Wachtel and Betsey (1972) therefore offer the following test for the existence of labour market duality. In order to explain individual earnings, they distinguish variables pertaining to individual characteristics, essentially labour supply variables, from 'structural' variables which are largely non-competitive labour demand variables (occupation–industry, region, union status and city size). Favourable structural characteristics, by implication, are associated with primary sector jobs so if these variables are significant in explaining individual earnings, then some implications of dual labour market theory are valid. They find that this is indeed the case. Nevertheless this test too does not offer a clear vindication of alternative theories because an orthodox theorist would use many similar demand-side variables in order to explain individual earnings. If there is an implication of these results, it is that attempts to reduce the inequality of income or to reduce poverty, whether among the employed or the unemployed, simply by improving supply-side characteristics (such as educational levels or greater government training) or a general increase in the level of aggregate demand will be limited in success by market imperfections. The implication of segmentation models is that industrial structure and the organization of labour markets is at fault and that measures such as minimum wage legislation and increased unionization, which may appear counter-intuitive in a competitive world, are the best ways of reducing pay disparities.

Orthodox theorists would respond that such policies may have detrimental effects on labour market efficiency if markets operate in a competitive way. An overall evaluation therefore needs to compare the evidence presented in the present section with that in section 5.3.

The second difficulty in using individual earnings distributions results from the use of data derived from cross-sectional surveys. An implication of dual labour market theory is that workers are trapped in the secondary labour market, being unable to benefit from having qualifications or other human capital. This suggests first that lifetime earnings should be the dependent variable and secondly that a test of dual labour market theory is whether the rate of return on human capital, especially education, differs in the two segments. Two further testable inferences from dual labour market theory, which are examined in later sub-sections, also stem from this – namely, that there is no significant mobility between the two sectors and that qualifications operate as screening devices. For the moment, the question of differential rates of return on human capital over the lifetime is considered.

Bosanquet and Doeringer (1973) use such an argument to infer that there is a dual labour market in Britain. They use evidence from the Department of Education and Science to show that age–earnings profiles for men and women for given levels of qualification are quite different (see also Phelps Brown, 1977, Figure 5.1). This is simply not evidence of a dual labour market, however, because it implies that labour market segmentation is identical to segregation by sex without providing theoretical justification. It is therefore unable to separate segmentation from discrimination, and does not consider the response of human capital theorists such as Mincer (1962) to this outcome in terms of 'role specialization', which is considered below.

A more pertinent test of differential rates of return in the two markets therefore is first to separate the two sectors by some criterion and then test for the different performance of the human capital variable in the two sectors. McNabb and Psacharopoulos (1978) divide jobs into the two sectors, choosing as their cut-off points jobs on average in the lowest decile of the pay distribution and, as a measure of 'bad' jobs, those jobs with a desirability rating of below 30 points on the Hope–Goldthorpe scale for both occupations and industries. Several studies have truncated the occupational distribution in such a manner in order to test for differential returns in the two sectors. But such a procedure is inappropriate for the statistical reason that if occupations are classified by their earnings, lower returns to education in the secondary sector simply reflect the definition of segmentation which ignores the effect of schooling on earnings via changes in occupations (Cain, 1976, pp. 1246–1247; Addison and Siebert, 1979, pp. 191–192). McNabb and Psacharopoulos (1978) use both earnings, in error given this argument, and occupational desirability as measures of segmentation. When the desirability variable is used to measure duality, they find no difference between the two sectors; indeed the human capital variable performs rather better in the secondary sector. But the force of their critique of the duality hypothesis is reduced by the arbitrary nature of the cut-off points by which they demarcate occupations. In practice, this whole test of segmentation seems to be of dubious value, since most human capital theorists argue that it is education in conjunction with training which raises lifetime earnings, whereas segmentation theorists argue that duality deprives those in the secondary market of any training. The question for policy-makers is whether better education will lead to a reduction in the inequality of earnings and here the evidence, at least from the United States, is mixed[11].

It was suggested that an alternative test for labour market segmentation would examine whether individuals are able to move freely between the two sectors. Substantial mobility would suggest that the dual labour market theory is wrong and provide support for a neoclassical model of wage determination. Mayhew and Rosewell (1979) provide one such test for Britain. They use data from the Oxford survey of social mobility which investigated whether people remain in the same occupation over various periods. Again, Mayhew and Rosewell (1979) allocate jobs to the two segments by their own assessments of status and by use of the Hope–Goldthorpe scale. On the first criterion, they find that around two-thirds of those classified in the secondary labour market remained there ten years later. Using the Hope–Goldthorpe scale, the proportion of stayers was even higher (1979, pp. 91–92). They conclude that there is a good deal of mobility but the mobility is far from random.

Metcalf and Nickell (1982) also test for mobility, among 400 occupational groups over the 10-year period 1965–1975. The occupational structure is ranked according to average pay, and movements are investigated which involve shifting to an occupation with the higher or lower average pay. Since the pay ranking of occupations may itself have shifted over the period, 1975 pay rankings are used throughout. They find that about two-thirds of individuals were in the same occupational band in both 1965 and 1975, that greater training and education increased the likelihood of upward movement, and that sickness and unemployment increased the probability of downward movement within the period. They then allocate occupations to primary and secondary segments by a number of factors including average earnings, and find that for individuals aged 30 and over, 60–70% in the secondary sector were still there 10 years later. This reflects a decline in the numbers employed in these occupations in this period, and provides some evidence for immobility, but there is no clear evidence for a strict segmentation in mobility patterns when the whole pay structure by occupation is considered.

These studies provide interesting evidence, but again cannot be considered as the final word on tests of segmentation. A problem with both studies is that they do not provide a satisfactory account of how much mobility is to be expected over such a period according to orthodox theories in contrast to market segmentation theories. If a *rate* of movement could be predicted theoretically, then a *pattern* of movement could be derived which could then be compared with observed movements. Unfortunately, deriving a predicted rate of movement is a tall order. Thus it is only possible to interpret these results as showing, in the case of Mayhew and Rosewell (1979), that once in the primary sector, few workers move down and, in the case of Metcalf and Nickell (1982), that workers tend to get trapped in the secondary sector unless they have some education and training. A second problem mentioned by Metcalf and Nickell is that such tests do not consider intraoccupational movements. These are alternative forms of mobility which should both be incorporated in the model of segmentation. The problem is less serious in the case of Metcalf and Nickell because occupational earnings bands are defined fairly narrowly. Nevertheless, the conclusion concerning these studies must be that they are illuminating but not conclusive proof or disproof of the dual labour market hypothesis.

Screening and job competition

An implication of a number of unorthodox theories is that earnings do not reflect differences in productivity. There is an empirical correlation between education and earnings, but this reflects the use of education as a screening device by employers, not the fact that educated individuals embody higher productivity as human capital theorists suggest. Within the primary sector, the internal labour market pays screened individuals either according to an institutionally given hierarchy (Doeringer and Piore, 1971) or according to on-the-job-training (Thurow, 1976) or according to ability (Wachter, 1974).

Taubman and Wales (1973) provide indirect support for a version of the screening hypothesis. They use American data on earnings from follow-up surveys in 1955 and 1969 of Army Air Force applicants who were tested for mental and physical ability in 1943. They find that individual earnings are related to both education and ability, although if anything the latter is more important. They then test the screening hypothesis in the following manner. If the wage structure reflects differing individual productivities, individuals will be distributed through the earnings hierarchy according to their education and ability (measured from the original 1943 tests). In fact, allowing for all productive characteristics, individuals with higher qualifications are over-represented in higher paying jobs and individuals with fewer qualifications are over-represented in lower paying jobs. Because education and ability do affect earnings over the lifetime, Taubman and Wales (1973) conclude that education is used as a screening device. But once employed both ability and education play their part in 'filtering up' more productive individuals through the hierarchy. Educational investment is necessary to maintain the place in the queue, but some educated individuals do not get jobs consonant with their overall productivity. The consequence is over-investment in education, which is reflected in the low rates of return on education found by Taubman and Wales (1973) once individual earnings are adjusted for differential ability.

Layard and Psacharopoulos (1974) oppose the screening hypothesis. They argue, against Taubman and Wales (1973), that if people are paid according to their ability and education once employed, then there is no difficulty in judging productivity and thus screening is unnecessary. But it is surely possible to argue, with Wachter (1974), that the internal labour market is a way of judging efficiency of employees without arguing that the employer has sufficient information to select applicants for vacancies without recourse to a screening procedure. Secondly, they argue that it is not the qualification itself that raises earnings since drop-outs perform as well as qualifiers over the lifetime. Therefore screening must include college entry as well as certification, which admittedly seems implausible. Thirdly, they suggest that returns to education do not diminish over the lifetime, which suggests that education has a lifetime effect as human capital theory would predict. On the other hand, a number of reasons could be adduced as to why the earnings of educated individuals continue to rise over the lifetime, and not all of them are consistent with the human capital story. Finally, since education is an expensive screening device to maintain, they argue that an alternative cheaper method of screening ability could be found.

This final criticism goes to the heart of the difference among various theoretical frameworks. A neoclassical theorist would argue that screening exists because of imperfect information about individual productivity and that employers would search for the screening device that is most consistent with a pay structure that selects individuals according to their expected productivity. Thus employers probably do use alternative screening devices, such as the aptitude tests in 1943 described by Taubman and Wales (1973), if the specific skills of the job so require, although in general employers do not bear the costs of education, so that using qualifications as a screen is probably a satisfactory procedure in many circumstances. Nevertheless a more generalized critique of the neoclassical position would argue that pay structure is not in general related to individual productivity, and is governed by institutional inertia, notions of equity and custom, imperfect knowledge and other structural constraints. In so far as education measures an individual attribute, it is not the human capital embodied in that individual but his or her general 'trainability' which lies at the heart of the screening process. The type of education received by an individual is a generalized measure of potential performance such as his or her acceptance of the work ethos, reliability, discipline and so on (Bowles and Gintis, 1976). The implications of such an approach for an understanding of the role of education and the functioning of the labour market are quite distinct, and it is difficult to think of any satisfactory test procedure that would allow the researcher to discriminate between the two theoretical approaches.

Labour market discrimination

It was suggested previously that both orthodox and unorthodox accounts of the pay structure are consistent with the existence of discrimination, whether on racial grounds or against women. The question to be considered here is whether investigations of discrimination cast any light on the predictive power of these various accounts of pay determination. Two recent studies concerning Britain, that of McNabb and Psacharopoulos (1980) on racial earnings differentials, and that of Greenhalgh (1980) on male –female differentials, are now examined.

McNabb and Psacharopoulos (1980) use data from the General Household Survey to isolate the sources of differences in earnings between white and coloured employees. By regressing earnings of the two groups on a set of characteristics, they find that the major cause of differences in earnings is differences in the return on education. In addition, the regression for coloured employees is unaffected by the industry in which they are working, unlike white employees. This latter point, as they suggest, provides some support for the idea that wages are roughly homogeneous for coloured individuals, perhaps because they are crowded into a few industries or jobs. The implication of this is to provide some support for the dual labour market hypothesis.

The differential rate of return on education also appears to support one of the contentions of labour market segmentation theorists. However, McNabb and Psacharopoulos (1980) proceed to disaggregate the schooling variable to take account of type of schooling and find that differential returns are most apparent for those coloured workers who obtained only a secondary modern educaton. Further the return on various qualifications for coloured workers varies widely. Finally, once this disaggregation is undertaken, the return on experience (a proxy for on-the-job-training) is also lower for coloured groups. In conclusion, coloured workers appear to be largely segregated into jobs that offer little training, a conclusion backed up by Stewart (1978), and obtain a lower return on education not through differential attainment but through lower returns on a basic secondary modern education. Although the authors might not wish to accept this view, it appears in the light of the earlier discussion that their evidence provides substantial support for some of the predictions of dual labour market theory.

The case of women is more complex. It was argued earlier that the evidence presented by Bosanquet and Doeringer (1973) for different male–female lifetime earnings profiles did not constitute an adequate test of dual labour market theory because, unlike a racial minority, it seems implausible to assign the majority of the female labour force to the secondary market. Moreover the neoclassical theory of household behaviour pioneered by Becker (1965) and others might predict, on the basis of 'role specialization', that women would obtain lower returns on education and other measures of individual productivity because of an interrupted working life stemming from marriage and child-minding (that these roles may illustrate more general forms of discrimination in society is an important issue, which is not pursued here).

Greenhalgh (1980), also using data from the General Household Survey, presents earnings functions for men and women, disaggregated by marital status. Her object is to find out what proportion of the earnings differential between men and women is attributable to discrimination in the labour market, and what proportion attributable to marriage, which she hypothesizes may heighten the work effort of the husband and reduce that of the wife. The analysis was performed on heads of households and wives to obtain similar age distributions. She shows that the earnings of single women were only slightly lower than for single men, but that there was a much greater disparity between married men and married women (1980, Table 1, p. 756). She finds that much of the diference in age–earnings profiles is attributable to marriage, but that even for single women, especially those who are unqualified, there is evidence for differential age–earnings profiles, particularly in relation to the experience variable. The earnings differential against single women had narrowed between 1971 and 1975, which she attributes to the effect of the Equal Pay Act of 1970, but the position of married women had not improved, which she hypothesizes is because many married women work part-time where the Equal Pay Act is less effective[12].

The evidence of Greenhalgh therefore provides some support for both the neoclassical and alternative models of the pay structure. A model of family behaviour can explain part of the difference in earnings between men and women, and qualified women appear to benefit from investments in human capital as such a theory would predict. On the other hand, differences in earnings among less qualified women appear to stem, as with racial minorities, from crowding into sectors with little on-the-job-training and into part-time employment where legislative protection is less stringent. Investments in education provide lesser benefits to female workers in such sectors. Again this gives some support to the concept of a secondary labour market where individual productive characteristics play a diminished role in pay determination and overall it may be concluded that studies of discrimination suggest that dual labour market theory has some validity.

Poverty and unemployment

It was suggested in the previous discussion of the various theories that observed inequalities of income and unemployment do not offer a satisfactory means of comparing the predictions of alternative theories. Furthermore, the literature in this area is now vast and accordingly this section concentrates on just a few of the specific issues.

The first test to consider is whether an improvement in supply side characteristics reduces income inequality and the unequal incidence of unemployment. Section 5.3 suggested that some levelling of average pay for broad occupational categories has come about, and that this might be attributed to the increased educational attainment of the labour force. Nevertheless the inequality of individual pay in Britain has remained roughly constant, although some reduction in the share of the highest percentile has taken place. In the case of training, Mincer (1976) shows a positive correlation between experience, which is his measure of training, and earnings. All the models of pay structure seem to agree that increased training raises earnings, subject to the qualification of Thurow (1976), that outside training by the government may substitute for, rather than complement, informal on-the-job-training. For if the informal training relationship is broken and job security threatened by an external supply of trainees, employers may be encouraged to dishoard trained labour in recessions (Cheshire, 1981), and greater training may simply lead to a more equal 'sharing-out' of poverty and unemployment rather than a reduction in the level of either.

A second issue relates to the supply characteristics of unemployed workes. All theories agree that individuals with inferior supply side characteristics will, on average, experience shorter job tenure, more frequent job changing, and higher rates of unemployment than other groups. There is no easy way of discriminating between alternative hypotheses. An implication of non-orthodox theories is that unemployment is highest among groups with inferior supply or other perceived characteristics. Disney (1979) suggests that the experience of unemployment is highly concentrated in Britain once allowance is made for recurrent spells of unemployment and Creedy and Disney (1981) show that the tenure of workers in given labour market states in Britain, defined by level of work interruption, is larger than would be predicted from models of random movement. Clark and Summers (1979) describe similar but more detailed results for the United States which cast doubt on job search explanations of unemployment.

Nevertheless, these results point to inequalities which are difficult to incorporate, although not capable of refuting, an orthodox account of poverty and unemployment which emphasizes supply-side factors. On the other hand, although a concentration of unemployment experience fits in well with market segmentation theories, the difficulty in establishing a specific test of such theories, in relation to unemployment and poverty, limits conclusive proof of their validity. A true longitudinal study of the

relation among employment instability, unemployment and lifetime earnings would offer interesting evidence, but the real test
among such theories in this area probably lies in their alternative
predictions concerning the success of orthodox policies to reduce
poverty and unemployment.

5.6   Conclusions and some policy implications

The alternative theories of the pay structure examined in preceding sections are based on quite distinct views concerning the
operation of labour markets and the rewards to individuals within
them. Underlying the central concepts of orthodox theory is a
competitive model in which individuals are rewarded on the basis
of their productivity characteristics and the nature of the job to
which they are attached. Alternative theories are heterogeneous
but share the belief that markets are basically not competitive, and
that individuals are rewarded by criteria other than their individual
productivity. The evidence suggests that in so far as these various
theories yield testable hypotheses, there is some justification for
both sets of theories. Nevertheless the difficulty in testing the
underlying postulates of orthodox and alternative theories is one
reason why much of the recent literature in labour economics has
been econometrically-oriented and catholic in its theoretical
assumptions.

Ironically, in some respects the broad predictions of the two
broad theoretical frameworks are not dissimilar. Crossley (1966,
p. 230) believes that the pay structure broadly reflects the predictions of a competitive framework, and that therefore there is little
need for government intervention in the context of pay relativities
to eliminate distortions and 'imperfections'. Many institutionally-
orientated economists would come to the same conclusion, but
argue from a quite distinct theoretical framework in which intervention is likely to be ineffective. This ineffectiveness is because
relativities are long-standing; they are institutionally determined
by 'distortions', like socially-established notions of fairness and
'imperfections' such as unions, and by informal training and
hierarchical pay structures.

There is probably most disagreement among the schools of
thought on microeconomic policies. Orthodox theories emphasize
policies towards supply-side characteristics and the overall demand for labour, whereas theorists in alternative frameworks
emphasize the nature of job characteristics and in particular, the
need to expand the number of 'good' jobs, and to share them out

more equitably. Expanding 'good' jobs involves not just increasing the supply of jobs by aggregate demand management but also by intervention in the labour market to improve 'bad' jobs, presumably by such measures as minimum wage legislation, improvements in working conditions and unionization of low paid sectors. Sharing out more equitably involves such measures as positive discrimination in favour of minorities in job hirings.

The role of minimum wage legislation in attempting to improve 'bad' jobs and to reduce the incidence of low pay in Britain has been examined by a number of authors. An inter-industry analysis of low pay for male manual adult employees was undertaken by Woodward and McNabb (1978) who found that the low-paid proportion was positively related to the proportion on shift work, the proportions unskilled, aged under 20 and female, and to the lack of industrial concentration. Metcalf (1980) examined by how much the workforce fell short of a low pay bench-mark of £60 per week and found that for men the proportion of the total wage bill that would be necessary to bring all workers up to this bench-mark is 0.68%. For women the corresponding figure is 10.13% and for the total labour force the proportion of the total wage bill is 2.83%. At first sight this would suggest that the extra wage costs resulting from the institution of a minimum wage would be rather low, if differentials above the minimum remain unchanged. But the incidence of low pay is uneven among industries, being as high as one-third of the female labour force in distributive trades and a quarter in clothing and footwear (Baines et al., 1981) and employment implications of minimum wage legislation in such industries may be substantial. Thus Metcalf suggests that national pay policies and existing Wages Councils have been rather unsuccessful in improving the position of the lowest paid. Finally, if both orthodox and alternative theorists suggest that pay relativities are slow to change, in the absence of competitive shifts or changes in notions of 'fairness' respectively, minimum wage legislation may do little to narrow relativities.

There has been little attempt at positive discrimination in favour of minorities in Britain, other than in the case of the disabled, and this has not been particularly successful. While legislation to protect existing workers has now been passed in most countries, including Britain, measures to affect hiring practices have a chequered history. The weakness of such policies is that serious unemployment problems among distinct minorities are most apparent in recessions, when fewer hirings are taking place and there is little scope for government intervention. On the other hand, there is evidence that legislation, prohibiting discrimination in the forms of both wage differentials between races and sexes and employment refusals for discriminated groups, has had some effect. Landes (1968), for instance, finds that in states with fair employment laws in America, racial differences in earnings were lower although, as neoclassical theory would predict, the difference in unemployment rates between blacks and whites were greater than would otherwise have been the case. As mentioned previously, Greenhalgh (1980) finds some evidence for a reduction in discrimination against single women after the passing of the Equal Pay Act, but also finds that occupational segregation, or indirect discrimination, against married women persists. There is, therefore, further scope for econometric testing of the effect of various policies to combat inequalities of pay. Whether such evidence will lead to a clear victory for one of the alternative frameworks for analysing pay structure must, however, remain open to doubt.

Notes

1. The data quoted in this section are taken from the Department of Employment's *New Earnings Survey, 1980.*
2. Disney (1981, section 6.4). The variance of weekly or annual earnings may therefore be a poor measure of the riskiness of an occupation.
3. See Lydall (1968, Chapter 4). Professional labour markets are examined in Chapter 7 of the present book.
4. In 1978 33.9% of girls gained five or more higher grade 'O' level GCEs or CSEs compared with 31.1% of boys, although the subjects studied differed between the sexes (NCCL, 1980).
5. For discussion and further references see Brown (1976), Lydall (1968), Pen (1971), Phelps Brown (1977) and Thatcher (1976).
6. For a discussion of adjustment mechanisms see Thomas (1981). The influence of trade union bargaining on the pay structure is examined in Chapter 6 of the present book.
7. See, for example, Metcalf (1973).
8. In the view of this author, Addison and Siebert (1979), for example, can be criticized for taking a one-sided view of the methodological pitfalls of non neoclassical theory. Routh (1980), with some justification, suggests that the 'outcome' of the Lester–Machlup debate on marginal productivity is another example of implicit double standards.
9. The role of imperfect information is also discussed in Chapters 4 and 7 of the present book.

10. See Phelps Brown (1977, sections 5.2 and 5.3).
11. See, for example, Weiss and Williamson (1972), and also the discussion of human capital theory in section 5.3.
12. Since anti-discrimination legislation relies on the existence of comparability and part-time work is almost entirely female, discrimination is hard to prove in law. My thanks to Erika Szyszczak for pointing this out.

References

Addison, J. T. (1975). On the interpretation of labour market earnings dispersion: a comment. In *Readings in Labour Economics* (ed. by J. E. King), pp. 311–320. Oxford; Oxford University Press

Addison, J. T. and Siebert, W. S. (1979). *The Market for Labor: An Analytical Treatment.* California; Goodyear

Ashenfelter, O. (1972). Racial discrimination and trade unionism. *Journal of Political Economy* **80,** 435–463

Baines, B., Halliwell, M. and Richards, J. (1981). The determination of low pay in UK manufacturing industry. University of Kent at Canterbury (mimeo)

Becker, G. (1965). A theory of the allocation of time. *Economic Journal* **75,** 493–517

Becker, G. (1971). *The Economics of Discrimination.* Chicago; The University of Chicago Press

Bosanquet, N. and Doeringer, P. B. (1973). Is there a dual labour market in Great Britain? *Economic Journal* **83,** 421–435

Bowles, S. and Gintis, H. (1976). *Schooling in Capitalist America.* London; Routledge and Kegan Paul

Brown, J. A. C. (1976). The mathematical and statistical theory of income distribution. In *The Personal Distribution of Incomes* (ed. by A. B. Atkinson), pp. 72–97. London; George Allen and Unwin

Cain, G. G. (1976). The challenge of segmented labour market theorists to orthodox theory: a survey. *Journal of Economic Literature* **XIV,** 1215–1257

Cairnes, J. E. (1874). *Some Leading Principles of Political Economy Newly Expounded.* London; Macmillan

Casson, M. C. (1981). Unemployment and the new macroeconomics. In *The Economics of Unemployment in Britain* (ed. by J. Creedy), pp. 48–98. London; Butterworths

Cheshire, P. C. (1979). Inner areas as spatial labour markets: a critique of the Inner Area Studies. *Urban Studies* **16,** 29–43

Cheshire, P. C. (1981). The regional demand for labour services: A suggested explanation for observed differences. *Scottish Journal of Political Economy* **28,** 95–98

Clark, K. B. and Summers, L. H. (1979). Labour market dynamics and unemployment: a reconsideration . *Brookings Papers on Economic Activity* **1,** 13–72

Creedy, J. (1977). The distribution of lifetime earnings. *Oxford Economic Papers* **29,** 412–429

Creedy, J. and Disney, R. (1981). Changes in labour market states in Great Britain. *Scottish Journal of Political Economy* **28,** 76–85

Creedy, J. and Hart, P. E. (1979). Age and the distribution of earnings. *Economic Journal* **89,** 280–293

Crossley, J. R. (1966). Collective bargaining, wage-structure and the labour market in the United Kingdom. In *Wage-Structure in Theory and Practice* (ed. by E. M. Hugh-Jones), pp. 159–235. Amsterdam; North Holland

Department of Employment (1980). *New Earnings Survey 1980.* London; HMSO

Disney, R. (1979). Recurrent spells and the concentration of unemployment in Great Britain. *Economic Journal* **89,** 109–119

Disney, R. (1981). Unemployment Insurance in Britain. In *The Economics of Unemployment in Britain* (ed. by J. Creedy), pp. 150–185. London; Butterworths

Doeringer, P. B. and Piore, M. J. (1971). *Internal Labor Markets and Manpower Analysis.* Lexington; Heath

Dunlop, J. T. (1957). The task of contemporary wage theory. In *New Concepts in Wage Discrimination* (ed. by G. W. Taylor and F. C. Pierson), pp. 117–139. New York; McGraw Hill

Edwards, R. (1979). *Contested terrain.* London; Heinemann

Evans, A. W. and Richardson, R. (1981). Urban unemployment: interpretation and additional evidence. *Scottish Journal of Political Economy* **28,** 107–124

Goldthorpe, T. H. and Hope, K. (1974). *The Social Grading of Occupations.* Oxford; Oxford University Press

Gordon, D. M. (1972). *Theories of Poverty and Underemployment.* Lexington; Heath

Greenhalgh, C. (1980). Male–female wage differentials in Great Britain: is marriage an equal opportunity? *Economic Journal* **90,** 751–775

Hicks, J. R. (1932). *The Theory of Wages.* London; Macmillan

Hirsch, F. (1977). *The Social Limits to Growth.* London; Routledge and Kegan Paul

Hood, W. and Rees, R. D. (1974). Inter-industry wage levels in United Kingdom manufacturing. *The Manchester School* **42**, 171–185

Humphries, J. (1977). Class struggle and the persistence of the working-class family. *Cambridge Journal of Economics* **1**, 241–258

Kerr, Clark (1954). The balkanization of labour markets. In *Readings in Labour Economics* (ed. by J. E. King), pp. 305–311. Oxford; Oxford University Press

Keynes, J. M. (1936). *The General Theory of Employment, Interest and Money.* London; Macmillan

Landes, W. M. (1968). The economics of fair employment laws. *Journal of Political Economy* **76**, 507–552

Layard, R. and Psacharopoulos, G. (1974). The screening hypothesis and the return to education. *Journal of Political Economy* **82**, 985–998

Lydall, H. (1968). *The Structure of Earnings.* Oxford; Clarendon

McNabb, R. and Psacharopoulos, G. (1978). Further evidence on the relevance of the dual labour market hypothesis for the UK. *London School of Economics, Centre for Labour Economics Discussion Paper No. 38*

McNabb, R. and Psacharopoulos, G. (1980). Racial earnings differentials in the UK. *London School of Economics, Centre for Labour Economics, Discussion Paper No. 76*

Mayhew, K. and Rosewell, B. (1979). Labour market segmentation in Britain. *Oxford Bulletin of Economics and Statistics* **41**, 81–116

Metcalf, D. (1973). Pay dispersion, information and returns to search in a professional labour market. *Review of Economic Studies* **40**, 491–505

Metcalf, D. (1980). Low pay, occupational mobility and minimum wage policy in Britain. *London School of Economics, Centre for Labour Economics Discussion Paper No. 80*

Metcalf, D. and Nickell, S. (1982). Occupational mobility in Great Britain. *Research in Labor Economics* **5** (forthcoming) (ed. by R. Ehrenberg), Greenwich, Connecticut; JAI Press

Metcalf, D., Nickell, S. and Richardson, R. (1976). The structure of hours and earnings in British manufacturing industry. *Oxford Economic Papers* **28**, 284–303

Mill, J. S. (1848). *The Principles of Political Economy.* London; Longmans

Mincer, J. (1962). Labour force participation of married women: a study of labour supply. Edited and reprinted in *The Economics of Women and Work* (ed. by A. H. Amsden), pp. 41–51. London; Penguin

Mincer, J. (1976). Progress in human capital analysis of the distribution of earnings. In *The Personal Distribution of Incomes* (ed. by A. B. Atkinson), pp. 136–192. London; George Allen and Unwin for the Royal Economic Society

National Council for Civil Liberties (1980). *Education and Training*. Rights for Women Unit. London

Nickell, S. (1977). Trade unions and the position of women in the industrial wage structure. *British Journal of Industrial Relations* **15,** 192–210

Pen, J. (1971). *Income Distribution*. London; Penguin Books

Phelps Brown, H. (1977). *The Inequality of Pay*. Oxford; Oxford University Press

Psacharopoulos, G. (1978). Labour market duality and income distribution: the case of the United Kingdom. In *Personal Income Distribution* (ed. by W. Krelle and A. F. Shorrocks), pp. 421–444. Amsterdam; North-Holland

Reder, M. W. (1962). Wage differentials: theory and measurement. In *Readings in Labour Economics* (ed. by J. E. King), pp. 280–295. Oxford; Oxford University Press

Routh, G. (1980). *Occupation and pay in Great Britain 1906–79*. London; Macmillan

Royal Commission on the Distribution of Income and Wealth (1975). *Report No. 1,* Cmnd 6171. London; HMSO

Sawyer, M. C. (1973). The earnings of manual workers: a cross section analysis. *Scottish Journal of Political Economy* **20,** 141–155

Steward, M. (1978). Racial discrimination and occupational attainment. *London School of Economics Centre for Labour Economics Discussion Paper No. 89*

Taubman, P. J. and Wales, T. J. (1973). Higher education, mental ability and screening. *Journal of Political Economy* **81,** 28–55

Thatcher, A. R. (1976). The New Earnings Survey and the distribution of earnings. In *The Personal Distribution of Incomes* (ed. by A. B. Atkinson), pp. 227–259. London; George Allen and Unwin for the Royal Economic Society

Thomas, R. B. (1981). Labour market adjustments. In *The Economics of Unemployment in Britain* (ed. by J. Creedy), pp. 17–47. London; Butterworths

Thurow, L. (1976). Generating inequality. London; Macmillan

Wachtel, H. M. and Betsey, C. (1972). Employment at low wages. In *Readings in Labour Economics* (ed. by J. E. King), pp. 320–334. Oxford; Oxford University Press

Wachter, M. L. (1974). Primary and secondary labour markets: a critique of the dual approach. *Brookings Papers on Economic Activity* **3,** 637–680

Weiss, L. and Williamson, J. G. (1972). Black education, earnings and interregional migration. *American Economic Review* **LXII,** 372–383

Wood, A. (1978). *A Theory of Pay.* Cambridge; Cambridge University Press

Woodward, N. and McNabb, R. (1978). Low pay in British manufacturing. *Applied Economics* **10,** 49–60

Wootton, B. (1955). *The Social Foundations of Wages Policy.* London; George Allen and Unwin

Wragg, R. and Robertson, J. (1978). Post-war trends in employment, productivity, output, labour costs and prices by industry in the United Kingdom. *Research Paper No. 3.* London; Department of Employment

Chapter 6

Unions and the labour market

6.1 Introduction[1]

Trade unions are a major feature of the labour market. Well over half the labour force belong to them and their behaviour often arouses strong views. Hayek (1980), for example, has argued that trade unions have become the biggest obstacle to raising the living standards of the working class and that they are the chief cause of unemployment and the main reason for the decline of the British economy. Others assert the virtues of unions with equal vigour. The element of passion which invades much popular discussion of unions arises from the fact that they apparently influence economic efficiency and the distribution of income.

In this chapter some aspects of the behaviour and significance of unions are considered. The focus is on economic aspects though it is evident that a comprehensive analysis of unions would also require political and other perspectives. The growth of unions and the nature of collective bargaining are briefly discussed in this section and in section 6.2 the questions of why unions exist and how economists have modelled them are discussed. The effects of unions on allocation and on pricing are dealt with in sections 6.3 and 6.4. A number of interesting and important questions have had to be excluded. There is no discussion of the role of unions in determining aggregate money wages and of their influence on distributive shares in the national product, nor of government intervention in industrial relations[2].

The growth of unions

There has been a pronounced growth in union membership. Union density, which is defined as the percentage of the labour force belonging to unions, now stands at 56% as shown in *Table 6.1*[3]. The growth of membership has, however, been uneven and Bain and Price (1980, p.163) show that over this century the annual rate of change of density in Great Britain has fluctuated between

173

TABLE 6.1 Union membership and density in the UK, 1892–1979

	Union membership	Potential membership	Union density
1892	1 576	14 803	10.6
1900	2 022	15 957	12.7
1910	2 565	17 596	14.6
1920	8 348	18 469	45.2
1930	4 842	19 096	25.4
1940	6 613	19 992	33.1
1950	9 289	21 055	44.1
1960	9 835	22 229	44.2
1970	11 187	23 050	48.5
1979	13 498	24 169	55.9

Note
Density is union membership as a percentage of potential membership. Potential membership is employees in employment plus unemployed. (It excludes self-employed and HM Forces.)
Sources: Bain and Price (1980, Table 2.1) and *Employment Gazette*, January 1981, Table 2, p.23 and Table 1.1, p.57.

−21.4% and +27.0%. The longer-term movements show a very pronounced upward trend between 1910 and 1920 and a subsequent fall until a new upward trend began in the mid-1930s. A plateau of about 44% was reached in the years following the Second World War and a new upsurge began in the 1960s. Within this pattern of overall growth there have been some notable differences. Males are more heavily unionized than females though the gap in their levels of unionization has tended to narrow. The density of white-collar workers is about two-thirds of that for manual workers, though the rate of growth of white-collar membership has increased rapidly in recent years. Significant differences occur among industries in the level of unionization. In particular, the public sector tends to be much more fully unionized than the private sector. Deaton and Beaumont (1979), for example, show that the density figures for mining and quarrying are 90%; gas, electricity and water, 92%; public administration, 88%. High figures in the private sector are engineering, 70%; food, drink and tobacco, 51%; chemicals, 51%; at the lower end are agriculture, 23% and distributive trades, 11%[4].

The growth of union membership since the 1960s has been accompanied by increasing concentration in unions[5]. Between 1969 and 1979 the number of unions fell by 20% whereas membership increased by 29%. *Table 6.2* shows that almost 90% of the membership is accounted for by 9% of the unions[6].

A prominent feature of British union structure is its complexity. There is a mixture of 'open' unions which recruit over a fairly

TABLE 6.2 Concentration of union membership, 1979

Size	Number of unions	% of unions	% of membership
Under 1000 members	244	53	<1
1 000–9 999	125	28	3
10 000–49 999	43	10	8
50 000–99 999	15	3	7
100 000–249 000	16	4	18
250 000 and over	11	2	64
	454	100	100

Source: *Employment Gazette*, January 1981, p.23

broad range of grades of worker and 'closed' unions which restrict membership to one or two grades of workers[7]. The traditional pattern of organization has been along occupational lines because workers are generally most interested in the type of work they do, whereas employers have tended to organize on industrial lines since they are mainly concerned with the product they produce[8]. Industrial unions are rare in Britain.

Collective bargaining

The typical method of setting pay and conditions is by collective bargaining. In the case of manual workers in manufacturing industry, only 10% of establishments, employing 4% of the workforce, had no discussions or negotiations over pay, and these tended to be the smaller establishments[9]. In the case of non-manual workers in manufacturing collective bargaining has become more important; only 25% of establishments, employing 15% of the workforce, had no bargaining.

Collective bargaining is a process of rule-making[10]. These rules are of two kinds: substantive rules relating to pay, hours, and other conditions; and procedural rules which govern the way substantive rules are made and interpreted. Much of the subsequent discussion in this chapter is concerned with the role of unions in this rule-making process and the outcomes which are achieved, but two general remarks about collective bargaining are in order here. The first is that the substantive rules may be very wide-ranging indeed and it is therefore naïve to suppose that the employment contract is simply a question of setting prices and quantities, as in the case of other commodities[11]. It is much wider than the typical transaction in market exchanges and its substantive content is almost never fully defined at the moment of engagement. The terms are implicit and are often defined by practice[12]. One consequence of this is that prescriptions for the reform of collective bargaining which are based purely on moves towards greater formalization may have very limited success.

The second point is that the administration of rules may occupy as much or more time than the making of rules. The whole process of rule making and administration involves substantial transaction costs and in this sense bargaining may be an inefficient decision procedure. Johansen (1979, pp.519–520) has pointed out that

> it tends to distort the information basis for decisions, it tends to use or waste resources in the process, partially by delaying decisions for reasons which are not technically necessary, it will more or less frequently break down or fail to realize the potential gains and threats will sometimes be carried out . . . bargaining has an inherent tendency to eliminate the potential gain which is the object of bargaining.

The British system

A number of features of the collective bargaining system in Britain are described before examining the role of unions in this process. One of the most obvious developments in the last decade has been the rise of single-employer bargaining, and it is now the most important means of pay determination for two-thirds of manual workers and almost three-quarters of non-manual workers[13]. Single-employer bargaining has become particularly important in larger companies, and to a lesser extent, in companies that are foreign-owned. All this is not to imply that multi-employer bargaining is dead. It is still important in industries such as printing, where 84% of manual workers are covered by national agreements, clothing (63%) and textiles (61%). For many industries, however, the proportion of the workforce covered by single-employer bargaining is large; for example, mechanical engineering and shipbuilding (88%), vehicles (90%), metal manufacture (83%) and instrument and electrical engineering (82%). It is more difficult to be certain whether single-employer bargaining implies local bargaining.

Table 6.3 shows that the pay of about a quarter of manual workers was set by industry agreements, and the proportion was much smaller for non-manual workers. Employers' associations have thus tended to become advisers rather than negotiators and, as Brown and Terry (1978) have argued, the role of industry-wide rates has changed from providing a 'floor' which raises all earnings to providing a 'safety net' whereby only earnings of the relatively low-paid are affected.

TABLE 6.3 Bargaining in manufacturing industry

Level of agreement	Manual workers		Non-manual workers	
	% of establishments	% of employees	% of establishments	% of employees
Industry-wide	33.2	24.0	17.2	8.3
Regional	3.0	2.7	1.3	0.9
Sub-total	36.2	26.7	18.5	9.2
Corporate	11.3	21.1	14.9	28.6
Establishment	41.6	46.5	39.5	44.7
Sub-total	52.9	67.6	54.4	73.3
Other	1.2	1.3	2.0	2.8
No bargaining	9.7	4.4	25.1	14.7
	100.0	100.0	100.0	100.0

Source: Brown (1981, Tables 2.1 and 2.3)

Another feature of British industrial relations over the last decade has been the growth of the closed shop. The proportion of workers in manufacturing industry covered by such arrangements increased from 25% in 1962 to at least 39% in 1978[14]. Although the decline in manufacturing employment has been most pronounced in areas where the closed shop has been strongest, that is shipbuilding, steel and heavy engineering, there has been a rapid spread to new areas such as chemicals, food, drink and tobacco, and clothing and footwear. Closed shops are found more frequently in larger establishments and are more common for manual workers than for non-manual. A remarkable feature of the closed shop is that it is massively supported by management. Three-quarters of closed shops in the survey reported by Brown (1981, p.57) were found to have open and formal support by management and in most other cases there was tacit support. Such support is a relatively recent phenomenon and stems from the fact that the closed shop is seen as a procedural device which increases the representativeness and stability of collective bargaining. Managers regarded the chief disadvantages as the increased strength of unions, the tendency to restrict recruiting and inflexibility in dealing with individuals.

The growth of the closed shop and of single-employer bargaining has been accompanied by a pronounced increase in the role of shop stewards in the formal negotiating arrangements. Full-time stewards are now far more numerous than the full-time officials on the unions' own payrolls[15]. But all this does not necessarily reflect any real growth in union power. Brown (1981, p.120) concluded that

> where shop steward organizations have sprung up in factories with little tradition for workplace bargaining they may owe the superficial sophistication of their facilities and procedures more to the administrative needs of management than to the bargaining achievements of the workforce. . . . Furthermore, the heavy emphasis that has been placed on formalizing the role of shop stewards in recent years makes them poorly equipped to cope with managerial decision-making above the level of the factory.

The structure of collective bargaining has a number of consequences. First, as Clegg (1976) has argued, it may affect union behaviour. For example, strikes tend to be fewer where collective bargaining is conducted at higher levels and more numerous where there is plant-level bargaining. At lower levels of bargaining unions probably have a greater effect on relative wages (reported in section 6.4), and the power of shop stewards is likely to be greater where there is more enterprise bargaining and less centralization of union government.

Secondly, the bargaining structure may affect the efficiency with which labour markets operate if the coverage of collective agreements does not coincide with areas of labour market pressure. For example, if there is market pressure to increase the wage of some particular type of labour this may be a very costly form of adjustment if the increase spills over to the other workers covered by the same agreement[16]. But bargaining arrangements do not invariably override the market pressures; they sometimes crumble when market forces are strong. The move towards company-level bargaining away from national-level bargaining may represent some improvement in the degree of coincidence between bargaining structure and labour markets.

6.2   Economic models of unions

The importance of unions in the economy has naturally led to attempts to model their behaviour, but this has proved a more formidable task than modelling the behaviour of firms or consumers. Some of these attempts are considered in this section, though bargaining models are not explicitly covered since most of them are not yet sufficiently tractable or close to reality to have much operational content[17]. It is useful to consider two questions before examining these models. The first is 'why do unions exist?' Although their strength varies from one country to another, unions are sufficiently prevalent to suggest that there are good reasons why such institutions invariably emerge in capitalist economies. The second closely related question is 'what are the goals of unions?' Neither question has a simple answer and this accounts for some of the evident shortcomings of the models of unions.

Why do unions exist?

There are several reasons why unions exist. Perhaps the most obvious is that individual workers are at a serious disadvantage in bargaining with employers. Since pay is the main source of income for most workers they have been anxious to avoid interruption to this flow of income by strikes, sickness or unemployment. Early unions therefore performed some of the 'insurance' functions of friendly societies and attempted to enhance the individual's bargaining power by collective action and the organization of strike funds. Some form of cartelization or monopoly offers potential gains over what individual sellers of labour services could achieve.

In addition to securing better terms, unions may be better able to monitor these terms for employees. Alchian and Demsetz (1972) argue that many aspects of employer performance are relatively easy to check, such as whether the correct wage is being paid, but other aspects such as non-pecuniary contingent fringe benefits (for example, redundancy payments, accident compensation, retirement pensions) may be more difficult to judge. In high-trust situations there would be no need for workers to employ specialist monitors but usually there will be little effective sanction which individual employees can bring to bear on employers who will thus have an incentive to default in the absence of unions.

In some types of production unions may be seen as advantageous from both the employees' *and* the employer's points of view. The fact, noted in section 6.1, that closed shops are often regarded benignly by employers may not therefore be totally surprising. Where there is substantial interdependence among workers in production[18], and between workers and a large capital stock, then production may be greatly increased by having the work period, the pace of work and the conditions of work fixed for all workers.

Duncan and Stafford (1980) have developed this view and suggested that there are some 'public good' aspects of work in the sense that its consumption by workers is non-rival. An example of this is physical conditions such as a comfortable temperature. Another example is effort input. Where each worker's effort input is highly complementary, as on an assembly line, then if one worker were to obtain reduced effort input by unilaterally buying more leisure, than other workers could also enjoy more leisure without the firm losing any further output.

Securing a workforce which is agreed on major aspects of the organization of work may require the firm to search for workers with near-homogeneous preferences. But if search costs are high then collective agreements may be reached as a means of overcoming the problem of individual agreements where there are public goods. It may be cheaper for the firm to recognize a union and compensate those workers who have to trade-off the restrictions on their individual behaviour, in order to conform with the common workplace standards, by the payment of higher wages. Duncan and Stafford (1980, p.369) note that there will thus be a tendency to generate economic rents for some workers 'though unions can reduce the level of these rents by better identifying the preferences of the median worker'. In this sense unions may actually aid efficient resource allocation. For example, when new technology is introduced, the firm with an interdependent production process might have to hire a new set of workers and engage in costly search to find them if unions did not do the searching.

This view suggests unions are more likely to exist where the production process is characterized by interdependencies[19], and incidentally that there will be higher wages under collective agreements to compensate workers for thier acceptance of a more structured work setting where they have less discretion over such matters as the pace of work and the scheduling of hours of work.

Some of the rationale for the existence of unions rests on non-economic factors. Moral and political factors are sometimes relevant. Any gains which a union obtains over the non-union position are public goods which are available for both union and non-union members so why is there not extensive 'free riding' leading to the collapse of the union? Part of the answer (Olson, 1965) lies in the fact that unions do attempt to prevent this by coercion and the closed shop. It may also be possible to provide selectively some benefits such as representation in unfair dismissal or accident cases. It is important, however, to recognize that the closed shop is not

> merely a form of industrial terrorism. It derives its strength from, and could not be sustained without, the deeply-felt sentiment that free-riding is *wrong*, and the belief that one is morally obliged to share the costs of trade-unionism so long as one enjoys the benefits, even if – perhaps especially if – one is not actually compelled to do so. (King, 1980, p.160).

This suggests that non-economic dimensions of unions are important.

Union goals

Some of the *effects* of unions' behaviour are examined in sections 6.3 and 6.4. If one were only interested in the effects there would be no need to discuss objectives, but it would not be possible to say anything about the effectiveness of unions, and it is therefore of interest to comment on their goals. It is not, however, easy to identify these.

Reference has been made to the fact that unions are both political and economic institutions. There are several aspects of the political dimension.

First, the internal organization of unions is often a complex pattern of national, district and branch officials, shop stewards at the workplace and rank and file members. There are marked differences among unions in these matters and this highlights the fact that there may be no simple answer to the question of who decides goals and tactics. There are likely to be several different answers and the 'leadership' and 'members' may have different goals. The former, for example, may stress long-term survival more than short-term improvements and conditions. Ross (1948), in his celebrated study of unions as political institutions, argued that the leadership is likely to be better informed than the members and thus able to secure a higher priority for its own goals rather than those of its members. In Britain, where company bargaining and shop steward involvement have become prominent, the force of this argument may have lessened but it is still apparent that a union can be considered less of a holistic concept than the firm.

Secondly, unions may pursue their goals through political channels as well as through bargaining. For much of its history the union movement has been actively engaged in trying to influence legislation. Thomson and Hunter (1978) argued that unions have projected the industrial relations system in the larger economic and political systems and in some instances have been able to dominate national economic decisions and institutions. Thomson (1979) goes on to claim that as a result of the wide channels through which unions exert their influence a corporate state has emerged in which bargaining among the major interest groups forms the basis of most decision making.

Thirdly, unions sometimes pursue purely political causes. Conference debates on such issues as nuclear disarmament, South Africa, and education are common and resolutions are sometimes translated into action.

A feature of political studies of unions is that they tend to infer purpose from observed behaviour. This is the reverse of the usual procedure in economics where behaviour is deduced from postulated objectives. This latter mode of thought is paramount in most models of the economic behaviour of unions. They often assume maximizing behaviour though it has long been recognized (Reder, 1952) that unions may not in fact be maximizers. It is also frequently assumed that there is a *single* maximand. This is convenient for multiple goals make the problem of modelling complex if not intractable, but it scarcely reflects the political as well as economic character of unions.

Further difficulties arise because the goals are subject to change. This may be partly because of what Hyman (1971) calls goal displacement. Unions, like other organizations, are created to achieve some specific purpose or purposes, but these original goals tend over time to become supplemented and extended. Procedures devised for the efficient attainment of these goals assume such importance that the union leaders become committed to 'institutional goals' which are considered necessary for the union's security and stability. The organization becomes an end rather than a means. Survival and growth each become important objectives in their own right. Change in goals over time may also be attributable to the achievement of some of the initial aims. Major advances in minimum standards of employment on matters such as unfair dismissal, guaranteed minimum wages, time off for union duties, and unemployment and redundancy compensation have been secured through legislation.

Despite these difficulties it is possible to be reasonably confident about some of the goals of unions. It is undeniable that unions are interested in the material welfare of their members, and this provides some justification for the focus of some models on narrow economic goals. Unions are especially concerned with wage advance and their achievements in this respect are examined in section 6.4. The predominance of the wage objective has sometimes been questioned. Students of industrial relations have often observed that unions are concerned with *all* aspects of job regulation rather than just pay, and some economists (Johnson, 1975, p.25) have taken the view that the major function of unions is to regulate *non-wage* conditions of employment. But attempts to control such things as output, the pace of work, hours and recruitment, can be viewed as an indirect means of achieving higher pay and it is therefore reasonable to focus on pay as a major objective[20].

Other goals are achieving recognition by employers for collective bargaining purposes, survival, and growth *per se*. These of course are important political aims of the union leadership and they are closely linked. Bain's (1970) analysis of the growth of white-collar unions showed that recognition was a crucial factor in growth.

The service union

The relationship between workers and unions is often thought to be a direct parallel with that between customers and firms[21]. Individuals will join a union if perceived benefits outweigh costs. The union is seen as a business organization, producing services for members such as collective bargaining, education and political action. The pure service union, to use Berkovitz's (1954) term, is concerned on the one hand with revenues from selling membership subscriptions, and on the other with the costs of providing the services[22]. Survival requires that revenues are at least equal to expenditure and this may explain why growth is apparently a major objective of unions since there are some fixed elements in the costs of services. Negotiating on behalf of 100 000 members requires a less than proportionate increase in costs compared with negotiations on behalf of 1000 members, though revenues would be increased considerably[23].

More particularly, unions may be thought of as intermediaries in the labour market in the same way as investment trusts are intermediaries in the financial markets. Fisher (1971, p.133) has argued that workers require a whole range of information and advice on such things as pay, rights at work, and grievance procedures, and the union exploits economies of scale in this information collection. This is very much in the spirit of the Alchian and Demestz (1972) view of monitoring, which was noted earlier. Fisher also suggested that unions, as intermediaries, may act as insurers against certain contingencies such as unemployment or redundancy though with the growth of the welfare state these functions have become much less important. One of the difficulties of viewing unions as pure intermediaries, pointed out by Crossley (1973), is that it does not account for the fact that unions are invariably organizations of the workers themselves. Pure commercial organizations do not have this feature.

A simple monopoly model

An obvious alternative way of looking at unions is in terms of their ability to control the supply of labour. The focus is on the income of members rather than of the union *per se*. An early model by Dunlop (1944), which has appeared widely in the subsequent literature, assumed that unions try to maximize revenue. Revenue in this case is taken to be the income of members and costs are assumed to be zero so the union aims to maximize the total wage bill for the membership[24]. The union leaders' perception of the number of workers who will identify with the union at different wage rates is shown as the membership function, *M*, in *Figure 6.1*.

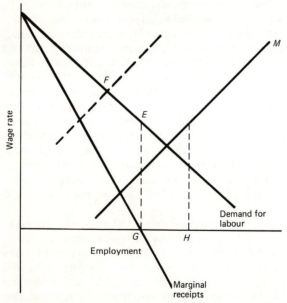

Figure 6.1 A simple monopoly model with maximization of the wage bill

It is positively sloped. The only constraint on the union's behaviour is the firm's downward-sloping demand curve for labour. The wage bill is maximized at the point of unit elasticity, E, since this is where the marginal receipts function is zero. If the intersection of the membership function and the demand curve had been to the left of E, as at F, then this would be the union's optimum position.

This type of model does give some interesting general qualitative predictions but it can hardly be directly translated into empirically testable propositions. There are some severe problems. It is not clear to what time period the analysis relates, and the effect of uncertainty characterizing the demand curve may make it extremely difficult, perhaps impossible, to identify the wage rate that maximizes the wage bill. Ross (1948), for example, argued that the slope and position of the demand curve are likely to change markedly during the life of an agreement so the employment implications of any wage become impossible to assess. This argument is still valid though it may have lost a little of its force now that the life of an agreement is typically one year only[25].

Another problem arises from the fact that many unions are not complete monopolists. Some workers may be non-members and maximization of the members' wage-bill becomes less certain. In any event the model implies that some union members may be unemployed (*GH* in *Figure 6.1*). It is not obvious that self-interested employed members could be persuaded to compensate unemployed members and resulting dissatisfaction of unemployed members would have to be considered by union leaders. All this adds up to a considerable question mark over the relevance of the wage-bill maximization model, though it does show clearly the possibility of monopoly wage gains. An elaboration of the Dunlop-type model would be to take account of the costs of achieving the maximum wage bill, such as strikes, so the *net* revenue would be maximized.

Two developments which meet some of these criticisms are first to recognize that unions are interested in both wages and employment and secondly to consider the role of employer preferences.

The wage–employment trade-off

Using an analogy with consumer behaviour Cartter (1959) has drawn an indiferrence map for a union, specifying its preferences between the level of wages and the level of enployment. These are competing goods. The optimum position for the union is that combination of wages and employment that maximizes utility given the constraint of the labour demand curve. This is shown as *E* in *Figure 6.2*. The shape of the union's indifference curves has been the subject of much speculation; they will be more rectangular the more complementary are wages and employment. The emphasis on each of these will be the outcome of political struggles within the union. As the demand for labour shifts, the optimum

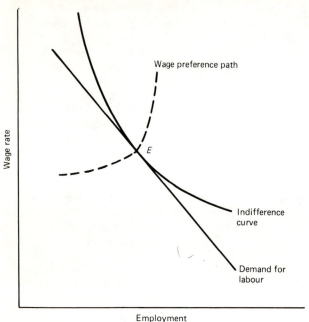

Figure 6.2 The wage–employment trade-off

point will change and the locus of such points is what Cartter (1959) has called the wage preference function. He suggests that it will be kinked as shown in *Figure 6.2* because the response to increases in the demand for labour is likely to be a preference for wages increases whereas the response to falls in the demand for labour is likely to be resistance to wage reductions[26].

Explicit consideration of employer's preferences is necessary if one is to determine the boundaries of the outcomes of the collective bargaining process. A useful elaboration of the simple monopoly model has been given by McDonald and Solow (1981) who demonstrate that the presence of unions may lead to inefficiencies in the sense of raising wages in excess of the marginal revenue product.

Consider a partial equilibrium analysis of a single profit-maximizing employer and a fixed pool of labour which is entirely controlled by a monopoly union. The firm will be faced with different combinations of wages and employment which yield the same level of profits. Such combinations can be represented by an isoprofit curve such as *CEKD* in *Figure 6.3*. The firm will be indifferent between points on any one such curve. For any given wage the firm will choose that level of employment which maximizes profits. The firm's sales proceeds are derived from selling the output produced by its labour force so its revenue will vary with employment and the revenue function can be written as $R(L)$. Profits are

$$\Pi = R(L) - wL \qquad (6.1)$$

where w is the wage rate and L the level of employment[27]. The slope of the isoprofit curve, dw/dL, can be found by setting the total differential of the profit function to zero. That is,

$$0 = (\partial R/\partial L)dL - wdL - Ldw$$

hence $dw/dL = \{(\partial R/\partial L) - w\}/L \qquad (6.2)$

The partial differential $\partial R/\partial L$ is the marginal revenue product of labour. When this is equated with the wage the slope of the isoprofit curve is zero, as at E in *Figure 6.3*. The isoprofit curve has a positive slope when $w < \partial R/\partial L$ and a negative slope when $w > \partial R/\partial L$. Lower isoprofit curves represent higher levels of profit and at a given wage of say w_1 the lowest isoprofit curve (highest profits) attainable is that which passes through E. Employment is then set at L_1. With the wage w_1 any other level of employment would lie on a higher isoprofit curve (lower profits). At different wages there will be different profit-maximizing points and the locus of these is the demand curve for labour. This has a negative slope[28].

The union's preference map is represented by the indifference curves in *Figure 6.3*. Given the labour demand curve the union will choose E[29]. *JEG* represents the highest possible level of satisfaction. Point E is an equilibrium for both parties; the firm is a wage-taker and sets employment unilaterally, and the union is assumed to set the wage and has to accept the quantity. It is apparent, however, that both parties could be better off if they moved to some point inside the shaded area. The union could reach *HKF* with no impairment of the firm's profits.

Points of tangency between the isoprofit curves and the union's indifference curves form the contract curve, shown as *NKM*. Both

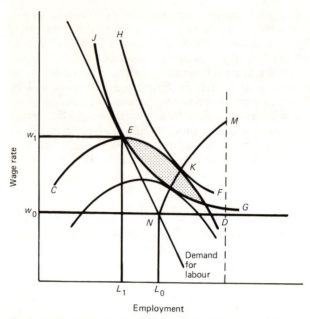

Figure 6.3 The determination of wages and employment in a firm
where there is a single union controlling a fixed pool of labour

parties will try to move on to this and thus w_1 appears too high and
L_1 too low. The union will try by devices such as agreements on
manning arrangements and the pace of work, to influence the level
of employment beyond that given by the demand curve for labour,
and the employer will try to influence wages. Bargaining takes
place over prices and quantities (and the model has thus been
transformed from a situation where one party was a price-taker
and the other a quantity-taker), but there is no determinate
solution on the contract curve.

Some features of the contract curve are known. It will cut the
demand curve at a wage w_0, which represents the supply price of
labour to the employer in the absence of unions. This can be seen
by assuming that the union wishes to maximize the memberships'
aggregate gain from employment, which can be expressed as the
product of the number of members in employment and the
individual member's gain in utility over the level derived from the
basic income with which each member begins; that is
$L\{\bar{U}(w)-\bar{U}\}$, where $\bar{U} = U(w_0)$. $\bar{U}$ is the level of utility obtainable
elsewhere in the economy and w_0 is the basic non-union wage; that
is, the supply price of labour. The slope of the indifference curve

can be found by setting the total differential of $L\{U(w) - \bar{U}\}$ equal to zero then

$$0 = L(\partial U/\partial w)\mathrm{d}w + \mathrm{d}L\{U(w) - \bar{U}\}$$

hence $\mathrm{d}w/\mathrm{d}L = -\{U(w) - \bar{U}\}/L(\partial U/\partial w)$ (6.3)

The indifference curves are asymptotic to w_0. On the contract curve the slope of the isoprofit curves and the slope of the indifference curves are equal, so that

$$\{U(w) - \bar{U}\}/(\partial U/\partial w) = w - (\partial R/\partial L).$$ (6.4)

Along the demand curve the right hand side of equation (6.4) is zero, because wages are equated with the marginal revenue product. The left hand side of (6.4) is zero only when $\{U(w) - \bar{U}\}$ = 0; that is when $w = w_0$. Thus the contract curve cuts the demand curve at w_0. The contract curve is bounded at the lower level by this intersection with the demand curve since no bargains can be struck with $w < w_0$, and it is bounded at the upper level by the total union membership, shown as M.

Points on the contract curve are, for both parties, superior to points such as E. It is not possible to say where on the contract curve the bargaining outcome will be. It will depend on bargaining power and if bargaining breaks down the outcome may not even lie on the contract curve. The model does, however, show clearly that there are pressures to move away from the competitive solution $w_0 L_0$, so bargains on the contract curve are only efficient from the viewpoint of the two parties concerned. Since all the points on the contract curve lie to the right of the demand curve the wage must exceed the marginal revenue product[30]. The existence of a union seems therefore to be advantageous for both parties in collective bargaining but does not, other things being equal, promote efficiency generally taking the competitive solution as the yardstick.

Bargaining power

The influence of the unions on pricing and allocation will depend on their bargaining power; that is on their ability to fix or alter the terms of exchange in their favour by imposing losses on employers through the exercise of sanctions. It is clear, as Bain and Price (1980, p.160) note, that power is not an independent absolute concept but is best viewed in terms of a specific relationship in a specific context since it depends on employer resistance and the

way this is affected by a whole range of economic and sociopolitical environmental variables such as product demand, technology,
legislation and public opinion. The difficulty of quantifying bargaining power has limited the operational usefulness of the
concept though a number of measures have been tried[31]. These
have included union membership, density, the rate of change of
density, and various measures of strike activity[32]. All of these have
rather obvious shortcomings, such as the lack of congruence
between labour market boundaries and the areas to which statistics on these measures refer, and the failure to account for
employers' resistance and the bargaining environment. The following remarks are therefore limited to a general discussion of the
sources of power and the way it is exercised.

The most propitious circumstances for the union to exercise
bargaining power are those associated with an inelastic labour
demand schedule. Marshall's famous rules, subsequently amended
by Hicks (1963), state that the demand will be more inelastic
where

(1) the elasticity of substitution between inputs is low;
(2) the elasticity of product demand is low;
(3) the share of wages in the total costs of production is low[33];
(4) the elasticity of supply of other inputs is low.

These rules describe conditions which give rise to once-for-all
gains. Fisher has argued that the rules relate to planning decisions.

> They imply that a union already formed will appreciate the
> advantages open to it . . . or, that a group of persons can detect
> the advantages of forming a union that can exploit the market
> situation. . . . If, in either case, the plan becomes operative,
> and is correct in its main features, the market position will be
> closed in the sense that it becomes no longer possible for further
> gains to be secured in this way. . . . Further unanticipated
> disequilibria, exhibiting these features, must arise before a
> union can gain further increases in wages in this way. (1971,
> p.146).

It is not, however, clear how far unions tend to organize and
achieve most in circumstances where the demand for labour is
inelastic and how far they themselves create inelasticity. They may
be able to do this by limiting the elasticity of subsitution between
labour and other inputs and by influencing the product demand
and the supply of other inputs. These strategies often involve
co-operation with other unions in order to exploit the economic

links among industries (for example, the triple alliance of miners, steelworkers, and railmen).

A popular view is that union power has increased over recent years. This view would be supported if one accepts measures of power such as union membership or density, but there is also the possibility that the demand for labour may have become more inelastic thus enhancing union power. Addison (1978) notes that this is often thought to be the case. On the basis of the Marshall rules it is attributed to capital-deepening, which raises the capital –labour ratio; to increasing concentration in industry which lowers the elasticity of product market demand; and to increasing division of labour which reduces the elasticity of substitution between inputs.

The three principal ways in which unions may exercise their bargaining power are by controls on the supply of labour, by the use of sanctions and by political activity. The latter includes attempts to lower employer resistance by altering the operating environment of the firm, for example by trying to influence governments to place contracts with the firm or to impose restrictions on the import of substitute products. Controls on labour supply and sanctions are usually of greater importance and these are dealt with in turn.

Attempts to restrict labour supply and make it less elastic above the prevailing wage, by entry controls such as apprenticeships, licensing rules and the limiting of dilutees, are well-known features of craft and professional workers' behaviour. Demarcation rules serve a similar purpose, and the closed shop is an obvious device to acquire monopoly power. Similarly, regulation of the supply of effort by controls on the pace of work, manning requirements and overtime is likely to secure advantage for the workers. Within the firm there may be complex sets of rules, often of an informal nature based on 'custom and practice', which govern internal allocation. Seniority rules governing redundancy and promotion affect the supply of labour to the firm.

Strikes

The third way in which unions exercise bargaining power is through strikes and other sanctions. As a response to offered terms and conditions in the labour market strikes are a form of protest behaviour. This contrasts strongly to the mobility behaviour, described in many economic models, where the response to unacceptable terms is movement. This so-called 'exit-voice' dichotomy is discussed in section 6.3. Most strikes are directed against employers, but at times they are called for other purposes. Sometimes they are protests at government actions such as incomes policies or particular attempts to legislate on industrial relations. They may be the result of inter-union disputes on recognition rights, job demarcation or wages differentials, and they may occasionally be used for internal political purposes. Union leaders may, for instance, need to demonstrate that the rank and file have unrealistically high expectations, or they may use a strike as a focal point of activity to produce a more cohesive and committed membership.

Sanctions may be used to secure bargaining goals, such as a wage increase, directly or indirectly. The latter is exemplified by the case of a union taking action to secure recognition, which will then place it in a stronger position to exert other pressures. Unions will normally attempt to minimize the cost of sanctions for any given degree of pressure exerted. There is frequent use of the so-called 'cut-price sanctions' such as working to rule (where there is an unnecessarily meticulous observance of work rules), overtime bans and 'go-slows', all of which can sometimes cause as much or more disruption than a strike. Threats of strikes may sometimes be sufficient to exert desired pressure though such threats will only be credible if strikes do sometimes occur.

Much empirical work has concentrated on the effects of strikes rather than on their effectiveness[34]. The effectiveness in achieving bargaining goals has so far proved too difficult to measure empirically.

> Bargaining theories often assume that there would never be a strike . . . [where the parties] . . . are perfectly rational and . . . have complete information about possible outcomes, about each other's utility function, and hence the payoff matrix . . . strikes are the result of either irrationality or mistakes. (Mayhew, 1979, p.2).

The probability of a strike actually being called will thus depend on each side's expectations and perception of the other side's position. Any strike, on this view, is 'accidental' (Siebert and Addison, 1981), resulting from mistakes. It is largely an information problem and they identify a number of circumstances where there will be a lower strike probability. Examples are, first, where there are cheaper channels of communication, as in small firms where communications may be easier; secondly, where there is less to communicate, as in times of high unemployment when management and unions' expectations are likely to be closest and each side appreciates better where the other stands; thirdly, where the costs of striking increase, assuming the increase in costs affects both sides. The duration of strikes will depend on knowledge available. Hicks (1963) argued that there will always be some unique wage that will make a settlement possible and the strike process is one of finding this settlement wage.

Empirical analysis of the determinants of strikes has not been wholly satisfactory[35]. In the first place there is a measurement problem though there is now general agreement that the number of stoppages recorded is more useful than the number of working days lost or the number of workers involved since the latter two measures show pronounced variations as a result of particular strikes. More importantly, the results of econometric studies have to be treated cautiously. They have shown the relevance of economic variables, such as the rate of change of wages, prices and productivity and the level of unemployment, which attempt to capture factors such as the degree of frustration with real wage increases and the likely costs and benefits of striking. Unfortunately, the estimating equations have often been consistent with a number of hypotheses. Variables have sometimes been included on an *ad hoc* basis. Moreover, when Mayhew carried out a regression analysis in which strike frequency was made dependent only on a linear time trend and seasonal dummy variables he found the results compared well with equations incorporating several economic variables. He concluded that 'there is a strong suspicion that such equations might be saying little more than that strikes have increased over time, and that they have a seasonal pattern' (1979, p.10).

Industries differ in their strike record. These differences, which have been described by Clegg (1979) and Brown (1981), are largely explicable in terms of the nature of the bargaining structure and by the size of plant. Where there is highly fragmented bargaining, especially where this is associated with payment-by-results systems and fluctuating earnings, strikes tend to be more frequent. Statistical investigations by Prais (1978) have shown the relevance of plant size, a fact which he attributes to the increases in the number of communication links as size increases. He found that the average number of strikes per year was almost directly proportional to the size of plant, though his use of official data on strikes, which cover only the larger stoppages, almost certainly exaggerates the effect of plant size on strike proneness. Survey data (Edwards, 1980) show a definite but less pronounced size effect. Other suggested explanations of inter-industry differences in strikes are that where there is a higher proportion of females, strikes may be fewer (Shorey, 1975) and that where the production technology is of a process kind there may be less strikes. Such notions did not, however, receive any support from the survey reported by Brown (1981).

6.3   Unions and allocation

Unions have direct and indirect effects on the allocation of labour. The indirect effects occur through their influence on wages. The size of this influence is considered in section 6.4. If wages are raised above the competitive market level, then some workers may be displaced from the high-paying unionized jobs. If these workers supply their labour to the non-union sector, then employment in the non-union sector increases and wages fall. This may give rise to a welfare loss because union labour is now being used less productively if it is assumed that wages reflect marginal products. The union sector has become more capital-intensive and the non-union sector more labour-intensive. Rees (1963) made a rough estimate of the size of this welfare loss in the US and found it to be only about 0.14% of GNP. He argued that these welfare losses

> are rather small relative to losses that involve labour's being completely idle or non-productive, that is, relative to losses from unemployment or from restrictive work practices. (Rees, 1979, p.151)

The more direct effects of unions on allocation are through these restrictive practices.

The closed shop is a source of control on employers' hiring policy which gives the union monopoly power. If there were no closed shops the employer would be able to hire non-union labour. It is therefore a means of controlling the elasticity of substitution between different types of labour though such control is obviously limited by the degree of product market substitution that is possible. Consumers may be able to buy from non-unionized firms. Unions may also affect the capital–labour ratio by 'overmanning'. This may take several forms such as specifying a minimum level of workers or a fixed number of workers per machine[36] or resisting new technology embodying more capital. These affect the production function which thus becomes determined by institutional as well as technological factors. It is often asserted (Clark, 1981, p.229 and Hayek, 1980, p.53) that the fall in productivity will lead to a fall in real incomes, but in fact the welfare effects are sometimes hard to determine because they may only involve *redistribution* of monopoly profits to workers.

There can be little doubt about the success of unions in constraining the elasticity of substitution. In the US Freeman and Medoff (1977) have estimated such elasticities in unionized and non-unionized firms in the US. Scale effects were held constant so there was a constant output demand. A range of estimates was found depending on the particular functional forms used. These are shown in *Table 6.4*. It is clear that the elasticities were lower in

TABLE 6.4 Elasticities of substitution in unionized and non-unionized firms

Elasticity of substitution	Range of estimates
Non-union firms: production/non-production workers	0.176 to 2.065
Union firms: production/non-production workers	−0.711 to 0.556
Non-union firms: production workers/capital	0.912 to 1.418
Union firms: production workers/capital	0.349 to 1.054

Source: Freeman and Medoff (1977)

union firms and suggest that it is easier to constrain labour–labour substitution than capital–labour substitution[37]. The greatest effect in the latter case is likely to be an *ex ante* substitution, for once capital is in place unions will have less chance of altering the input combinations. Obviously some care is needed with this argument since it is difficult to establish the extent to which unions actually cause the elasticity of substitution, and hence of demand for labour, to be lower. It may be that they tend to locate and prosper best in environments where these conditions already pertain.

Where unions are present there is likely to be more stability in the workforce. In internal labour markets rules such as the seniority principle govern allocation, and workplace union organizations are likely to institutionalize the informal custom and practice rules[38]. The general effect is to impart a degree of stability to the workforce, and there is evidence (Freeman, 1980) that there is an increase in the degree of attachment of workers to firms stemming from changes in worker behaviour arising for example from well-defined grievance procedures and seniority rules. Unions impede the use of quits at the same time as resisting cuts in real wages and restraining firms' ability to reduce hours. Thus lay-offs are more common in unionized firms (see Feldstein, 1978; Medoff, 1979).

Whether these effects of unions add up to a serious welfare loss is a matter of dispute. The closed shop is often seen as a pernicious institution though some claims about the size of welfare loss, such as Burton's (1978, p.51) view that the combined effect of union wage effects and effects on allocation could be as much as 6% of GNP, are clearly exaggerated (see Yarrow, 1978). A prevailing assumption in current policy discussions is that unions and the closed shop are harmful but this assumption should not be accepted unquestioningly. In addition to the efficiency argument that closed shops are a way of dealing with the 'public-goods' nature of work and the fact that unions may take on some of the inevitable search and transaction costs in the market by 'demonstrating to workers the advantages of forming themselves into suitably classified systems for bargaining purposes' (Fisher, 1971, p.147), there are a number of reasons for supposing unions may not have unambiguously harmful allocative effects.

First, the statistical evidence on the effect of unions on productivity is flimsy. Ball and Skeoch (1981), in a cross-industry regression analysis using UK data, found that the influence of unions as proxied by the proportion of the industrial workforce covered by collective agreements, was consistently negative but very weak. In the US Clark (1980) found that in the cement industry unionization led to large productivity gains deriving from changes in management personnel and procedures, and Brown and Medoff (1978) concluded from a study of manufacturing that under certain assumptions unionization had a substantial positive effect on output per worker.

Secondly, the development of worker attachment to firms and of internal labour markets based on union-imposed rules may actually serve to promote efficiency. In Williamson's (1975, p.81) words,

> the wage structure reflects objective long-term job values rather than current bargaining exigencies. Internal promotion ladders encourage a positive worker attitude toward on-the-job training and enable the firm to reward co-operative behaviour. A grievance procedure, with impartial arbitration as the usual final step, allows the firm and the workers to deal with continually changing conditions in a relatively nonlitigious manner. Contract revision and renewal take place in an atmosphere of mutual restraint in which the parties are committed to continuing accommodation. Unionization commonly facilitates the orderly achievement of these results.

Further, it is evident that the closed shop itself is preserved partly by employer acquiescence. In section 6.1 the high degree of employer support for the closed shop was noted.

Thirdly, and perhaps most important, unions may act as the institution of 'voice' in the labour market. The 'exit-voice' model developed by Hirschman (1970) contrasts two types of behaviour. 'Exit' is when workers who are dissatisfied with pay and conditions quit and seek better terms elsewhere. 'Voice' is the attempt to alter terms by protest rather than mobility. Individuals are unlikely to express discontent to managers because it is easier for employers to retaliate against a single worker. And individuals cannot bargain over plant-wide pay and conditions so it may be difficult to get workers to reveal preferences. 'Voice' thus tends to be a collective activity and unions provide a direct channel of communication between workers and management thus preserving information about work conditions which might be lost through individual quits.

'Voice' and 'exit' behaviour have different implications, and it is quite possible, as Freeman (1976) has argued, that 'voice' may be superior to 'exit'. 'Voice' reduces turnover and training costs and increases firm–specific investments in human capital. These may have efficiency gains which could outweigh the adverse consequences of the monopoly power of unions and the 'loss' of the resources which are used in the very act of collective bargaining. Further, to quote Freeman it

> transforms the supply side of the job market by *making median (or some other average) rather than marginal preferences the 'determinant' of the labour contract.* (1976, p.366, emphasis original).

Optimality criteria usually require marginal rather than average first-order conditions so this might seem to imply inefficiency. There are however several instances, such as situations where the provision of desirable work conditions or fringe benefits involves substantial fixed costs, where average rather than marginal criteria may be more appropriate, and it must remain an open question whether unions impair efficiency.

6.4   Unions and wages

The effects of unions on wages has been studied intensively. Their effect on aggregate money wages and on the share of wages in the national income lie beyond the scope of this chapter and the discussion here is confined to their effects on wage differentials. Unions are interested in securing wage increases for their members. They are also interested in fairness. The notion of 'the rate for the job' has always been of central importance and unions have rarely been willing to accept intra-occupational differences in pay except where these are based on some objective criterion such as length of service or level of qualifications[39].

There are therefore strong forces for equalizing the pay of given occupations in different employments. Differentials between occupations are often accepted and indeed preserved. Customary differentials are often sufficiently strong to override market forces at least in the short run.

These equality considerations relate to differences in pay among unionized groups but most of this section is concerned with whether unions can secure any real gain in pay above what would have occurred due to the ordinary workings of the market, that is in the absence of unions altogether. If they can raise pay in this way there may be implications for the allocation of labour and for the distribution of income.

Estimation of the union wage effect

In practice the question has usually been posed in the form of asking whether the pay of union members is higher than that of non-members. This assumes that the pay of non-unionists is the same as that which would have prevailed in the absence of unions altogether. It is not at all obvious that this is the case but for the moment remarks will be confined to what studies have in fact done. A number of early studies in the US tried to assess the union/non-union differential by making comparisons of wages in industries before and after unionization, or comparisons of similar occupations in unionized and non-unionized areas or industries. The main problem with such studies was that they were not sufficiently able to hold other things constant. Many of the highly unionized industries for example were also the most concentrated and had the highest capital–labour ratios so it was never clear how far, if at all, wage differences were attributable to unionism.

In recent years almost all studies have followed a procedure set out by Lewis (1963), which is apparently more rigorous. The most common form of the procedure is to estimate the union mark-up from a single equation model based on the identity

$$W_i = T_i W_i^T + (1 - T_i) W_i^N \tag{6.5}$$

where W_i is the average wage in sector i (an occupation or industry), W_i^T is the average union wage, W_i^N the average non-union wage, and T_i the proportion of the labour force which is paid the union wage. The identity simply says that the average wage in any sector is a weighted average of union and non-union wages. It can also be expressed in terms of the logarithms of the geometric means, w_i.

$$\ln w_i = T_i \ln w_i^T + (1 - T_i) \ln w_i^N \qquad (6.6)$$

This can be rearranged to give

$$\ln w_i = \ln w_i^N + (\ln w_i^T - \ln w_i^N)\, T_i$$

or

$$\ln w_i = \ln w_i^N + \ln(1 + M_i)\, T_i \qquad (6.7)$$

where M_i is the mark-up of union over non-union wages; that is $(w_i^T - w_i^N)/w_i^N$. Since data are usually only available on w_i and T_i a vector of variables which 'determines' w_i^N is used and the estimating equation becomes, assuming that M_i is the same in all sectors,

$$\ln w_i = \alpha X_i + \beta T_i + e_i \qquad (6.8)$$

where X_i is the vector of determinants of w_i^N such as education, sex, experience, age, and e_i is an error term. The estimated value of β, which equals $\ln (1 + M)$, is then used to find the effect of unions on relative wages.

The results of empirical studies

For manual workers in British manufacturing industry many studies, summarized with a commentary in Metcalf (1977), have reported mark-ups in the region of 25%. There is however considerable doubt about the size of the mark-up because, as will be argued below, the procedure used is questionable.

There is some evidence from the US that the differential varies cyclically. Lewis (1963) found that the effect of unions is relatively large during periods of deflation. Such a result is plausible because unions may well be able to resist cuts in money wages to a greater extent than non-unionists but in periods of rising prices employers are unwilling to grant exceptional increases in money wages. This reduces the union wage advantage in times of high employment. Moreover, with fixed-term bargaining the very process of collective bargaining may lead to slower adjustments than individual bargaining thereby causing cyclical movements in the differential.

It would however be wrong to suppose that employers are not restrained from also cutting non-union wages in a recession. Phelps Brown (1962, p.184) has argued that respect for custom and for the good opinion of the neighbourhood and especially the work people themselves will limit the widening of differentials in depression. It is not therefore surprising that evidence on movements over time is not strong. For the UK Layard et al. (1978) claimed that the differential has increased over the period 1961 –1975, and regression analysis showed the differential to be positively related to unemployment[40].

Attempts to relate the size of the differential to the skill level are mainly from the US. The studies, which are reported in Ashenfelter (1978, p.37), have shown the surprising result that the union mark-up is higher for less skilled workers. This does not accord with the view that craft unions are likely to have greater power than unskilled workers' unions because the essential non-substitutable skills of craft labour makes the demand for their labour less elastic than that for unskilled workers. The result may be attributable to the fact that unskilled workers are frequently in the same unions as skilled workers. In such industrial unions skilled workers would secure a smaller advantage especially if, as Turner (1952) has argued, these unions pursue egalitarian policies of seeking the same absolute increases in pay for all skill levels.

TABLE 6.5 Differential over 'no agreement' average gross hourly earnings for adults in Great Britain, 1973 (%)

	National plus supplementary agreement	National agreement only	Company agreement only
Manual males manufacturing	11.3	2.5	11.3
non-manufacturing	16.2	16.2	16.2
Manual females manufacturing	17.4	8.7	13.0
non-manufacturing	31.6	28.9	15.8
Non-manual males manufacturing	–16.7	–16.7	–9.1
non-manufacturing	–2.4	0.8	–6.4
Non-manual females manufacturing	– 1.7	– 5.2	3.4
non-manufacturing	24.6	36.8	5.3

Source: Thomson et al. (1977, p.184)

There is no evidence of any sex differences in the mark-up in the UK. Nickell (1977) looked explicitly at this question and found that the result was about the same for both men and women. The evidence in favour of a lower mark-up for women is very slightly stronger in the US.

A finding on which there is a firmer measure of agreement amongst empirical studies is that the mark-up is likely to be greater the more local bargaining there is. At least in the case of manual workers in manufacturing an early study by Mulvey (1976) showed that workers covered only by national agreements appear to have little or no observed advantage over uncovered workers whereas those with local bargaining, instead of or in addition to national bargaining have a substantial advantage. *Table 6.5* shows however that this result does not appear to hold for the non-manufacturing sector and indeed there are negative differentials reported for non-manual workers in manufacturing. This uncertainty in the result may partly reflect the fact that local bargains are not entirely independent but are linked through shop stewards' combine committees and similar arrangements. The study by Thomson *et al.* (1977) indicated that unions have their greatest effect on components of pay other than the basic rates; that is, such items as on overtime, shift premiums and bonuses.

There is then a broad consensus that unions do raise pay though the size of this influence is the subject of considerable dispute. Much of the uncertainty stems from the problems relating to the method of estimating differentials.

One of the basic problems is that the non-union wage may not be the wage that would prevail in the absence of unions altogether. The observed non-union wage may not be independent of the union wage. This is partly because of threat effects, under which employers of non-union labour may pay higher wages than the purely competitive level in order to buy-off the threat of organizing, and partly because any fall in the demand for highly paid unionists would increase the supply of labour to the non-union sector thereby lowering non-union wages.

Another problem is that the use of average weekly earnings does not give any reliable guide to the effectiveness of unions. Creedy (1979) has demonstrated that changes in the hourly rates of pay and in the number of hours worked will have different effects on weekly earnings, and since unions will normally be concerned with both of these the priorities they attach to each must be known before evaluating effectiveness of unions on weekly earnings[41]. Of course, if the concern is only with the effects of unions rather than their effectiveness then this would not matter.

Data problems in the empirical work on Britain have been serious[42]. Some of these have been overcome by the widespread use of data relating to workers covered by agreements rather than to union membership *per se*. This partly overcomes the problem of controlling for spill-over effects between union members and non-union members who are covered by the agreement. There are also difficulties in interpreting the coefficients from which the mark-up is calculated because there are several sources of bias. Creedy (1979) has demonstrated that the decomposition of average wages in a sector into a weighted average of the average union wage and the average non-union wage is not so simple as most studies imply. A consequence is that the use of the estimated value of β in equation 6.8 leads to an overstatement of the size of the union mark-up. Mulvey and Abowd (1980), using different arguments, also suggest that the estimates in most British studies are very greatly exaggerated.

Other problems arise because of possible non-linearities in the union–wage relationship (see Rees, 1979, p.143) and, as suggested below, wages and unionism may well be simultaneously determined. Yet there are no UK studies which use a simultaneous equation approach. Finally, it is worth noting that although it has been usual to use a logarithmic specification for the estimating equations, on the grounds that proportionate differences in pay are more significant from an allocative point of view, unions sometimes may be more concerned with absolute differentials (Turner, 1952)[43].

The nature of these problems suggests that extreme caution is necessary in interpreting the results of the empirical studies though there can be little doubt that unions do have an impact effect on wages.

The link between unionism and high wages

It is evident that the procedure described for estimating the size of the union mark-up offers no indication as to why there should be such a differential. It is simply based on the manipulation of an identity. How then can the association of unions and high wages be explained?

First, the observed union wage effect may simply be a result of the exercise of monopoly power. But it may be that wages and union membership are simultaneously determined. The credit for high wages will be claimed by unions: this will lead to workers having a greater propensity to join unions and enable them to pay union subscriptions more easily.

Secondly, the higher union wages may simply be compensating differentials for having to accept particular work regimes. As Metcalf (1977, p.163) noted, union members tend to work in larger plants with more formal procedures. The public goods characteristics of work require acceptance of plant-wide conditions.

Thirdly, both unions and wages may be related to some other variable. One possibility here is the level of industrial concentration. Larger firms are more heavily unionized and there is considerable empirical support for the view that larger firms pay higher wages. Unions find it easier to gain recognition and to be organized in large firms because of economies of scale in organization. Some of the relationship between unions and wages may thus be attributable to high concentration. The quality of workers hired may also be systematically related to both union membership and wages. Where for example there is firm specific training, firms may pay high wages to secure low quit rates. Employers who choose such a strategy are likely to have a stable, skilled workforce giving rise to a low elasticity of substitution. This is likely to be associated with a high degree of unionization and again the observed link between wages and unions may be partly because of a common association with the quality of labour. There is evidence from the US (Lee, 1978; Kalachek and Raines, 1980) that unionized firms do tend to select more productive workers and, incidentally, that union membership is determined mainly by wage gains.

Unions and the dispersion of wages

The relative wage effect means that highly unionized industries are likely to pull ahead of less unionized ones. The inter-industry dispersion in wages is thus likely to increase. Lewis (1963) found this to be the case in the US though it was not a strong effect.

Unions may also have an effect on widening wage differences between persons when firms respond to union-forced wage increases by upgrading their workforce. This will increase the demand for high-quality labour, whether unionized or not, and raise the wages of such workers. The wages of low-quality labour will fall and the wage differential between high and low quality workers is thus greater than under perfect competition. The differences in wages have been estimated by Pettengill (1980) to exceed differences in productive capacity by as much as 50%.

More generally however, it seems likely that unions have a strong conservative effect on the wage structure. Unions' concern with preserving relativities and insisting on a uniform rate for the job has contributed to a long-run tendency to reduce regional differentials and to narrow inter-plant differences. By collecting and disseminating information on what is being paid in other plants unions ensure that the internal pay structure becomes less insulated; in this way the effect of trade unions is to reduce rather than protect or create differences in pay between firms for the same work. There are many examples of this in the UK[44] and in the US Freeman (1980) has suggested that such an effect often dominates the impact of unionism on the dispersion of wages across industries, so that the net effect of unionism is to reduce rather than increase inequality in pay.

This section has shown that unions may be able to raise the pay of their members above the competitive level. This is a once-for-all effect and so there is no continuing source of gain. Particular groups of workers may enjoy considerable power to raise their pay but the overall effect of unions on the wage structure is probably small. There are some pressures to widen and some to reduce the inequality of pay and there still seems no reason to challenge the conclusion Phelps Brown reached in the mid-1960s.

> In sum, collective bargaining distorts the structure of wages and salaries at a few points while making it more orderly and equitable at many others and leaving its main proportions unchanged. (1967, p.1616).

6.5 Conclusions

Union structure in Britain is complex. This is partly because of historical factors and partly because unions do not have a single objective or *raison d'être*[45]. This complexity of structure and aims has made it difficult to develop general models of union behaviour. There are sociopolitical as well as purely economic aims and characteristics. Unions are concerned to

> protect not only their [members'] material standards of living, but equally their security, status and self respect – in short, their dignity as human beings. (Flanders, 1970, p.21).

Given this broad view it is no surprise to find unions lending support to wider political movements. In this chapter stress has been placed on the existence of political aspects of unions but there has been no explicit discussion of these, for unions are not simply vehicles for pursuing political causes. They develop as responses to *employers* and have their base firmly in specific employment situations. Attention has thus been limited to models of unions' economic behaviour and to their effect on wages and allocation.

Unions affect wages and other aspects of employment. The wage effects command principal attention because unions are more concerned with setting prices rather than quantities in the labour market. Bargaining is primarily about the wage-rate and the employer is left free to determine how many workers he will hire[46]. The state of demand does not always figure centrally in collective bargaining and it is a common observation that large wage claims and settlements occur even where there is high unemployment.

Once-for-all monopoly gains have been achieved by unions. Despite the formidable problems in estimating the size of their influence there is a strong consensus that unions do raise their members' pay above that which would prevail in the absence of unions. It is quite possible that nobody actually loses by this if, for example, union pressure on management forces increased efficiency, or if wage increases generate higher aggregate demand and increased output. It seems likely, however, that some redistribution of income does take place. In addition to raising the level of pay unions are concerned with fairness. They make some wages more uniform and have a conservative effect on the wage structure.

The non-wage effects of unions are important and some writers, such as Addison and Siebert (1979, p.293), have argued that the main effects of collective bargaining are in the areas of discrimination, job regulation, and restrictive practices rather than in determining the level and structure of pay. These effects, particularly those in the field of what Freeman (1980, p.60) calls 'industrial jurisprudence' may provide subtle but wide-ranging effects.

These wage and non-wage effects may affect efficiency adversely. The models described in section 6.2 showed that there is scope for monopoly wage gains and suggested that when employers and unions each adopt maximizing behaviour then both the level of wages and of employment may be greater than those which would prevail under competitive conditions. The use of restrictive practices lowers productivity and competitive labour market prices may be 'distorted' by exploiting monopoly positions and by setting pay according to equity criteria. Where pay is set on the basis of fairness, then non-wage adjustments to imbalances of supply and demand in the labour market become necessary.

Whether unions impair efficiency in practice is not so certain. In some cases higher wages paid to unionists may be compensated for by higher productivity. More significantly the extent to which wages do perform an allocative function is debatable, so it may matter little if the wage structure is based on fairness. There have been major changes in the deployment of the labour force without marked changes in relative wages, though this observation does not imply that changes in differentials would not have exerted a powerful influence on allocation if they had occurred. In any case it may be that by reducing the differences in pay among firms unions may actually bring the market closer to its underlying equilibrium positions[47].

This tendency towards equal wages in different plants would, under competitive market conditions, come about through the movement of employees but unions may achieve the result without mobility. 'Voice' may be a more relevant description of behaviour than 'exit' and unions are the main institution of 'voice'[48]. It is not self-evident that 'voice' is inferior to 'exit'; this remains an open question. Indeed, the whole issue of whether unions are socially harmful is unresolved. There is systematic evidence that unions have a harmful effect on economic performance, but it has been argued in this chapter that some of the effects of unions may be beneficial[49].

The state has played an increasingly prominent role in industrial relations. It has attempted to regulate the structure, conduct and performance of collective bargaining. The Donovan Commission (1968) saw structural reform as the key to influencing behaviour and debates on incomes policies and wage inflation are increasingly turning to the consideration of reform in the structure of pay bargaining (Blackaby, 1980). Attempts to change the behaviour of unions have been largely by restrictions on closed shops, picketing, and various legal immunities which unions enjoy. More positively the state has taken an important role in trying to facilitate the process of collective bargaining through such agencies as the Advisory Conciliation and Arbitration Service[50].

Formulating government policy in this area is difficult because of the unsettled state of many of the questions about the overall effects of unions. More adequate modelling of unions to incorporate equity objectives and political dimensions of unions is desirable. There is also a need for more convincing empirical work on the extent to which union conduct is dependent on structure and on the effects and welfare implication of this conduct.

Notes

1. I am grateful to J. Graham for helpful discussions during the preparation of this chapter.
2. See Ashworth (1981), Phelps Brown (1968) and Thomson and Hunter (1978) on these issues respectively.
3. This is considerably higher than the USA, 25%, and Germany, 37%., but less than the Scandinavian countries where the figures are Sweden 87%, Denmark 67% and Norway 61%. The figures are for 1975 and are taken from Bain and Price (1980, Table 10.1).
4. This is the largest single factor contributing to variations in density among industries in establishment size. In large establishments union recognition and density tend to be higher, though the sensitivity of unionization to size diminishes the larger the establishment size. See El Sheikh and Bain (1980).
5. Bain and El Sheikh (1976) show that the growth of union membership is positively related to the rate of change of money wages and of prices and negatively related to the level of unemployment. For a discussion of their model see Richardson (1977) and El Sheikh and Bain (1979).
6. This concentration may be partly a response to the growth in concentration in industry, reflecting a need for greater bargaining strength when faced with larger employers. But this argument can easily be overstated. Clegg (1979, p.176) shows that amalgamations of unions have occurred in bursts following changes in the law which eased the legal requirements for amalgamations.
7. This 'open', 'closed' terminology is attributable to Turner (1952). More traditionally unions have been described as craft, industrial or general.
8. The fastest growing unions in recent years have been those which have diversified their membership, so there has been some tendency for unions to become more open. The largest white-collar unions such as the Association of Scientific, Technical and Managerial Staffs have diversified and the major blue-collar unions such as the Transport and General Workers' Union, the General and Municipal Workers' Union and the Amalgamated Union of Engineering Workers have all formed or incorporated white-collar sections.
9. See Brown's (1981) report of an authoritative survey of 970 establishments in manufacturing. Firms employing fewer than 50 workers were excluded but this is not very serious given that only 15% of the labour force is employed in such establishments.

10. Joint regulation of terms and conditions has not, however, always been the norm. Unilateral regulation by unions, as in the case of nineteenth century craft unions which controlled the supply of skilled labour, or by employers, as was the case with the mass of unskilled labour in the last century, and statutory regulation have also been prominent at various times.

11. Coker and Stuttard (1976) discuss the scope of bargaining and show that it includes not only pay (including all the various components) and hours (including all the particular working arrangements such as shifts, overtime and holidays) but also such factors as job security, pensions, health and safety, productivity, discipline, training and education, union facilities, power sharing and participation, work satisfaction and physical conditions.

12. The concept of implicit contracts has figured prominently in the literature on macroeconomics in recent years. See Azariadis (1981) for a survey.

13. Multi-employer negotiations involving employers' associations were common during the 1960s. The Donovan Commission (1968) described this as the formal system and noted that it was supplemented by an informal system of company bargaining. The Commission recommended more formalization of this company bargaining. This in fact is what has happened though Brown (1981, p.24) notes that the move has been largely the unplanned consequence of piecemeal reform rather than any deliberate rejection of established multi-employer arrangements. It is more because of the increases in industrial concentration and in the size of firms, the growth in specialist industrial relations management (partly resulting from the increase in legislation in this field), and the growth of the public sector where single-employer bargaining is of course the norm.

14. The term 'closed shop' is here used to mean a practice under which workers have to be members of unions to keep their jobs. The 1962 estimate is from McCarthy (1964) and the 1978 figure from Gennard et al. (1980).

15. Management itself has been drawn into direct involvement in workplace union administration through closed shops, full-time stewards, check-off arrangements and consultative committees.

16. The market for school teachers provides a striking example where uniform salary scales have meant that the pay of say maths and science teachers could not be raised without raising

the pay of the whole teaching force. See Thomas and Deaton (1977).

17. For example, formal theories of bargaining usually assume that the outcome of the bargaining process is efficient and many models postulate solutions such as Nash's where the outcome is that point that maximizes the product of the employer's and union's gains over the no-contract outcome. This provides little insight into real bargaining situations.

18. This is characterized by Duncan and Stafford (1980) as

$$E = \min (e_1/\alpha_2, e_1/\alpha_2, \ldots e_n/\alpha_n)n$$

where E is total effort of the workers, e_i is effort per worker and α_i is an adjustment for efficiency differences across workers. This contrasts to the situation where the effort inputs of workers are separable and E can be expressed as

$$E = \sum_{i=1}^{n} \alpha_i e_i$$

19. Duncan and Stafford (1980) provide some empirical support for this view using US data.

20. In some cases unions may be interested in non-wage forms of remuneration. Farber's (1978) study of the United Mine Workers in the USA, for example, found that members valued an extra dollar spent on fixed fringe benefits more highly than an extra dollar on discretionary income. The tax advantages were of course relevant.

21. See Ashenfelter and Pencavel (1969) and Sharpe (1971).

22. In practice unions are likely to face special sets of prices for their inputs since some people are prepared to work at lower than market rates because they derive non-pecuniary satisfaction from working for an ideological cause.

23. Block (1980) has argued that as unions increase the extent of their organization they devote more of their resources to representation and less to organizing so there are increasing returns to membership.

24. Dunlop (1944) discusses several alternative maximands such as the amount of employment, the average wage income of members, the sum of the private wage bill plus public payments to unemployed members. The spirit of each model is similar but these maximands are regarded as less plausible by Dunlop.

25. There is some evidence that the *goals* of bargaining may not change in response to variations in product demand. See Farber's (1978) study of the United Mine Workers in the USA.

26. This raises the interesting question of the relative importance of price and quantity adjustments in the labour market in response to demand changes but it is beyond the scope of this chapter to consider this question. Some discussion can be found in Thomas (1981). Much depends on the risk-averseness of workers and there is some evidence (Farber, 1978) that union members tend to be risk-averse in that they discount future benefits at a relatively low rate.

27. A constant product price is assumed in $R(L)$ but this can easily be relaxed without altering the argument.

28. The slope must be negative. This can be seen from the fact that the maximum point on any isoprofit curve must lie to the left of the maxima of lower curves because for any given L the slope, $\{(\partial R/\partial L) - w\}/L$, of higher curves falls (and becomes negative) as w rises (and eventually exceeds $\partial R/\partial L$). This implies that the isoprofit curves are as shown in *Figure 6.3*.

29. It is assumed that there is a unique point of tangency; that is, the demand curve for labour is less convex than the indifference curve.

30. This follows from the fact that the isoprofit curves have a negative slope to the right of the demand curve, that is $dw/dL < 0$ which implies $(\partial R/\partial L) < w$.

31. One of the best-known conceptual expressions of bargaining power is that of Chamberlain (1951). He suggested that the bargaining power of unions is the ratio of the 'costs of disagreeing with the employer' to the 'costs to the employer of agreeing on the union's terms'. The bargaining power of employers is the ratio of the 'costs to the union of disagreeing with the employer' to the 'costs to the union of agreeing on the employer's terms'. These ratios, however, whilst offering some interesting hypotheses, are not susceptible of measurement.

32. See Armstrong *et al.* (1977) for a discussion of desirable attributes of any suitable proxy for bargaining power. For quite different types of measure see Edwards (1978).

33. This holds provided the elasticity of product demand exceeds the elasticity of substitution, i.e. where consumers can substitute products more easily than employers can substitute inputs.

34. Much of this work is reviewed in Creigh (1978). He concludes that the present state of knowledge is not sufficiently firm to conclude that strikes have a strong effect on the performance of the economy as a whole, though in particular sectors they may sometimes have profound effects. There is dispute over

the question of whether the tendency to strike is a cause or an effect of poor economic performance.

35. See for example Pencavel (1970), Knight (1972), and Davies (1979).

36. Addison and Siebert (1979, p.300) analyse the effects of different forms of overmanning on output. In some cases employers may have preferences about the desired labour –output ratio which is strongly supportive of union attitudes. See Thomas (1973) for an examination of this type of situation.

37. This will vary with the type of labour. Hamermesh and Grant (1979), for example, have some evidence that skilled labour and capital are complements rather than substitutes though raw labour and capital are substitutes. Constraints on labour –labour substitution are likely to be greater where there is multi-unionism and consequent demarcation.

38. Doeringer and Piore (1971) discuss the importance of custom and practice rules in internal labour markets. For illustrations and an account of the significance of such rules in the UK see Brown (1972). A fuller discussion of internal labour markets can be found in Chapter 7 of the present volume.

39. This applies equally to manual and non-manual workers. Many white-collar groups such as teachers and lecturers press for common salary scales across different subject groups. Metcalf (1973) discusses the reasons for this.

40. A major limitation of the study was that the variable relating to the percentage of the workforce covered by unions was for one year only and it was assumed that this coverage did not change over the period.

41. There is some slight evidence (Metcalf et al., 1976) that workers in unionized jobs work fewer hours than non-unionists.

42. The problems arise mainly from the fact that in the UK there are no single data sources which give both an individual's union membership status and his personal characteristics such as age and skill level. Studies which have used data on individuals have had to use *average* levels of unionism.

43. The specification is usually in terms of the logs of the geometric means though arithmetic means have had to be used in practice.

44. Phelps-Brown (1977, p.274) has put this argument forcefully. In the UK it is illustrated by the study by Brown and Sisson (1975) of the close movements in pay among different firms in Coventry and among different newspaper houses in Fleet Street.

45. See Clegg (1979, Chapter 5) for a discussion of these.
46. One consequence of this is that some union members will be employed and some unemployed, thereby entailing a redistribution of income among members. This redistribution has been modified by the introduction of state unemployment benefits but rarely by pure work-sharing on the part of unions.
47. This view is argued by Phelps-Brown (1977, p.274) who shows that Lydall (1968) developed similar arguments.
48. The revelance of 'voice' may not be confined to union members. The ability to raise pay, for instance, will depend on 'conditions of inelastic demand *and permissive attitudes of other workers or the public*' (Phelps-Brown, 1967, p.1616, our emphasis).
49. See Caves (1980).
50. See Hunter (1977) for a discussion of these issues.

References

Addison, J. T. (1978). The balance of market advantage. In *Trade Unions. Public Goods or Public 'Bads'?* pp.34–36. IEA Readings 17. London; Institute of Economic Affairs

Addison, J. T. and Siebert, W. S. (1979). *The Market for Labor: An Analytical Treatment*. Santa Monica; Goodyear

Alchian, A. A. and Demsetz, H. (1972). Production, information costs and economic organization. *American Economic Review* **62**, 777–795

Armstrong, K. J., Bowers, D. and Burkitt, B. (1977). The measurement of trade union bargaining power. *British Journal of Industrial Relations* **15**, 91–100

Ashenfelter, O. (1978). Union relative wage effects: new evidence and a survey of their implications for wage inflation. In *Econometric Contributions to Public Policy* (ed. by R. Stone and W. Peterson), pp.31–60. London; Macmillan

Ashenfelter, O. and Pencavel, J. H. (1969). American trade union growth: 1900–1960. *Quarterly Journal of Economics* **83**, 434–448

Ashworth, J. (1981). Wages, prices and unemployment. In *The Economics of Unemployment in Britain* (ed. by J. Creedy), pp.186–234. London; Butterworths

Azariadis, C. (1981). Implicit contracts and related topics: a survey. In *The Economics of the Labour Market* (ed. by Z. Hornstein, J. Grice and A. Webb), pp.221–248. London; HMSO

Bain, G. S. (1970). *The Growth of White Collar Unionism.* Oxford; Clarendon Press

Bain, G. S. and El Sheikh, F. (1976). *Union Growth and the Business Cycle.* Oxford; Basil Blackwell

Bain, G. S. and El Sheikh, F. (1979). An inter-industry analysis of unionization in Britain. *British Journal of Industrial Relations* **17**, 137–157

Bain G. S. and Price, R. (1980). *Profiles of Union Growth.* Oxford; Basil Blackwell

Ball, J. M. and Skeoch, N. K. (1981). *Inter-plant Comparisons of Productivity and Earnings.* Government economic service working paper No. 38. Unit for Manpower Studies, Department of Employment

Berkovitz, M. (1954). The economics of trade union organisation and administration. *Industrial and Labour Relations Review* **7**, 575–592

Blackaby, F. (ed.) (1980). *The Future of Pay Bargaining.* London; Heinemann

Block, R.N. (1980). Union organizing and the allocaton of union resources. *Industrial and Labour Relations Review* **34**, 101–113

Brown, C. and Medoff, J. (1978). Trade unions in the production process. *Journal of Political Economy* **86**, 355–378

Brown, W. (1972). A consideration of 'Custom and Practice'. *British Journal of Industrial Relations* **10**, 42–61

Brown, W. (1981). *The Changing Contours of British Industrial Relations.* Oxford; Basil Blackwell

Brown, W. and Sisson, K. (1975). The use of comparisons in workplace wage determination. *British Journal of Industrial Relations* **13**, 25–53

Brown, W. A. and Terry, M. (1978). The changing nature of national wage agreements. *Scottish Journal of Political Economy* **25**, 119–124

Burton, J. (1978). Are trade unions a public good/'bad'?: the economics of the closed shop. In *Trade Unions. Public Goods or Public 'Bads'?* pp.41–52. IEA Readings 17. London; Institute of Economic Affairs

Caves, R. E. (1980). Productivity differences among industries. In *Britain's Economic Performance* (ed. by R. E. Caves and L. B. Krause), pp.135–198. Washington; The Brookings Instititution

Cartter, A. M. (1959). *The Theory of Wages and Employment.* Homewood; Richard D. Irwin

Chamberlain, N. W. (1951). *Collective Bargaining.* New York; McGraw-Hill

Clark, C. (1981). Do trade unions raise wages? *Journal of Economic Affairs* **1**, 228–229

Clark, K. B. (1980). Unionization and productivity. Microeconomic evidence. *Quarterly Journal of Economics* **95**, 613–640

Clegg, H. A. (1976). *Trade Unionism under Collective Bargaining*. Oxford; Basil Blackwell

Clegg, H. A. (1979). *The Changing System of Industrial Relations in Great Britain*. Oxford; Basil Blackwell

Coker, E. and Stuttard, G. (1976). *Trade Union Industrial Studies 2: The Bargaining Context*. London; Arrow Books

Creedy, J. (1979). A note on the analysis of trade unions and relative wages. *Oxford Bulletin of Economics and Statistics* **40**, 39–46

Creigh, S. W. (1978). The economic costs of strikes. *Industrial Relations Journal* **9**, 19–26

Crossley, J. R. (1973). A mixed strategy for labour economists. *Scottish Journal of Political Economy* **20**, 211–238

Davies, R. J. (1979). Economic activity. Incomes policy and strikes. *British Journal of Industrial Relations* **17**, 205–223

Deaton, D. R. and Beaumont, P. B. (1979). The determinants of the bargaining structure: some large scale survey evidence for Britain. *Discussion Paper No. 15 University of Warwick, SSRC Industrial Relations Research Unit*

Doeringer, P. B. and Piore, M. J. (1971). *Internal Labor Markets and Manpower Analysis*. Lexington; D. C. Heath

Donovan Commission (1968). *Report of the Royal Commission on Trade Unions and Employers' Associations 1965–1968*. London; HMSO

Duncan, G. J. and Stafford, F. P. (1980). Do union members receive compensating wage differentials? *American Economic Review* **70**, 355–371

Dunlop, J. T. (1944). *Wage Determination under Trade Unions*. New York; Macmillan

Edwards, C. (1978). Measuring union power: a comparison of two methods applied to the study of local union power in the coal industry. *British Journal of Industrial Relations* **16**, 1–15

Edwards, P. K. (1980). Size of plant and strike-proneness. *Oxford Bulletin of Economics and Statistics* **42**, 145–156

El Sheikh, F. and Bain, G. S. (1979). The determination of the rate of change of unionization in the UK: a comment and further analysis. *Applied Economics* **11**, 451–463

El Sheikh, F. and Bain, G. S. (1980). Unionization in Britain: an inter-establishment analysis based on survey data. *British Journal of Industrial Relations* **18**, 169–178

Farber, H. (1978). Individual preferences and union wage determination: the case of the United Mine Workers. *Journal of Political Economy* **86**, 923–942

Feldstein, M. (1978). The effect of unemployment insurance on temporary lay-off unemployment. *American Economic Review* **68**, 834–846

Fisher, M. R. (1971). *The Economic Analysis of Labour*. London; Weidenfeld and Nicolson

Flanders, A. (1970). *Management and Unions*. London; Faber and Faber

Freeman, R. B. (1976). Individual mobility and union voice in the labor market. *American Economic Review* **66**, 361–368

Freeman, R. B. (1980). The effect of unionism on worker attachment to firms. *Journal of Labor Research* **1**, 29–61

Freeman, R. B. and Medoff, J. (1977). *Substitution between production labor and other inputs in unionized and non-unionized manufacturing*. Discussion Paper No. 581, Harvard University, Department of Economics

Gennard, J., Dunn, S. and Wright, M. (1980). The extent of the closed shop arrangements in British industry. *Employment Gazette* **88**, 16–22

Hamermesh, D. S. and Grant, J. (1979). Econometric studies of labor–labor substitution and their implications for policy. *Journal of Human Resources* **14**, 518–542

Hayek, F. A. (1980). *1980s Unemployment and the Unions*. Hobart Paper 87. London; Institute of Economic Affairs

Hicks, J. R. (1963). *The Theory of Wages*. London; Macmillan

Hirschman, A. O. (1970). *Exit, Voice and Loyalty*. Cambridge, Mass; Harvard University Press

Hunter, L. C. (1977). Economic issues in conciliation and arbitration. *British Journal of Industrial Relations* **15**, 226–245

Hyman, R. (1971). *The Workers' Union*. Oxford; Clarendon Press

Johansen, L. (1979). The bargaining society and the inefficiency of bargaining. *Kyklos* **32**, 497–522

Johnson, G. (1975). The economic analysis of trade unionism. *American Economic Review* **65**, 23–26

Kalachek, E. and Raines, F. (1980). Trade unions and living standards. *Journal of Labor Research* **1**, 95–114

King, J. E. (ed.) (1980). *Readings in Labour Economics*. Oxford; Oxford University Press

Knight, K. G. (1972). Strikes and wage inflation in British manufacturing industry, 1950–68. *Oxford Bulletin of Economics and Statistics* **34**, 281–294

Layard, R., Metcalf, D. and Nickell, S. (1978). The effect of collective bargaining on wages. In *Personal Income Distribution* (ed. by W. Krelle and A. F. Shorrocks), pp.445–468. Amsterdam; North-Holland

Lee, L. (1978). Unionism and wage rates: a simultaneous equation model with qualitative and limited dependent variables. *International Economic Review* **19**, 415–433

Lewis, H. G. (1963). *Unionism and Relative Wages in the United States*. Chicago; University of Chicago Press

Lydall, H. (1968). *The Structure of Earnings*. Oxford; Oxford University Press

McCarthy, W. E. J. (1964). *The Closed Shop in Britain*. Oxford; Basil Blackwell

McDonald, I. M. and Solow, R. M. (1981). Wage bargaining and employment. *American Economic Review* **71**, 896–908

Mayhew, K. (1979). Economists and strikes. *Oxford Bulletin of Economics and Statistics* **41**, 1–20

Medoff, J. L. (1979). Lay-offs and alternatives under trade unions in US manufacturing. *American Economic Review* **69**, 380–395

Metcalf, D. (1973). Some aspects of the university teachers' labour market in the UK. In *Essays in Modern Economics*. Proceedings of the conference of the Association of University Teachers 1972 (ed. by M. Parkin and A. R. Nobay), pp.192–211. London; Longman

Metcalf, D. (1977). Unions, incomes policy and relative wages in Britain. *British Journal of Industrial Relations* **15**, 157–175

Metcalf, D., Nickell, S. and Richardson, R. (1976). The structure of hours in British manufacturing industry. *Oxford Economic Papers* **28**, 284–303

Mulvey, C. (1976). Collective agreements and relative earnings in UK manufacturing in 1973. *Economica* **43**, 419–428

Mulvey, C. and Abowd, J. M. (1980). Estimating the union/non-union wage differential: a statistical issue. *Economica* **47**, 73–79

Nickell, S. (1977). Trade unions and the position of women in the industrial wage structure. *British Journal of Industrial Relations* **15**, 192–210

Olson, M. (1965). *The Logic of Collective Action*. Cambridge, Mass; Harvard University Press

Pencavel, J. H. (1970). An investigation into industrial strike activity in Britain. *Economica* **37**, 239–256

Pettengill, J. S. (1980). *Labour Unions and the Inequality of Earned Income*. Amsterdam; North-Holland

Phelps Brown, E. H. (1962). *The Economics of Labor*. New Haven; Yale University Press

Phelps Brown, E. H. (1967). *Royal Commission on Trade Unions and Employers' Associations. Minutes of Evidence* **38**, 1603 –1621. London; HMSO

Phelps Brown, E. H. (1968). *Pay and Profits*. Manchester; Manchester University Press

Phelps Brown, E. H. (1977). *The Inequality of Pay*. Oxford; Oxford University Press

Prais, S. J. (1978). The strike-proneness of large plants in Britain, *Journal of the Royal Statistical Society*, Series A (General) **141**, 368–384

Reder, M. W. (1952). The theory of union wage policy. *Review of Economics and Statistics* **34**, 34–45

Rees, A. (1963). The effects of unions on resource allocation. *Journal of Law and Economics* **6**, 69–78

Rees, A. (1979). *The Economics of Work and Pay* (2nd edn.). New York; Harper and Row

Richardson, R. (1977). Trade union growth, *British Journal of Industrial Relations* **15**, 279–282

Ross, A. M. (1948). *Trade Union Wage Policy*. Berkeley; California University Press

Sharp, I. G. (1971). The growth of Australian trade unions: 1967–1969. *Journal of Industrial Relations* **13**, 140–161

Shorey, J. (1975). The size of the work unit and strike incidence. *Journal of Industrial Economics* **23**, 175–188

Siebert, W. S. and Addison, J. T. (1981). Are strikes accidental? *Economic Journal* **91**, 389–404

Thomas, B. and Deaton, D. (1977). *Labour Shortage and Economic Analysis*. Oxford; Basil Blackwell

Thomas, R. B. (1973). On the definition of 'shortages' in administered labour markets. *Manchester School* **41**, 169–186

Thomas, R. B. (1981). Labour market adjustments. In *The Economics of Unemployment in Britain* (ed. by J. Creedy), pp.17–47. London; Butterworths

Thomson, A. W. J. (1979). Trade unions and the corporate state in Britain. *Industrial and Labour Relations Review* **33**, 36–54

Thomson, A. W. J., Mulvey, C. and Farbman, M. (1977). Bargaining structure and relative earnings in Great Britain. *British Journal of Industrial Relations* **15**, 176–191

Thomson, A. W. J. and Hunter, L. C. (1978). Great Britain. In *Labour in the Twentieth Century* (ed. by J. T. Dunlop and W. Gatenson), pp.85–146. London; Academic Press

Turner, H. A. (1952). Trade unions, differentials and the levelling of wages. *Manchester School* **20,** 227–282

Williamson, O. E. (1975). *Markets and Hierarchies*. New York; The Free Press

Yarrow, G. (1979). Trade unions and economic welfare. In *Trade Unions. Public Goods or Public 'Bads'?* pp.55–57. IEA Readings 17. London; Institute of Economic Affairs

Chapter 7
Professional labour markets[1]

7.1 Introduction

The occupations which have been designated as the professions are to be found at the upper end of the occupational hierarchy. Members of the professions are generally accorded high incomes and it has been estimated that the median earnings of British professional occupations in 1970 were between 1.8 and 3.7 times the median earnings of all male employees[2] (Norris, 1980, p.258). This privileged economic position is reflected in the status which is granted to professional workers. The top of the Goldthorpe–Hope scale of occupational status is reserved for members of the medical and legal professions and the top six ranks are dominated by professional occupations (Phelps Brown, 1977, p.106).

Many occupations strive to obtain the status of their professional counterparts in the hope of gaining similar rewards. However, this status has been accorded to only a select group of occupations and there is little evidence that society is witnessing the 'professionalization of everyone'[3]. Further, while the status of occupations is closely related to the level of earnings received, there is little evidence of a causal mechanism running from status to pay. Thus attempts to raise status in the expectation of an improvement in remuneration are not likely to be fruitful. Economic analysis of the relationship between the two variables indicates that pay is determined independently of status, according to the operations of the labour market, and that variations in the supply of labour to differing occupations are of crucial importance in determining relative pay (Phelps Brown, 1977, Chapter 4).

There is evidence that the absolute number of professional workers in the working population has increased quite rapidly in recent years. *Table 7.1* shows data from the 1961 and 1971 Censuses, which indicate that the number of workers classified as professional increased by 42% over the period. However, the definition of professional adopted by the Office of Population and Census Surveys – self-employed persons or employees engaged in work normally requiring qualifications of university degree standard – is considerably broader than alternative definitions, including that adopted in this chapter. Moreover, it is possible that the Census data reflect the expansion of tertiary education rather than any change in the occupational distribution itself.

TABLE 7.1 Number of professional workers in England and Wales, 1961 and 1971

| | 1961 | | 1971 | |
	In self-employment	In salaried employment	In self-employment	In salaried employment
Males	128 300	426 740	139 990	644 960
Females	6 080	55 940	11 350	76 750
Total	134 380	482 580	151 340	721 710

Sources: Table 19 of Census 1961, England and Wales Occupation Tables, London, HMSO (1966). 'Persons stating a present or former economic activity.' Table 29 of Census 1971, (GB) Economic Activity, Part IV; London, HMSO (1976). 'Economically active and retired': England and Wales.

There are in fact several distinct types of professional worker. This chapter begins by examining the distinctions between those professions in which market exchange is based on the practitioner–client relationship and those in which it is based on the employee–employer relationship. It then investigates the characteristics of market exchange which distinguish the professions from other occupations, and which result in the development of particular institutional structures.

Section 7.2 indicates that there is a certain paradox in the manner in which many economists have analysed professional labour markets. In their examination of markets in which exchange is based on the practitioner–client relationship, economists concentrate upon the existence of institutional structures, such as occupational licensing and professional codes of conduct, which seriously limit the degree of competition which these markets exhibit. It is contended that these institutions evolve because of the difficulties associated with market exchange where the commodity is information. A further suggestion is that certain of these institutions are used to control the supply of labour in an attempt to raise occupational remuneration. However, in their examination of markets in which exchange is based on the employee–employer relationship, economists assume that such markets exhibit a highly competitive nature and that they closely resemble the markets of the 'standard textbook commodity'. No allowance is made for the problems associated with market exchange where the commodity is information.

The assumption that labour markets composed of professional scientists and engineers are competitive is based on extremely fragile evidence concerning the mobility of scientists and engineers. The aim of section 7.3 is to re-examine this evidence in the light of two mobility surveys which were undertaken by the Royal Institute of Chemistry in the mid-1970s. The most important aspect of the job mobility of professional chemists is a lifetime-specific movement into positions of managerial responsibility, often without a change of employing organization. It is demonstrated that the mobility characteristics, when viewed in a longitudinal framework, show much resemblance to the form of mobility which has been associated with the internal labour market, the subject of section 7.4.

The internal labour market concept is based on the notion that the overall labour market is segmented. Within each segment the pricing and allocation of labour is determined independently of the operations of the overall or 'external' labour market. The essential characteristics of the internal labour market are a high degree of employment stability, emphasis upon internal promotion and a close regard for internal relativities in wage determination. It has been viewed by economists as an institution which reflects the possession by employees of knowledge which is highly specific to, say, a given organization. However, section 7.4 suggests that it could also be regarded as a functional institution which aids the exchange of services in all markets which exhibit informational-inequality, whether this inequality emanates from the possession of specific or general knowledge by the employees concerned.

Section 7.5 then examines the development of trade unionism among professional workers and suggests that the hierarchical nature of the salaried professions has prompted the development of 'professional unionism'. However, the professional union has been prevented from developing in Britain by the opposition of established white-collar, but non-professional, unions.

Section 7.6 examines the rationale behind the male-domination of the professions. It is suggested that many women have considerable difficulty in reconciling commitments to their families and to their careers. It would seem that this dilemma is most acute in the hierarchical salaried professions.

Types of professional market

This chapter emphasizes the importance of distinguishing between those professions in which market exchange is predominantly based on the practitioner–client relationship and those in which it is based on the employee–employer relationship. The distinction is similar to that between the supply of labour in a contract for service and the supply of labour in a contract of service. In the former the supplier of professional expertise provides a defined service as part of a temporary relationship with the purchaser. In the latter the supplier of professional expertise provides unspecified service as part of a permanent relationship with the purchaser.

The distinction between professions based on the practitioner –client relationship and those based on the employee–employer relationship might be expected to follow closely that between independent practice and salaried employment. While these dichotomies do show some degree of congruency, the relationship between them is complicated by a number of factors.

First, a number of professional workers are employed as salaried employees of principals. A principal is a person who supplies professional services either as an individual or as a partner of a firm; for example, a solicitor operating as a partner in private practice. Some salaried employees of principals are working, for example, as articled clerks in law practices so as to acquire experience or capital before becoming principals in their own right. Viewed from a cross-sectional perspective they are salaried employees; viewed on a longitudinal framework they are independent practitioners. Other salaried employees of principals have neither the opportunity nor the potential of becoming principals, and are to be regarded as synonymous with the salaried employees of non-principals.

Secondly, the existence of the National Health Service means that doctors, who supply professional services on a practitioner –client basis and so would be expected to show a high degree of independent practice, are in salaried employment to a degree greater than in comparable countries (for example,USA and Australia). Thus the British medical general practitioner supplies services on an individual basis but is paid independently of each market exchange.

Table 7.2 summarizes information collected by the Monopolies Commission on the Supply of Professional Services. This shows for each professional institution, the distribution of members among individuals supplying professional services as principals, employees of principals, and directors or employees of companies, public corporations or local government departments (or, in the case of doctors and dentists, for the National Health Service). On the basis of this information professional institutions can be classified into the following three main types:

(1) Institutions with a predominance of independent principals; the Law Society and the British Dental Association are examples. In the absence of the National Health Service the British Medical Association (BMA) would probably be in this group, and thus resemble the US pattern.

(2) Institutions with large proportions of both principals and salaried employees; this group includes the BMA and the professional institutes relating to accountancy. Accountancy has exemplified the trend, noted by Kornhauser (1964, p.4), for formerly independent professions to find their members' skills increasingly valued by large corporations. The Institute of Chartered Accountants, which has traditionally been the professional body of the independent accountants, now has more members working as employees than as principals[4].

(3) Institutions with a predominance of employees; in this group are the medical Royal Colleges (mainly hospital doctors) but it is dominated by the scientific and engineering institutions. Less than 10% of the members of these institutions work as principals supplying professional services.

It has been conventional to equate the professions with independent practice despite the fact that a large and growing proportion of professionals work as salaried employees. For example in the US it has been found that there is a positive relationship between the growth of professions and the proportion of members who are salaried. It would seem that this results from the development of new professions based on salaried employment, the tendency of established professions to show increasing proportions of non-independent practitioners and from the greater degree of control over supply enjoyed by the independent professions[5].

The data shown in *Table 7.1* suggest that approximately three-quarters of professional workers in England and Wales worked in the salaried employee capacity and that only one-quarter were self-employed. Further, between 1961 and 1971 the growth rate of the salaried employee group was four times as fast as that of the self-employed group. The same relationship therefore applies to England and Wales as to the US[6].

Training and information inequality

Professional status is closely associated with the possession by practitioners of a set of skills of a theoretical nature. These skills have been acquired during a lengthy training process which is usually concentrated at the beginning of the individual's career.

TABLE 7.2 Distribution of members of professional institutions between independent practice and salaried employment

Professional institute	% of professionally active members		
	Supplying professional services as principals	Working as employees of principals in col (1)	Working as directors or employees
Law Society	73	15	12
British Dental Association	77	7	16
Institute of Chartered Accountants in England and Wales	33	22	45
Association of Certified and Corporate Accountants	21	11	68
British Medical Association	44	–	56
Royal College of Physicians of London	–	–	great majority
Royal College of Surgeons of England	–	–	great majority
Institute of Civil Engineers	7	17	77
Institution of Mechanical Engineers	4		96
Institution of Electrical Engineers	2	10	88
Royal Institute of Chemistry	1	1	98

Note
All rows sum to 100.
Source: Monopolies Commission on the Supply of Professional Services (1970, Table IX)

Thus part of the higher income obtained by professional workers represents a return on the costs of this training, as would be predicted by human capital theory, which is discussed in more detail in Chapter 4. Many occupations require lengthy training before they can be entered, but not all would be regarded as professions. For example, craft occupations have apprenticeships and hairdressing requires considerable training. What distinguishes the professions is the theoretical or intellectual nature of the skills acquired. The training of the professional develops his understanding of a body of theoretical knowledge which he applies to concrete situations when qualified. The most important aspect of this training is that it provides the professional with privileged access to a body of knowledge and so generates the development of informational inequality in those situations in which he is selling his services. Greenwood (1957) illustrates this characteristic by comparing the customer of a member of a non-professional occupation, for example a retail grocer, with the client of a member of a professional occupation. The former shops around until he finds the services and/or commodities required, having sufficient knowledge to judge the potential of the service or commodity. However, the latter lacks the requisite theoretical knowledge to discriminate among the range of possibilities and so the professional is left a great deal of discretion in deciding what is best for the client.

One of the distinctive characteristics of the professional occupation is the code of conduct, which attempts to guarantee that the professional practitioner will serve the best interests of clients. The need for a code can be seen to emanate directly from the informational inequality which is inherent in the supply of professional services. It provides some assurance that the practitioner will not abuse privileged access to information. The professional code of conduct is one of several distinctive structural characteristics deriving from this source. A related institution which generates a higher degree of trust for the client is the system of occupational licensing which a number of professions have been accorded. Occupational licensing will be considered in more depth in section 7.2 below. Briefly, it refers to the situation in which an individual must obtain a licence to practise from a state-recognized authority. Thus the client of a given practitioner is guaranteed that the latter has attained a given level of competence and has completed a minimum level of training.

Taking a broad definition of the term 'institution' it could be said that the favoured economic and social standing of the professional worker is an institution which develops trust where there is informational inequality in market exchange. In a quote which has perplexed many economists, Adam Smith stated that,

> The wages of labour vary accordingly to the small or great trust which must be reposed in the workmen. . . . We trust our health to the physician; our fortune and sometimes our life and reputation to the lawyer and attorney. Such confidence could not safely be reposed in people of a very mean or low condition.

Their reward must be such, therefore, as may give them that
rank in society which so important a trust requires. (1970, p.207).

The suggestion that relative wages have a role in developing
trust has two important implications for wage theory. First, the net
advantages of occupations which rely on trust will not tend to
equality with the net advantages of other occupations because of
the need for practitioners to maintain a high social standing.
Secondly, conventional ideas of fairness are likely to be a major
influence upon wage relativities (Wood, 1978, pp.16–18).

Alternative theories of wage determination can be seen to have
developed directly from the analysis of Smith. The orthodox or
neoclassical framework is based upon Smith's model of net
equalization. However, economists working within this framework
have paid little attention to the role played by trust in wage-
determination[7]. Such considerations have been most fully examined by institutional economists and by sociologists. In consequence labour economics has developed two competing
frameworks. This subject is examined in more depth in section 7.2
below.

Degrees of professionalism

Some writers have suggested that professionalism should be seen
not as a matter of kind but as one of degree; that is, professional
status should be seen as a continuum rather than as a quality which
some occupations possess and others do not. This reflects the fact
that most, if not all, jobs possess some privileged access to
information but some, and particularly those based on theoretical
knowledge, show this tendency to the greatest degree. Those who
have analysed degrees of professionalism have concentrated upon
differences in the institutional structures of differing professions
and upon differences in the income and status accorded to
members of differing occupations.

For example, Hickson and Thomas (1969) produced a scale of
professionalism based on the structural characteristics of the
professions, such as length of training period, explicit ethic of
confidentiality and recognized disciplinary procedures. In terms of
the resultant professionalization-score, the medical and legal
professions showed the greatest degree of professionalism. The
authors interpreted their findings as consistent with two major
hypotheses. First, professionalization is an historical process. This
approach can be said to have developed from the classic work of
Carr-Saunders and Wilson (1933, p.3) which indicated that there

are two types of profession – those of ancient lineage which are commonly regarded as the 'typical professions' and those which, while commonly regarded as professions, are 'younger and therefore less firmly established'.

Secondly, professionalism is a reflection of the nature of the relationship between the professional and the purchaser of his services. Hickson and Thomas noted that there is evidence of a positive relationship between professionalization-score and the proportion of members of an institution in private practice. Because this relationship depends on the age of the profession, it is difficult to distinguish between the two hypotheses.

A prime example of the approach that considers degrees of professionalism according to differences in income and status is in the *Finniston Report* which stated that, 'the professional status of engineers is not generally acknowledged in this country by the public and by employers to the extent that it is for, say, doctors and lawyers' (HMSO, 1980, p.125). This is reflected in the occupational status and average income of engineering relative to medicine and law. While the medical and legal professions dominate rank order one of the Goldthorpe–Hope scale of occupational status, engineering ranks only sixth. According to Norris (1980, p.258) the median earnings of medical general practitioners and solicitors who are partners in practice are more than three and a half times the median earnings of all male employees. The equivalent figure for engineers is 1.8 – only half as much. The evidence therefore shows that engineering, one of the younger and less firmly established professions of Carr-Saunders and Wilson's analysis, has not been able to attain a more established status relative to the vocations of ancient lineage in the half century since their study. This suggests that variations in the degree of professionalism reflect the nature of the relationship between the professional worker and the purchaser of his services rather than the age of the profession.

7.2   Competition in professional markets

One of the major requirements for entry into a profession is that the individual undertakes specialized training. It has become part of the conventional wisdom of economic analysis that the above average incomes received by professional workers represent returns on the costs of this training. Some economists, however, have suggested that the high incomes of such workers are greater than can be justified on the grounds of training costs alone and that the professions constitute a non-competing group, reflecting the social and economic stratification of society (Friedman and Kuznets, 1945, p.391). It is extremely difficult to test for the existence of non-competing groups and in consequence it has not been possible to prove whether professional workers receive more than would be justified on the basis of the greater costs and/or risks associated with their occupations[8].

Entry into some professions requires that the individual obtains a form of licence from the state which indicates the attainment of minimum standards of education and competence. In other professions entry is much less structured and requires that the individual attains a certain standard of education and obtains a job supplying the relevant professional services. The essential difference between the two types of profession is that the former offers a licence to practise whereas the latter does not; that is, the state decides upon the qualities of the suitable practitioner rather than the purchaser of the services.

Friedman (1962, p.144) has indicated that an occupation may be accorded special status by the state in three main ways:

(1) *Registration*   In order to engage in certain activities individuals are required to list their names in an official register. However, non-registrants may still be allowed to practise the activity.
(2) *Certification*   Whereby the state issues a certificate indicating that a given individual has certain skills. It may still be possible for those not possessing certificates to practise.
(3) *Licensing*   Under which an individual must obtain a licence from a recognized authority, usually after obtaining some minimum standard of competence in the activity, in order to practise. Non-licence-holders are barred from practising.

The accordance of special status to certain occupations reduces the degree of competition in the market for professional services. On the one hand, professional practitioners are required to obtain a level of qualifications which might be different from that which they would freely choose on economic grounds. On the other hand, the freedom of purchasers of such services to choose among practitioners of differing competence levels (and therefore prices) is reduced. It has been suggested that the development of these institutions reflects a market response to the difficulties associated with exchange where the commodity is information. For example, Arrow (1963, p.947) has hypothesized that, 'the special structural characteristics of the medical care market are largely attempts to overcome the lack of optimality due to the non-marketability of the bearing of suitable risks and the imperfect marketability of information'.

Occupational licensing

The essence of Arrow's argument is that a number of characteristics of medical care distinguish it from the usual commodity of economics textbooks. First, an individual's demand for medical services is irregular and unpredictable. Secondly, medical care belongs to that category of commodities for which the product and activity of production are identical. Therefore the consumer cannot test the product before consumption. Thirdly, even after treatment the patient is not certain of its quality; this is a consequence of the informational inequality which is inherent in professional market exchange (Arrow, 1963, pp.948–951).

The high degree of uncertainty and the attendant informational inequality mean that patients have to rely on a large degree of trust. Occupational licensing and rigid entry requirements can be seen as institutions which are designed to guarantee a minimum of quality and so reduce the consumer's uncertainty of the quality of the product as much as possible. It is further argued that the pricing practices in the medical care market result from the same factors. In particular, the restrictions placed on competition among physicians through advertising and price-reduction result from the requirement that the treatment should be seen to be dictated by the objective needs of the case and not by financial considerations.

The uncertainty that is associated with medical care is also likely to lead to the profession itself calling for licensing. Where trust between doctor and patient improves the quality of care an important externality arises. In this situation it is possible for the activities of poorly trained practitioners to lower the reputation of the profession as a whole and thereby reduce the degree of trust in the doctor–patient relationship (Siebert, 1977, p.31). The lower the degree of trust that patients accord doctors the less easy is their communication and the more difficult is diagnosis and treatment.

The concentration of the analysis upon the medical care market is a reflection of the fact that the majority of registered professions in Britain are in the medical area (Lees, 1966, p.13). In general it would seem that two factors are predominant in determining whether an occupational grouping is able to attain registered status or at least be regarded as possessing a legitimate claim to such status. The first is that the producer–consumer relationship must be of the practitioner–client variety rather than the employee–employer type. The second is that the worker must be dealing with matters that are closely associated with health and safety. The recommendations of the Finniston Committee (HMSO, 1980, pp.135–138) are instructive in this respect. While they were opposed to the licensing of the bulk of (salaried) engineers, they did recommend forms of licensing for workers in jobs where health and safety considerations arise, and for consulting engineers.

In Britain medicine does not possess the full licensed status under the terms of Friedman's definition. Any individual is free to practise medicine as long as he does not call himself a doctor, imply that he is qualified practitioner, prescribe drugs or sign death and certain other statutory certificates. The same status is possessed by veterinary surgery and architecture (Lees, 1966, pp.9–11). These professions are more akin to certificated or registered professions than licensed. However, it is doubtful whether the distinction means anything in reality for the number of unqualified doctors and architects practising is small. Thus it is contended by Lees (1966, p.11) that 'By and large, it would seem, once a profession is registered, it is difficult for those not on the register to make a living.' The status of licensed occupation in Britain is confined to barristers, patent agents, midwives, dentists, opticians and pharmacists in the dispensing of drugs (Lees, 1966, p.11).

While state registration, occupational licensing and other social institutions that are designed to generate trust emanate from the shared interests of the practitioner and the client, it has been argued that certain professions have used the legal or effective monopoly which such institutions generate to foster their own interests. It has been noted by Siebert (1977, p.32) that occupational pressure for ever increasing standards of entry and tight rules governing the distinction between qualified and unqualified medical practitioners (demarcation rules) are compatible with both the desire for entry limitation (private interests) and for improving standards (public interests). However, three factors indicated to Siebert that the call for increased training requirements contained in the *Merrison Report* resulted from the former rather than the latter. First, the general desire to raise entry standards was accompanied by opposition to the imposition of the higher standards on established practitioners by a 'grandfather clause'. Secondly, the net present value of lifetime earnings for general practitioners was seen to be far higher than is easily compatible with competition. Thirdly, there was substantial evidence of nepotism in the selection of medical school students –which suggests that doctors' actions are guided more by family income maximization than by regard to the public interest (Siebert, 1977, pp.32–36). Similar evidence has been collected by Friedman and Kuznets (1945), and by Freeman (1976) for the US medical profession. Moreover many analyses of professional occupations have indicated that the professional code of conduct and related fee-fixing practices are used as much, and possibly even more, in the interests of practitioners as in those of their clients[9].

The principal means by which a profession can raise its collective income is the restriction of entry into the occupation. The benefit of the restriction on labour supply will be confined to those individuals who are already members of the occupation; these workers will receive a windfall similar to a capital gain on a share (Fisher, 1971, p.142)[10]. Subsequent entrants will receive no such benefit for a major effect of the wage increase is to attract more individuals to the occupation, up to the point at which there is no advantage to be secured by training for this occupation rather than any other. The increased returns to occupational membership will be covered by increased costs of entry. Thus the wage increase is simply a once-for-all gain for existing occupational members and further increases can only result from further attempts to restrict supply.

The size of the wage increase which is received by the occupation, once the market has returned to its equilibrium level, will depend upon the degree to which the purchasers of the relevant services are able to undertake action to minimize the effect of the supply-restriction. A crucial condition for successfully raising wages by controlling supply is that there should be no easy alternative for the commodity that their occupation helps to produce.

The essence of occupational licensing is that it not only gives the occupation an important role in deciding upon the appropriate training for entry but that it also allows the occupation to reduce the degree to which consumers can substitute for the services of its members. A system of occupational licensing effectively gives the occupation the power to reserve work for the qualified worker. In consequence the ability of the consumer to substitute for a less expensive factor is reduced.

Most professional bodies are qualifying associations and, while this does offer them the possibility of controlling the standards of entry into their occupations, they do not possess the power to reserve work for the qualified worker. The situation is particularly acute for the scientific and engineering professions which would seem to exhibit a great deal of substitutability among members of the varying disciplines and between off-the-job and on-the-job trained workers[11]. Even if all of the professional bodies in this field were able to work in concert to raise entry standards in the hope of raising collective incomes, employers could use technician engineers and non-degree scientists to overcome problems in those areas of short supply. In order to be effective, control over the supply of labour to an occupation needs to be complemented by the existence of a set of demarcation rules which define tasks that can only be undertaken by members of that particular occupation[12].

Professional scientists and engineers

Labour markets composed of professional scientific and engineering manpower have not witnessed the development of those overt institutions that are designed to generate trust, such as occupational licensing, to the same degree as their medical and legal counterparts. Hence economists have generally considered it justifiable to treat them as being more competitive. However, it is expected that the problems of information exchange are as prevalent in these markets as in those that have developed accommodating institutional infrastructures. It might therefore be expected that the technology-based professions have developed alternative institutions to aid exchange and that these structures transform their basic competitive nature.

A great deal of the economic analysis of labour markets for qualified scientific and engineering manpower has been based upon the assumption that such markets are highly competitive. This reflects the influence which the seminal work by Blank and Stigler (1957) exerts upon the analysis of professional labour markets in the United States and Britain. The basic rationale behind their study was the investigation of the widespread belief that there was a shortage of technologists in the United States at the time of the Korean War. In a competitive market a shortage, defined as a situation in which 'the number of workers available increases less rapidly than the number demanded at the salaries paid in the recent past' (Blank and Stigler, 1957, p.24), would result in a rise in salaries, that is 'a salary rise shortage'.

On the basis of indirect evidence which suggested that engineers showed considerable mobility, the authors asserted that the relevant labour markets were competitive and that analysis based on the salary rise shortage concept was therefore valid. As a direct consequence, they interpreted information suggesting a substantial decline in engineering salaries relative to both the earnings of all wage-earners and to the income of independent professional practitioners between 1929 and 1950 as proof that there had been no shortage of engineers.

There are two fundamental difficulties with this interpretation. The first concerns the assumption that the markets are competitive in the conventional sense, which is based on extremely fragile evidence. This evidence is examined in more depth in section 7.3 below. The second difficulty relates to the implication which is drawn from the assumption of competition. While this is a necessary condition for the interpretation of a relative wage increase as indicative of a shortage, it is by no means sufficient. It must also be proved that those markets that form the basis of the comparison were also competitive, or at least showed the same degree of competition, throughout the period. The decline in the relative salary of scientists and engineers might have resulted, for example, from an increase in the degree of 'market imperfection' in other occupational markets between 1929 and 1950, for example from the development of trade unionism and/or control over supply[13].

Subsequent work on scientific and engineering labour markets has indicated that they exhibit characteristics which differentiate them to a significant extent from the textbook-like model upon which Blank and Stigler (1957) based their analysis. However, the majority of studies have accepted the basic notion that these markets are highly competitive. This assumption has been justified, in the main, by reference to the fragile evidence which was provided by Blank and Stigler; for example, see Arrow and Capron (1959, p.298) and Cain et al. (1973, p.66)[14].

Arrow and Capron (1959, pp.303–305) contended that the popular notion of a continuing shortage of scientists and engineers could be seen as a 'dynamic shortage' which reflected three factors. These were the failure of salaries to rise sufficiently rapidly to eliminate excess demand instantaneously, a continual increase in the level of demand, and the length of time it takes to train new personnel in these markets. The slow reaction speed of salaries to excess demand was the result of the prevalence of long-term contracts in the market, the slow diffusion of information (which reflected the heterogeneity of the market) and the dominance of a relatively small number of large firms which could slow down, but not eliminate, the salary rise. Thus Arrow and Capron (1959) suggested that there was a continuing shortage of scientific and engineering manpower during the early 1950s but that it only showed in salaries following a lag.

A further analysis which concentrated upon 'frictions' in the labour market for professional scientists and engineers was undertaken by Folk (1970). He suggested that certain salaries may not be free to rise in response to excess demand because of administrative constraints ('controlled price shortage') and because engineering students are slow to react to any changes that might occur. Therefore he contended that adjustment in this market moved along relatively elastic demand curves and inelastic supply curves (Folk, 1970, p.8). The analysis undertaken by Freeman (1971) was based upon the postulate that the most important characteristic of markets composed of scientific and engineering personnel was the existence of a lengthy training period. Thus career decisions made in response to changes in salary could be expected to influence supply conditions only three to five years later. It is possible that such patterns could set in motion the tendency for a 'cobweb' mechanism.

The cobweb model was tested against available data by Freeman (1971). Two supply equations (the first for the supply of freshman engineers and the second for the number of enrollees who graduate four years later) and a demand equation were specified. Each equation contained a number of crude proxies for the major theoretical variables. For example, the incentives to enter engineering were measured by starting salaries and not by discounted lifetime earnings. This approach was justified by evidence showing the stability of age–earnings profiles. Further, alternatives to engineering were represented by annual male professional earnings, which the author suggested to be a crude but plausible measure of the opportunities facing potential engineers (Freeman, 1971, p.59).

The resultant model indicated that the supply of engineering students was highly responsive to both the relative wage of engineering and to changes in job opportunities. On the demand side it was discovered that the change in salaries was closely related to changes in expenditure on research and development and on durable goods. Overall, the tests showed extremely good fits and high statistical significance. As a result the analysis has been extended to many other disciplines (Freeman, 1975a, 1975b, 1976).

The empirical work of Freeman has been criticized on a number of grounds. Firstly, it has been suggested that the results reflect a trial and error approach rather than an understanding of labour market operation (Mace and Wilkinson, 1977, p.109). The crude nature of Freeman's proxies lends some support to this argument. Secondly, it is highly likely that Freeman's results are open to identification error. In his equations both supply and demand factors are functions of the wage variable. Single equation estimates capture both demand and supply factors and are therefore not subject to unequivocal interpretations[15]. Finally, Freeman's work is not about professional labour markets as such but simply about entry into such markets. In his model mobility among established engineers in response to wage changes only dampens the cobweb cycles. A much more fundamental question concerns the mobility of established scientific and engineering workers, who form a much larger group than the entrants.

The majority of British work upon scientific and engineering labour markets has followed very closely the guidelines set by the American literature. The analyses have not been able to attain even the limited econometric sophistication of the American studies, however, because of a deficiency of suitable data. For example, there is little information relating to starting salaries and so studies have been required to use data based upon the median earnings of given age-groups.

Richardson (1969) attempted to assess whether there had been a salary rise shortage of engineers in Britain during the late 1950s and early 1960s. The data which he analysed (based upon the corporate memberships of the major engineering professional institutions) indicated that the earnings of engineers had increased more rapidly than those of other salaried employees and of manual workers between 1955 and 1962 but less rapidly than both between 1962 and 1965. On the assumption that the engineering market is competitive, Richardson concluded that there may have been an overall shortage of engineers in the former period but not in the latter[16].

This type of analysis was further extended (with extreme reservation concerning the data) by Wilkinson and Mace (1973), who concluded that if movements in the earnings of engineers relative to other groups are in response to changing market forces, the evidence suggests that there was neither a 'salary rise shortage' nor a 'dynamic shortage' of engineers during the 1960s. Additional evidence, such as a deceleration in the rate of increase in the stock of engineers, falling activity rates and falling vacancies, tended to point in the same direction.

The inadequacies of existing data prompted Wilkinson and Mace (1973) to undertake their own sample survey of engineers employed in 12 public and private British firms in a wide variety of industries[17]. A number of the findings of their survey suggested that the labour market for professional engineers in Britain was not competitive. First, none of the firms used salary adjustment as the principal adjustment mechanism. Further, two-thirds of the firms interviewed stated that if non-salary measures were unsuccessful they would leave vacancies unfilled rather than adjust the salaries that they offered. Secondly, graduate engineers of the same age were paid differently according to the firm for which they worked. Thirdly, every firm preferred internal promotion to external recruitment in their adjustment policies and, moreover, justified this preference by arguments relating to morale and other factors which are rarely made explicit in the orthodox or neoclassical framework.

Subsequent analysis of these data by Mace (1979) indicated that the internal labour market framework was more appropriate for the study of markets composed of professional engineers than the competitive model. First, turnover in all firms was below the 10% figure which Alexander (1974) adopted to identify the existence of internal labour market structures[18]. Moreover, the information showed that for nine firms, over half of their engineers had been with the firm all of their working lives. Secondly, entry ports into the firms were confined to junior jobs. Thirdly, there was a close relationship between the degree of promotion attained by the engineer and the length of time that he had spent with the firm. Fourthly, each firm rotated engineers vertically and horizontally through a number of jobs as part of a career development policy. Fifthly, a large proportion of the knowledge used by engineers was acquired on the job. Finally, it was found that internal comparisons were more important than external in the setting of salaries.

Bosworth and Wilson (1980) made the crucial distinction between the labour market for qualified scientists and engineers (the majority of whom do not work as scientists and technologists) and the labour market for scientists and technologists (the majority of whom are not qualified as scientists and technologists). Their analysis concentrated upon the market for qualified scientists and engineers, although their demand side variables are seeminly more applicable to the market for those working as scientists and technologists. The authors attempted to model supply and demand equations on the basis of non-wage variables, such as the number obtaining 'A' level qualifications and expenditure on research and development. Tentative approaches to integrating wage variables suggested that variations in pay do play a role in market-adjustment. However, in their interpretation of employer reaction to a situation of surplus, Bosworth and Wilson (1980, p.326) indicated that employers will respond by up-grading jobs and hiring standards. Such behaviour is compatible with internal labour market models in general, and Thurow's (1975) 'job competition' model in particular.

There is also evidence of the existence of internal labour markets within the market for professional chemists. It is argued by Whitehead (1981) that labour market segmentation will be reflected in inelastic supply curves, considerable volatility in the rank-order of industry wage-rates through time and a large dispersion of earnings. Using cross-sectional data from the Royal Institute of Chemistry Triennial Remuneration Surveys, the analysis shows that both the rank correlation coefficients for earnings and earnings dispersions reported in differing surveys are in general greater in the public sector, although they are both lower for the youngest age-group in this sector (Whitehead, 1981, pp.269–273). These differences can be attributed to a greater degree of specificity in on-the-job training and, in consequence, a more comprehensive development of internal labour markets in the public relative to the private sector (1981, p.274).

7.3   The mobility of professional scientists

The foregoing analysis has shown that the bulk of the early work upon labour markets composed of professional scientists and engineers was based upon the assumption that such markets are highly competitive. However, more recent work has suggested that these markets have developed internal structures which seriously constrain the degree of competition which they exhibit. This section examines mobility in professional markets and looks in particular at evidence from two mobility surveys which were undertaken under the aegis of the Royal Institute of Chemistry in the mid-1970s.

The question of whether the competitive framework is most appropriate for the analysis of professional labour markets has received scant attention. Many authors of studies of scientific and engineering labour markets have been prepared to accept the justification for this assumption which was advanced by Blank and Stigler in their seminal work. Others have justified the adoption of the competitive framework by recourse to evidence which suggests that these markets do not possess those 'imperfections', such as trade unions, which characterize other occupational markets.

The Blank and Stigler (1957) justification, however, is far from conclusive and is based (on the authors' admission) upon indirect evidence. It was asserted that analysis based on the competitive framework would be justified if engineers were mobile among employers. Lacking direct information on such mobility, they found that,

Of those members of the engineering profession in 1939 who remained civilians in the United States between 1939 and 1946, 25% changed at least once the industry in which they were employed during this seven-year period, 30% changed their state of employment at least once, 22% changed from one engineering activity to another . . . 14% changed their branch of engineering and more than 20% of all engineers worked at some time in their lives in a branch of engineering other than that in which they were trained. (Blank and Stigler, 1957, pp.29–30)[19].

On the basis of this information, Blank and Stigler concluded that engineers were sufficiently responsive to offers of higher wages for the market to be regarded as competitive.

The fact that considerable mobility exists in the overall labour market for engineers or scientists does not prove that the labour market is competitive. Such a proof requries evidence that the mobility process is of the type that underlies the orthodox theory of labour supply. For example, a large proportion of the changes which were noted by Blank and Stigler could have occurred without a change of employer. Changes in engineering activity, branch of engineering and even industry can take place without a change of employing organization[20].

Mobility in economic theory

The basis of the competitive model of the labour market is the theory of occupational choice which was propounded by Adam Smith. Its essential feature is that individuals will move between jobs until the net advantages of differing jobs are equalized. This model can only be tested against empirical information if operational content can be provided for the term 'job' and for the concept of net advantages. Economists have tended to define 'job' extremely narrowly, as synonymous with a continuous period of employment with a single employer[21]. Thus they ignore changes in both employment status and work-type that occur during this period of employment. This type of approach has been criticized for putting the researcher in the position of insisting that mobility only occurs when there is employer change (Cole, 1979, p.35). It effectively reduces mobility analysis to the study of labour market turnover. A further problem with the empirical testing of Smith's model is that it has proved extremely difficult to obtain information on the non-pecuniary aspects of the net advantages of differing jobs. In consequence most research has been based on the assumption that relative wages are a reasonable proxy for net advantages. Such an approach leaves the analysis open to the charge that the results would be considerably different if a more accurate representation of net advantages were adopted.

Many studies have suggested that the efficient operation of a dynamic economy requires a great deal of mobility among occupations, industries, establishments and geographical regions in response to changes in the relative attractiveness of differing jobs (for example Ross, 1958, p.904 and Burton and Parker, 1969, p.61). However, recent developments have suggested that both employers and employees benefit from organizational attachment. In such a situation the relationship between inter-organizational mobility and labour market efficiency is complex.

The most significant development of this type is the integration of the specific human capital concept into neoclassical theory. The development of this concept reflected the recognition that human capital can be acquired on the job as well as during formal education. The fact that a certain proportion of the capital so acquired is useful only in the organization of its acquisition provides a rationale for both employers and employees to value organizational stability (Becker, 1964). In this framework, on-the-job training can be divided into two main ideal types. First, there is general training, which increases the marginal productivity of trainees by exactly the same amount in the organization providing the training as in other organizations. Secondly, there is completely firm-specific training, which has no effect on the productivity of trainees in other organizations. While organizations will be willing to provide general training they will only do so if the trainee is willing to bear the costs of training by accepting a wage that is below that which would be obtained in a job with no general training by an amount equivalent to the training costs. If an organization bears part of the cost of general training by paying the trainee a wage above his marginal productivity during the training period, it can only recoup these costs by paying the individual a wage below his (improved) marginal productivity during the post-training period. However, it would be economically irrational for the trained person to receive a wage below that which he could receive in another organization; thus the organization would be unable to recoup the costs.

An employing organization would be more willing to finance the costs of specific training. As long as it paid the employee a wage during the post-training period which is at least as high as could be received in a job with no training, there would be no positive incentive for the employee to leave. However, there would be no certainty that the employee will remain with the organization and so the latter runs the risk of losing his services before the costs of specific training have been recouped. It can reduce this risk by sharing the returns from the training with the employee, so offering a positive incentive for the continuation of the employment relationship. Thus the existence of specific human capital generates a rationale for stability in the contract of employment.

The most fundamental difficulty with the specific human capital concept is that it is not readily amenable to empirical development. It has been noted by Parsons (1977, p.205) that, 'One major difficulty keeps these firm-specific human capital concepts from being vigorously exploited (or at least adequately tested) and that is the lack of a readily observable measure.' There are two major factors which underlie this problem. The first is that the specificity of a given training programme reflects not only the nature of the training content but also the degree of competition in the labour market facing trained workers. Secondly, a large part of on-the-job training takes the form of learning-by-doing and it is extremely difficult to isolate the costs of this process.

Becker was aware of the fact that specificity of training depended as much upon the nature of labour markets as upon training content. He stated,

> Very strong monopsonists might be completely insulated from competition by other firms, and practically all investments in their labor force would be specific. On the other hand, firms in extremely competitive labor markets would face a constant threat of raiding and would have few specific investments available. (1964, p.27).

Thus under conditions of less than perfect labour mobility firms would be willing to bear the costs of training which would be beneficial to the trainee in other firms. This renders the specific –general distinction unclear.

A further problem with the development of the specific human capital concept relates to the fact that a considerable proportion of on-the-job skill-acquisition results from learning-by-doing rather than from formal training programmes. The former is an unavoidable by-product of the production process and so, in one sense, it is costless (see Oatey, 1970, p.4). Further, it is not an easy process to identify and this poses the problem of how firms can apportion the costs, in terms of output forgone during the training period, of a process which is virtually immeasurable. Mincer (1976, p.140) has asserted that neither of these factors poses a problem for the human capital framework because variations in the supply of labour to jobs with differing opportunities for learning-by-doing will lower the initial earnings of the jobs with steeper profiles below the initial earnings of those with flatter profiles. This assumes considerable knowledge and foresight on the part of workers in a situation in which the acquisition of informtion poses problems for firms. Overall the extension of human capital concepts to cover learning-by-doing, while logically sound, strains the bounds of plausibility (Blaug, 1976, p.837).

The competitive model represents the application of analytical tools, which are derived from the general theory of price, to markets in which the commodity is labour, with suitable modifications for the idiosyncracies of labour as a factor of production. The internal labour market framework, on the other hand, represents the development of a more descriptive approach to labour economics, which reflects a dissatisfaction with analysis within the conventional framework. There are two main elements to this approach. The first is that the labour market develops structures which influence the degree and direction of mobility and which therefore severely constrain its competitive nature. The second is that emphasis is placed upon considerations of fairness in wage determination and labour allocation.

Kerr (1954) made the observation that labour markets develop rules, both formal and informal, which introduce structure beyond that which would emanate from the preferences of employees and employers alone. Movement into, within and out of labour markets is crucially influenced by these rules. Kerr (1954) distinguished three types of market according to the mobility patterns which they exhibited:

(1) *Open* A structureless and competitive market in which mobility is unsystematic.
(2) *Guild* In which movement is predominantly between firms or horizontal in the craft area.
(3) *Manorial* In which movement is mainly in the vertical dimension along well-defined job-ladders.

The manorial variant of Kerr's trichotomy has been subject to most development within the internal labour market framework. It has been asserted that the manorial or enterprise-specific internal labour market reflects job and skill specificity in the production-process (Doeringer and Piore, 1971, pp.13–22). Of particular importance in the generation of such structures is the form of on-the-job skill-acquisition which takes place through a process of 'osmosis' or informal on-the-job learning. The most extreme example is the line of progression in which work on one job develops skills which are necessary for the job above it in terms of complexity. In this case, workers on lower level jobs form the natural source of supply for higher level jobs (Kerr, 1954, p.99; Doeringer and Piore, 1971, p.58). The implication for mobility is that movement between firms (turnover) will be reduced, and vertical movement within firms will be enhanced. The net effect on mobility, broadly defined, is uncertain.

It has been suggested that the majority of job changes in a labour market may result from the form of internal mobility which has been emphasized by the internal labour market theorists. The hypothesis is that the most common type of labour mobility may result from change in the job performed rather than from any physical movement on the part of labour. While such change will involve some flexibility by the worker concerned, it will be of only a very small degree. Although this may be the most common type of labour mobility, 'it is possibly the part about which we have the least factual knowledge due to difficulties of identification and measurement' (Hunter and Reid, 1968, p.29).

Such a gradual form of labour mobility is distinct from the discrete job-change which forms the basis of the competitive model. Moreover it poses considerable conceptual problems for the conventional supply and demand framework. Where training for higher level jobs takes place in the performance of lower level jobs, it is impossible to distinguish between the supply and demand curves for the higher level jobs; in effect, the two curves become synonymous (Thurow, 1975, pp.79–80). The corollary of this situation is that the analyses (discussed in section 7.2), that attempt to identify supply and demand curves, are inappropriate for the study of labour markets composed of established rather than entrant engineers and scientists.

It is very difficult to choose among competing frameworks in economic theory, largely because they are so malleable as to be compatible with almost any set of findings (Mackay *et al.*, 1971, p.16). However a number of differences of emphasis can be suggested between the competitive and internal labour market frameworks. First, the latter puts considerable weight upon the importance of employment stability. Secondly, the competitive model concentrates its attention upon mobility between organizations. Thirdly, the dominant form of mobility in the internal labour market model is the gradual change in the bundle of job-duties performed whereas the dominant form in the competitive model is the discrete change of job.

Surveys of professional chemists

The Royal Institute of Chemistry (RIC) mobility surveys were undertaken between 1973 and 1975. Both surveys obtained retrospective work-histories from specially selected samples of the Institute's membership. The first survey was conducted in late 1973 and early 1974 among 435 members of the Institute who were aged 47 years on 1 January 1973[22]. The second was undertaken in late 1975 and was based upon 2000 members who were aged between 25 and 44 years at the time of the survey[23].

The most significant aspect of these surveys is that they permit an extremely detailed investigation of mobility from the employee's viewpoint. In contrast to many similar surveys, the decision as to what constituted a change of job was left to the respondent. It is more usual to delineate job-changes from mere changes in job-duties by reference to a code which is adopted by the researcher. While this self-reporting technique has many disadvantages, it has the advantage of concentrating the analysis upon those aspects of the mobility-process that are important for the respondent rather than upon those which are imposed by the classification which is adopted; that is, it taps individual perception of change[24].

Many mobility surveys define the characteristics of a job-change in such a manner as to ignore completely within-organizational mobility or define such mobility in a much more restrictive manner than its between-organizational correspondent[25]. The chemists' surveys left to the respondent the decision of whether such mobility was to be included. The questionnaire that accompanied the first survey made little explicit refererence to within-organizational mobility but the second survey's questionnaire requested information on job-changes that took place within the confines of a given establishment. The distinction between reported within and between-organizational job changing could be made by reference to the section on reasons for job-change, which included categories relating to transfer within organizations.

Both surveys also requested information on the characteristics of each job, such as type of work undertaken and level of responsibility held, at the beginning and end of the job. This allowed investigation of those changes in job-duties that were not regarded by the respondents concerned as being of sufficiently large scale to be deemed full job-changes. These changes are assumed to correspond closely to the osmotic forms of mobility which have been emphasized by the institutionalists.

Three types of mobility can therefore be isolated. First, there is non-reported or within-job mobility, which is most closely associated with the internal labour market framework. Second, there is reported within-organizational mobility, which is more closely associated with the internal labour market than the competitive framework, although a case can be made for regarding it as compatible with the latter. Third, there is reported between-organizational mobility, which is most fully articulated within the competitive model.

Employment stability

The frequency distributions of number of jobs held were positively skewed, with a median of four jobs in every group, suggesting considerable employment stability. Analysis of the second survey indicated that the degree of employment stability of labour market entrants declined during the post-war period; whereas 48% of those aged between 40 and 44 had remained in their first job for more than five years, only 30% of those aged 25 to 29 at the time of the survey (late 1975) remained in their initial employment for an equivalent period of time (Creedy and Whitfield, 1980, p.5)[26].

It should be borne in mind that these figures include reported within-organizational job-changes and so they underestimate the degree of organizational stability exhibited by the respondents. Information on this phenomenon can be obtained by dividing the number of between-organizational job-changes that were reported by the total number of man-years that the respondents have spent in the labour market. The statistic so obtained provides an indication of turnover rate which can be compared to those figures which were obtained by Alexander (1974) and Mace (1979). The turnover rate for the first survey is 0.075 organizational changes per man year of labour market experience and for the second survey it is 0.102[27]. Thus the former is below Alexander's figure of 0.100 for the identification of an internal labour market structure and the latter is slightly above it. The difference between the two statistics reflects the lower average age of the respondents to the second survey. While the respondents to the first survey were all aged between 47 and 48 at the time of the survey, the median age of the respondents to the second survey was 30. Both the secular decrease in employment stability (which was noted above) and the lifetime-specific increase in organizational stability, which will be examined below, point to a positive relationship between organizational-stability and age of respondent at the time of survey.

Within and between-organizational mobility

Both surveys showed that a considerable proportion of reported job changing took place without a change of organization. One-quarter of the job changes which were reported in the first survey and over one-third of those reported in the second survey took place within the confines of a given organization. The major reason for the greater relative importance of internal mobility in the latter would seem to be the request for such information in the second survey's questionnaire. This suggests that the degree of internal mobility which is reported depends crucially upon the composition of the questionnaire (see Whitfield, 1981, p.279).

There is a definite relationship between the incidence of the different types of mobility and the age of the respondent at the time of job-change. While the importance of between-organizational mobility declines with age, the importance of within-organizational mobility remains virtually constant. The decline in mobility among firms with increasing age has been discovered by so many studies that it has been termed a socioeconomic law (Byrne, 1975). It has been explained by reference to the greater costs of moving for older workers and the smaller the amount of time that such workers have to recoup the costs of the move. An alternative explanation is that the high degree of mobility at the beginning of working life represents a period of experimentation with jobs in an attempt to obtain information which can only be discovered after some experience on the job, that is 'job shopping' (Johnson, 1978). This approach implies that organizational stability is the norm and movement between organizations is exceptional.

The relative incidences of internal and external mobility vary not only on a lifetime framework but also on a cross-sectional basis. Within-organizational mobility is much more important in non-educational in comparison with educational sectors of employment and is most important in governmental sectors. Less than one-eighth of job-changes made by respondents in the university sector and just over one-quarter of those in the local authority sector were made internally to the organization. The equivalent figures for the industrial and governmental sectors were 37 and 41% respectively. The nationalized industry sector showed the greatest degree of within-organizational mobility with 56% of all reported job-changes being made in this manner.

These findings indicate that the educational labour market is considerably different in the manner of its operation from the industrial and governmental markets. Two economic analyses of educational labour markets (Williams *et al.*, 1974 on university teachers and Zabalza *et al.*, 1979 on school teachers) devote considerable attention to the nature and degree of mobility in the markets that are studied. Both studies define mobility as movement between establishments, however. While the quantitative evidence which has been presented above suggests that there is some justification for this approach in the case of educational labour markets, one should be wary of generalizing the analysis to non-educational labour markets.

Information relating to change in income upon job-change, which is summarized in *Table 7.3*, suggests that job-changing within the same organization is very different from job-changing on change of organization. While the majority of voluntary

TABLE 7.3 The percentage distribution of types of income change among mobile employment

	Type of mobility		
Type of income change	Between organizations (voluntary)	Within organizations	Between organizations (involuntary)
Increase	78	44	39
No change	11	53	29
Decrease	11	3	32
	100	100	100

Note
The distinction between voluntary and involuntary mobility follows traditional lines, and relates to whether the move was formally initiated by the employee or the employer respectively (Rees, 1973, p.102). In the present study involuntary moves resulted from plant closure, redundancy and dismissal.
Source: Creedy (1975)

external job-changes resulted in the mover increasing his salary, the majority of internal job-changes resulted in no change in salary. Thus while movement between organizations seems to take place in response to differences in net advantages narrowly defined, movement between jobs within the same organization would seem to have a different motivating force. It is important to distinguish between voluntary and involuntary movement in the analysis of labour market turnover. *Table 7.3* shows that *increases* in income were achieved by a much smaller proportion of respondents who moved involuntarily than of those who moved voluntarily. It is also the case that the size of the increase achieved was, on average, smaller for the involuntary movers.

Upward mobility

During the course of his working life the typical professional chemist experiences a considerable increase in the level of responsibility which he holds. It has long been noted that the move from purely technical functions into positions that involve administrative and managerial responsibility are of crucial importance in attaining financial success in a scientific or engineering career. This movement can take one of two forms; the chemist can move from purely technical work with little managerial input into management of technical work, or he can move into general management. Evidence from the RIC Remuneration Surveys indicates that, in each age group, those who are managers of technical work earn more than those who are non-managers involved in the same type of work, and that those in general management earn more than those in technical work of all descriptions.

The first survey gave some indication of the magnitude of this movement. It showed that between the beginning of the first job and the time of the survey, when respondents were 47 or 48 years old, the proportion in the main types of *technical* work (research and/or development and other scientific and technical work) declined from 77 to 59%, and the proportion in such work as production and education increased from 23 to 41%. When asked about the nature of their work it was found that the proportion in work that was primarily administrative or managerial increased from 2 to 60%.

The most important factor about the pattern of job mobility was that the majority of moves across the boundary between work that was primarily non-managerial and work that was primarily managerial were reported as being within-job changes and in job-duties. Two to three times as many moves into management took place within the same job as on a change of organization and the majority of moves across this boundary took place within the same organization rather than on change of organization. The category of reported within-organizational moves into management is much larger in the results for the second survey, and this again reflects the importance of the request for such information about internal mobility.

Similar evidence is obtained from analysis of changes in level of responsibility during the course of the working life. Respondents were asked to list the level of responsibility held at the beginning and end of each job in their work-histories. A six-part classification was used for this purpose. It was discovered that the modal level of responsibility held increased from level six (at which the respondent was directly responsible to the works chemist, team leader, research chemist or higher scientific officer) at age 21, to level two (at which the respondent was directly responsible to the managing director, divisional manager, deputy chief scientific officer or chief scientific officer) at age 44. As a proportion of the 1516 upward moves which were reported in the second survey, 35% took place within the job, 24% on change of job within the same organization and 41% on change of organization. The major difference among these forms of moving among positions on the responsibility ladder was that between-organizational mobility was much more likely to be associated with decreases in responsibility level than the two types of internal movement. Whereas only 23 within-job-changes and 42 job-changes within the same organization were of a downward magnitude on the responsibility ladder, 296 among-organizational changes were of this kind. Thus internal mobility is predominantly of the gradual and positive variety but external mobility is much more heterogeneous and a considerable proportion of such job-changes involve demotion.

Overall, evidence relating to the upward mobility of professional chemists suggests that a substantial fraction of the professional chemist's career-advancement takes place without a change of organization and that many of the relevant changes are regarded by the respondents as being simply changes in the duties of a given job rather than as job-changes in their own right.

Summary

The foregoing analysis indicates that it is extremely difficult to test whether the labour market for professional chemists is competitive. Such a test is much more complex than it was thought to be when Blank and Stigler (1957) made their evaluation. This is largely because the competitive model has been extended to include elements, such as internal mobility and learning-by-doing. The evidence discussed above shows that many of the changes in employment status which were used as evidence of mobility among employers by Blank and Stigler (1957) were as likely, and possibly more likely, to have taken place without organizational change.

However, although it is difficult to test whether a market is competitive, a number of differences in emphasis between the competitive model and its institutional counterpart, the internal labour market framework, were outlined.

On the one hand, there is evidence of considerable movement between organizations in response to economic incentives. Most external mobility is fruitful and cannot be likened to heavy drinking; that is, a symptom of unhappiness but not a cure for it (Sleeper, 1975, p.194). Further, most sectors of employment show a preponderance of reported external over internal mobility; this is particularly the case in the educational sectors, upon which much orthodox analysis has been based.

On the other hand, the respondents show mobility patterns which are akin to those that are emphasized by institutional labour economists. The majority of changes in job-situation which benefit the respondents take place without a change of organization and most of these are of the gradual type which pose most problem for orthodox theory. In this context it would seem most appropriate to attribute to between-organizational mobility the role of assigning labour market entrants to appropriate job-ladders in a setting in which within-organizational mobility predominates.

Overall, there is evidence to support versions of both the competitive and institutionalist models. This reflects, in the main, differences in level of concentration between the two frameworks. Whereas the competitive model concentrates upon the derivation of earnings profiles, the institutionalist approach aims at attaining descriptive reality. However, the analysis indicates that the labour market for professional chemists does contain features that limit its competitive nature. Further, there is considerable support for the more recent studies which have discovered that labour markets composed of professional scientists and engineers exhibit comprehensive internal labour market structures.

7.4   Internal labour markets

Many of the more recent studies examining the labour markets of professional scientists and engineers, the archetypal salaried professions, have shown that these markets have developed internal labour market structures. This poses two main questions for economic analysis. The first asks why markets that are based on the exchange of professional services between employee and employer should develop such institutions. The second relates to the consequences of internal labour market structures for analysis within the orthodox economic framework.

The rationale of internal labour markets

The internal labour market has often been considered an economically inefficient institution which constrains the operation of market forces. However, the plausibility of this approach has been questioned by Thurow (1975) who contends that any long-lasting 'market imperfection' cannot be inefficient at all but must be a functional element in the working of the economic system. There are always profits to be made from eliminating 'market imperfections' and therefore, if markets are basically competitive, someone will sooner or later discover a way around the imperfection (1975, p.xii). Thus many 'market imperfections' represent misconceptualization on the part of the theoretical framework rather than blemishes in an otherwise perfect system.

Analyses that have emphasized the efficiency aspects of internal labour market operations have concentrated upon the argument that they are institutions which facilitate the workings of labour markets in those situations in which knowledge and skill are acquired on the job and, in particular, through learing-by-doing. In the context of the labour market for professional scientists this would indicate that, during the performance of the technical work role, the scientist acquires skills that facilitate the assumption of managerial responsibilities.

Arguments which have attempted to give a rationale for the development of internal labour markets can be divided into two main types. First, there are those that concentrate upon the need to reduce labour turnover in the presence of skill-specificity. Secondly, there are those which emphasize the need for the organization to gain a high level of cooperation from employees in order to facilitate the training and/or production process.

The former school is exemplified by the work of Doeringer and Piore (1971) who contended that skill-specificity, which increases both the level of training costs and the proportion of these costs that is borne by the employer, provides firms with an incentive to reduce turnover. Further, the gradual acquisition of skill through experience makes it efficient for the firm to adopt a policy of internal promotion. Thus the internal labour market represents an attempt by management to maximize the benefits of skill specificity.

Doeringer and Piore stressed, however, that the actual structure which is adopted will not reflect management's interest in organizational efficiency alone. It will also be influenced by the interests of employees who will prefer, for example, policies based upon promotion by seniority as opposed to management's preference for promotion by ability. Moreover, a natural consequence of the employment stability which the managerial policy generates will be the increasing importance of custom in organizational operation. This will reduce the degree to which management will be able to reorganize the market structure in line with new organizational imperatives. Thus the internal labour market structure can be seen to reflect, in part but not whole, the dictates of organizational efficiency.

The school of thought that has concentrated upon the need of the organization to gain the cooperation of the workforce in the presence of on-the-job skill-acquisition implicitly contested the validity of the distinction between employee and employer interests which was adopted by Doeringer and Piore. It is contended by Thurow that the efficiency of on-the-job training depends crucially upon the willingness of incumbent workers to transmit their knowledge to new workers. Their cooperation in this process would be low if they thought that they were training potential wage or employment competitors. Thus, to facilitate training, employers must suppress wage competition within the plant, and they must provide employment security to those involved in the training process. In this context, promotion by seniority is an efficient institution which aims at maximizing the effectiveness of the training-process[28].

Williamson (1975) suggested that internal labour market structures develop because of the difficulty of developing individualistic contracting schemes where the tasks to be performed are of the idiosyncratic variety. Of particular importance in these settings is the need to structure the employment relation so as to develop a high level of cooperation among employees. The essence of the argument is that task idiosyncracies produce an informational inequality which offers employees advantageous positions from which they can bargain with their employers. Examples of task idiosyncracies are knowledge of equipment which is gained through experience, adaptations to the production-process which are made by the worker, the development of team relationships and the existence of codes of communication which are specific to the firm (Williamson, 1975, p.62). The possession of idiosyncratic knowledge by employees yields the risk to employers that they will hoard the information and disclose it strategically as part of a series of bilateral monopoly exchanges. The employment relation is therefore structured in a manner which reduces these bargaining costs and develops the consummate (as opposed to perfunctory) cooperation of employees. The former is achieved by attaching wage rates to jobs rather than individuals and the latter by the development of internal promotion practices which act as an incentive to disclose information in a non-strategic manner.

While the arguments which have explained the development of internal labour markets have concentrated upon the problems associated with the acquisition of skills in an on-the-job setting, it can also be argued that such structures will exist in all settings where there is an informational inequality in the employee–employer relationship. The essential characteristic of this line of analysis is that organizations develop hierarchical control structures, of which the internal labour market is the most sophisticated, to ensure that employees undertake their work-roles in a manner that is in the best interests of the organization. This aspect of the employment relation has been subject to most scrutiny within the radical tradition of economic analysis and builds upon the distinction between 'labour power' (the capacity to perform useful work) and 'labour' (the human effort expended in the production of a commodity), which was developed by Marx.

The hierarchy as a control structure

It is suggested that there is a fundamental conflict of interest within the employment relation which reflects the more fundamental conflict between capital and labour. In the absence of a system of control, the employee would define his work-role in a manner that was congruent with his own interests and therefore against those of his employing organization. In order to ensure that the employee complies with its requirements, the latter must develop a hierarchical structure which directs the work-role of its labour force.

Edwards (1975, p.58) has suggested that compliance can be gained on the following three distinct levels, each of which is more sophisticated than its predecessor

(1) *Rules orientation* The employee is aware of and unambiguously follows the rules.
(2) *Habits of predictability and dependability*   The employee performs his task according to the spirit of the work criteria and transcends the particular rules to carry out their intent.
(3) *Internalization of the enterprise's goals and values*   The employee identifies with the enterprise, is loyal and committed and is therefore self-directed or self-controlled.

It is further suggested that the organization encourages compliance with its criteria for work-performance by the differential distribution of rewards. Workers who behave 'properly' are rewarded accordingly, and this encourages the adoption of attitudes which aid the translation of labour power into labour.

When an organization employs a professionally trained worker, it is hiring someone who has privileged access to information which is useful when applied to the production of a given commodity. The informational inequality which is fundamental to the exchange of professional services makes it inevitable that there will be a considerable degree of discretion which is left to the professional employee in the performance of his work-role. This has two crucial implications for the translation of labour power into labour. First, the employee will have considerable latitude to undertake his work in a manner which is incompatible with the interests of the organization. Secondly, it is impossible for the organization to control the activities of the professional employee by laying down tight work criteria which must be followed in either the letter or the spirit. The organization must therefore attempt to gain the necessary degree of compliance by ensuring that the employee internalizes its goals and values. Fox (1975, p.58) has suggested that an important aspect of this process is to offer the professional employee a level of rewards, perquisites, opportunities and prospects which make it clear that he is seen as a member of the organizational community; that is, by providing a special employment relation which offers a guarantee of continuing employment, steady promotion and movement into upper managerial ranks given satisfactory performance.

The implication of this analysis is that one would expect to see the development of internal labour market structures wherever the employee possesses power over his employer in the sense of privileged access to information, whether it is based upon knowledge acquired during the production process or in a setting external to the organization. Professional labour markets will therefore be expected to contain internal labour markets.

It should be noted that the efficient translation of labour power into labour depends upon factors external to the employment-relation as well as those which are bound up with this relationship. There is considerable evidence that the educational process develops attitudes which facilitate the integration of the individual into a bureaucratic organizational structure and therefore aids the transformation of labour power into labour (Gintis, 1971). Further, the professional worker, through his professional association, is made aware that he is ethically bound to serve the best interests of his employer as part of a professional code of conduct. Thus the trained professional is likely to enter the organization with attitudes which are, in many respects, compatible with those of the latter and the special employment relationship both develops this congruency and relates it to a specific context[29].

The steady lifetime movement up the ladder of responsibility and the related increase in economic welfare which is characteristic of the employment relation in labour markets composed of professional scientists and engineers can be seen to reflect, on this interpretation, both the social assimilation and the development of commitment of the individual to the organization. This commitment is generated by promoting an individual through a series of posts each vested with greater responsibility and discretion than the one before. 'It is usual for an individual moving thus up the hierarchy to display an increasing commitment to, and identification with, the organization and its imputed values.' (Fox, 1975, p.114).

The major hypothesis which is suggested by this analysis is that the internal labour market reflects the difficulties associated with market exchange where there is informational inequality. In other words, it undertakes the same function in professional labour markets in which exchange of services is based on the employee –employer relationship as is performed by more overt institutions, such as occupational licensing and professional codes of conduct, in markets which are based on the practitioner–client relationship.

The internal labour market and neoclassical theory

Many of the proponents of internal labour market analysis have expressed the belief that its very existence casts doubt upon the efficacy of analysis within the orthodox or neoclassical framework. For example, Doeringer and Piore (1971, p.84) suggested that the internal labour market weakens the assumptions of the competitive model and interferes with the competitive determination of factor prices. Thurow (1975, p.78) similarly stated that the essence of efficiency in a dynamic economy where learning takes place on the job is different from that in static neoclassical models. However, other economists view the internal labour market as an institution which reflects the peculiarities of labour as a factor of production and which helps the market better achieve the conditions which are necessary for neoclassical efficiency. For example, Williamson (1975, p.78) suggested that the internal labour market aids the organization in equating wages and marginal productivity for higher-level jobs through the processes of continuous screening and differential rates of promotion.

The essential difference between the two approaches lies in the level of focus that is adopted. Those adopting the orthodox approach view the firm as an institution which operates according to certain laws which are derived from a set of concepts which have little descriptive reality. However, those using a more institutional approach concentrate their attentions upon the actual operations of the firm. The orthodox theorist is only interested in whether firms operate in aggregate as if they conform to the theoretical ideal and is therefore not concerned with micro-data which suggest that the actual processes are different from those of the model. Opponents of such an approach suggest that it is totally inadequate to take such a perspective in a situation in which firms are creators of employment opportunities, important sources of training and principal allocators of rewards (Loveridge and Mok, 1980, p.404).

The line of argument that views the internal labour market as a fundamental component in the process of translating labour power into labour can be integrated quite readily into the orthodox framework. For example, the degree to which the employee internalizes the goals and values of his employing organization can be defined as a specific skill which is acquired on the job. Thus the greater the cooperation of the employee (the greater the acquisition of specific skills), the greater the promotion which he is accorded. The internal labour market can therefore be viewed as an institution which aids the attainment of wage and marginal productivity in situations where there is informational inequality in the employee–employer relationship[30]. However, those economists who stress the importance of distinguishing between labour and labour power believe that such a rationalization bypasses the most important characteristic of the employment relation, the conflict between capital and labour, and effectively promotes the viewpoint that the structure of the capitalist organization is both natural and inevitable.

In general, a judgement as to whether the internal labour market approach represents a threat to the credence of the orthodox model or is merely an institution which aids the labour market in its pursuit of allocative efficiency rests on an article of faith. There is no doubt that the professional scientist's employment relation differs considerably from that of the relationship between a purchaser and seller of a standardized, physical commodity. Whether this requires modification of the orthodox theory or its complete replacement cannot be decided upon empirical grounds alone.

7.5   The development of professional unions

The trade union has been regarded by economists within the orthodox approach as the archetypal 'market imperfection'. Thus the presence of trade unions is seen to offer an important indication that a labour market is less than fully competitive. It has traditionally been assumed that professional labour markets show little evidence of trade union organization and can therefore be regarded as more competitive than many of their non-professional counterparts. However, recent years have seen the considerable development of trade unionism within the scientific and engineering professions. By the late 1970s 45% of chartered engineers who were members of the Council of Engineering Institutions (CEI), and 55% of the members of the Royal Institute of Chemistry, were members of trade unions.

The major factor which promoted this development would seem to be a decline in the average income of members of the scientific and engineering professions relative to skilled manual employees on one side and members of the independent professions on the other. The most likely explanation of this decline in income is that these professions lack a collective voice. It was shown in section 7.2 that many of the professions that sell their services on a practitioner–client basis have been able to gain control over the supply of entrants into the occupation and thereby improve the collective income of their memberships. The professional associations of these occupations can therefore be regarded as extremely effective trade unions which are able to improve the economic welfare of their members without recourse to the less subtle tactics, such as the strike, the overtime ban and the work-to-rule, of the general unions. Thus collective action can be regarded as a continuum from supply-restriction at one end to mass withdrawal of labour at the other (Lansbury, 1978, pp.31–32).

The scientific and engineering professions do not possess such a collective voice and have relied upon their privileged access to information, and the concomitant degree of discretion which it provides, to obtain their relatively privileged employment relations. In particular, salaried professionals have been able to obtain steady career advancement as a result of the information inequality associated with their work roles. There is, however, evidence that this special relationship was proving less effective during the late 1960s and early 1970s than the collective actions of other occupations. It has variously been suggested that this reflected a decline in demand for scientific and engineering specalists (Russell *et al.* 1977, pp.258–259) and a rationalization of the production-process which reduced the amount of discretion in some jobs, (Fox, 1975, p.111).

A major consequence of the decline in relative standards was pressure upon the various professional associations to undertake bargaining activities as part of an attempt to provide a collective voice for their members. Some institutes, notably the Royal

Institute of Chemistry, were already engaged in action which aimed at improving the economic welfare of their members but most stopped short of actual bargaining with employers. Professional associations in this area have justified this reticence to become more actively involved in bargaining by reference to their charters (which constrain them to act in the public interest) and to their position as charitable organizations (which yields financial benefits)[31]. Prandy (1965, p.70) suggested that the main reason behind this reluctance lies in the managerial status of a large proportion of members of professional institutes.

The peak councils of the scientific and engineering professions, the Council of Science and Technology Institutes (CSTI) and the Council of Engineering Institutions (CEI), have both attempted to aid the process of unionization of their members. In the early 1970s the CSTI was instrumental in establishing a 'professional union', the Asociation of Professional Scientists and Technologists (APST). In January 1976, the CEI issued a strong recommendation to its members that they should join a 'professional union'. It mentioned three main unions as being suitable for professional engineers – APST, the United Kingdom Association of Professional Engineers' (UKAPE), and the Association of Supervisory and Executive Engineers (ASEE) – and also stated that the Electrical Power Engineers' Association (EPEA) would be acceptable if it proved willing to recruit outside of its public sector base. Thus professional associations in the scientific and engineering area hoped that these unions would be able to undertake those bargaining functions which they were either unable or unwilling to accomplish.

Professional unions have not been able to attain the degree of coverage among professional scientists which was originally anticipated. Indeed, only 10% of professional chemists and chartered engineers have joined professional unions. The trade union membership figures of both professions are dominated by public sector unions and, further, a large proportion of professionals belong to non-professional white collar unions such as the Association of Scientific, Technological and Managerial Staffs (ASTMS) and the Technical, Allied and Supervisory Staffs section of the Amalgamated Union of Engineering Workers (AEUW/TASS).

The special character of professional unions

Members of the salaried professions have been reluctant to join trade unions. This reflects not so much an ideological antipathy towards these collective organizations as an instrumental attitude towards their employment relations. It is a matter of some concern to many professional workers that the action of joining a trade union could damage the special relation which they have with their employers. In those areas where employers have expressed a willingness to recognize and negotiate with unions composed of salaried professionals, a high density of union membership has been achieved. This is particularly apparent in the public sector (including the nationalized industries) where management has been at least tolerant of trade unionism and at most has actively encouraged its development. In such an environment there is less risk attached to joining a union and large numbers of salaried professionals have become union members. For example, the 1977 CEI Survey of Professional Engineers showed that 77% of chartered engineers in the public sector belonged to a trade union in contrast to 20% in the private sector.

The analysis of section 7.4 suggested that the career-advancement of the professional worker is closely associated with the development of cooperative attitudes. On the one hand, the prospect of future advancement contributes to the degree of cooperation which such workers exhibit in the present and, on the other, workers who show themselves to be more cooperative are likely to achieve a greater degree of advancement. Thus the professional worker can expect a steady increase in welfare during his working-life and a possibility of moving into highly remunerative managerial positions. However, the act of joining a trade union is an open indication that the worker sees a basic conflict between his interests and those of the organization. This will disturb the perceived shared interests upon which the 'special employment relationship' is based and will thereby reduce the possibility of upward mobility into the upper managerial ranks. Hence the professional worker who joins a trade union is trading future career prospects for the uncertain gains of collective action. In consequence there is a general reluctance to take this step.

The development of the professional union represents a compromise between the desire of professional workers to exert a collective voice and their hopes of maintaining a special relationship with their employers. The central characteristics of these unions is that they restrict membership to small bands of highly qualified workers, show a reluctance to engage in any action which breaches the professional code of conduct (in particular, strike action) and are non-political in the sense of stressing an absence of links with the Labour Party[32]. These features led to the CEI recommendation that professional engineers should join APST, UKAPE, ASEE or EPEA and that they should not join the more militant white collar unions, such as ASTMS or AUEW/TASS, which were unwilling to guarantee not to engage in any action which would infringe the professional code of conduct. There was a belief that these characteristics would appeal to the professional worker who showed reluctance to join the more aggressive trade unions and that they would suggest to the employer that the 'shared interest' had not been broken[33].

It has been contended that such unions would be largely ineffective without the ultimate threat of withdrawal of labour. Collective bargaining is more than just the mere representation of views and will only yield results if some pressure is placed on the party on the opposite side of the bargaining table. However, such pressure can take a variety of forms (Turkington, 1976), and it is possible that in the special case of the professional worker the less visible forms of industrial action may be the most effective. The majority of professional workers undertake functions in which the mass withdrawal of labour would have only a limited impact upon the company's output. Unless their work is closely tied to the production-process, it is likely that it would take a long time before the effects of a strike would be felt in terms of lost production (Goldstein, 1965, p.205; Dickens, 1972, p.7).

The main bargaining weapon that the majority of professionals possess is that any discontent on their part can break down any shared interest that exists between themselves and management. This could have subtle but far-reaching effects on the organization's efficiency. Not only would such workers show a lesser willingness to interpret discretionary aspects of their employment relations to the benefit of the organization but the latter would have also lost an important source of managerial material. Thus it is in the interests of both employers and employees to maintain the 'shared interest' as much as possible. In this respect the professional union can be seen as a mechanism to channel the discontents of these workers and so uphold the beneficial employment relation. In general, it is by no means certain that the reluctance to engage in overt industrial action represents the ineffectual nature of professional unionism rather than the particular employment situations of professional workers.

It has been suggested by Dickens (1972) that effective professional unionism requires that these institutions should operate in a manner which is similar to that of craft unions. In particular, they should ensure that certain types of work are reserved for the qualified worker and that entry into the occupation should be restricted. Such action would give professional unions the control enjoyed by professional associations in the independent professions. However, despite statements which are generally in favour of such a policy, it seems that professional unions are unwilling to take the necessary action in this direction (Dickens, 1972, p.8).

The major problems faced by the professional unions have stemmed not from any contradiction relating to their reluctance to engage in strike action, however, but from the difficulties which they have encountered in gaining negotiating rights from employers in the face of opposition from established white-collar (but non-professional) trade unions. While employers have generally welcomed the development of the non-militant professional unions and have preferred to recognize them when given the alternative of facing a recognition claim from, for example, ASTMS or AUEW/TASS, they are loathe to do so if a non-professional union already possesses some negotiating rights. This has proved to be particularly important in the engineering industry where many employees are party to the industry-wide agreement which is negotiated between the Engineering Employers' Federation and the Confederation of Shipbuilding and Engineering Unions. The non-professional white collar unions are party to this agreement but none of the professional unions have been able to achieve this status. Employers feared that recognition of the professional unions would arouse strong opposition from the established unions, who were keen to oppose any development which would limit their potential recruitment areas. Further, it was believed that such recognition might fragment even further what was regarded as an overly-fragmented bargaining structure.

Overall, professional unions have not been able to provide professional scientists and engineers with a form of collective voice which represents their views while, at the same time, respecting their special employment relationship. Thus they have been faced with the choice of remaining unrepresented or joining a union which threatens this advantageous status.

7.6   Women and the professions

Table 7.1 showed that only 10% of those workers classified as professional were female. However, evidence collected by social researchers such as Young and Wilmott (1973) and the Rapoports (1971) suggests that an increasing proportion of women desire to undertake a professional career. A development of particular importance is the desire of married women and mothers to undertake professional work.

Prior to the Second World War the typical professional woman was a spinster because many occupations barred married women from employment, either by an explicit marriage bar (for example, teaching and nursing) or by a combination of strong institutional and social pressures. The removal of these formal barriers and changes in attitudes towards female employment have been associated with an increase in the proportion of women marrying. As a result the typical career-woman is now the working wife rather than the spinster.

The most important effect of this development is to change the issue of conflict for professional women from career versus marriage to career versus family. While career spinsters show a similar career pattern to men (school – training – work – retirement), career wives show what has been termed a bi-modal career pattern of school – training – work – withdrawal – (re-training) – work – retirement (Ward and Silverstone, 1980, pp.10–18). The break in the middle of working life, caused by childbirth and child-care, poses major problems for the woman who has trained for a profession because of the conflict between career and family interests.

The demands of the professional work role are likely to make this conflict more acute for women in the professions than for women in other occupations. Young and Wilmott (1973, pp.177–178) collected considerable evidence of role strain within families in which the mother was of professional or managerial status.

The Rapoports (1971, p.20) noted that career wives reacted to this conflict in one of the following three ways.

(1) *Conventional* Where a woman drops her career when she has a child.
(2) *Interrupted* Where a career ceases while the children are young but is re-adopted later.
(3) *Continuous* Where the interruption to work is minimal during childbirth.

They find that the first is still the most common form of conflict resolution and that the third imposes a large degree of strain upon the women concerned.

The manner in which the conflict is resolved depends upon three main factors. First, there is the availability of alternative child-care facilities. Secondly, there is the degree to which each profession offers the opportunity for flexible employment conditions and, in particular, the provision of part-time work. Some professions, notably accountancy, dentistry, nursing and teaching, are fairly well advanced in this respect but others, particularly in the medical profession, seem to be less sympathetic to the career wife's needs (Silverstone and Ward, 1980, pp.212–213). Thirdly, the problems of the career-wife are most acute in those professions with well-defined hierarchical ladders; that is, the salaried professions in general and specifically the scientific and engineering professions. In such occupations a high income results from the development of skills during the years following the end of formal education (see sections 7.3 and 7.4) through the process of on-the-job training and the accumulation of experience. This contrasts, for example, to those occupations in which formal qualification in early-career provides the individual with a licence to supply professional services.

The career-wife suffers from a number of disadvantages in a hierarchical occupation. During childbirth and the pre-school years, the career mother will be forgoing possible training and promotion opportunities and so will be lagging behind her contemporaries. It is also likely that, on return to the labour market, the woman will not be able to obtain employment at her previous job and may be forced to accept a job at a lower level than the one which she left. Further, even during the pre-childbirth years (and even if she has no intention of having children) the career-woman is less likely to be trained for promotion than her male counterparts. Employers are reluctant both to recruit and to train women because of a belief that women have a greater likelihood of leaving the organization than men. Such an action would amortize any resources which had been invested in the training process. Evidence suggests that women do show a greater propensity to move in and out of the labour force but that they show a lower incidence of inter-organizational movement within the labour force than men and that this largely offsets the greater degree of extra-labour-force movement[34].

Lewis (1979) has found that personnel managers exaggerate the greater propensity of women to leave the labour force relative to the greater propensity of men to move among organizations within the labour force. In consequence they over-emphasize the degree of employment instability exhibited by women. This is likely to result in a lower provision of training and/or promotion than is justified on the basis of relative mobility rates. The final disadvantage suffered by women in the hierarchical occupations is that part-time work is less plentiful than in those occupations in which the acquisition of a licence is of crucial importance in gaining access to the labour market.

During the period 1961 to 1971 the proportion of professional workers who were female, according to the figures shown in *Table 7.1*, remained fairly constant. However, the proportion of the salaried professionals who were female declined from 13 to 12% while the proportion of females in the self-employed professions increased from 5 to 8%. It is possible that this reflects a response to the growing demand of women to find a job that shows a greater degree of compatibility between professional and familial roles. The very structure of the salaried professions does not allow for such compatibility.

7.7   Conclusions

The major aim of this chapter has been to examine the manner in which professional labour markets have been studied by economists. The analysis suggests a number of implications for economic analysis and these can be usefully sub-divided into the categories of theory, policy and further research.

The major theoretical implication of the analysis is that professional labour markets develop institutions which restrict the degree of competition which they exhibit. These institutions evolve because of the difficulties associated with market-exchange where the commodity is information and they reflect the need to develop a high trust relationship between the seller and purchaser of professional services. In markets in which the exchange of services is based on the practitioner–client relationship the relevant institutions are based on the market as a whole; for example, occupational licensing and professional codes of conduct. Markets in which the exchange of services is based on the employee–employer relationship have evolved employment relations which are highly advantageous to the workers concerned, such as those which are to be found in internal labour markets. The information upon which this relationship is based can emanate from either the acquisition of both specific knowledge, as emphasized by those explaining the development of internal labour market structures, or general knowledge, as suggested by those in a more radical tradition of economic thought. The analysis concluded by showing that the nature of this employment-relation has had important consequences for both the development of trade unionism and the employment of women within professional labour markets.

The efficacy of policy-prescriptions depends crucially upon an understanding of the operation of the labour market. Much early advice was based on the assumption that the market for salaried professionals bore a close resemblance to the idealized market of economics textbooks. Subsequent analysis has shown this position to be untenable. Employers purposively shield their employees from variations in external market conditions in order to obtain their consummate cooperation and thereby to increase the level of their contribution to the organization's output. In such a labour market major changes in employment status take place without a change of organization and such organizational changes as do occur reflect, in the main, early career attempts to move to a preferred job-ladder. The role of the price mechanism in this type of market is therefore limited. Analysis of the utilization of salaried professionals must therefore concentrate on factors which relate to their deployment within the employing organization rather than on those relating to the broader issues of their employment.

One of the major implications of this chapter is that there is a need to collect longitudinal data for a wide range of occupational groupings. It is also important that such studies concentrate on the processes which affect the utilization of highly-qualified manpower at the level of the organization. This form of analysis is fraught with technical and methodological difficulties but the information which it yields is invaluable for the testing of theoretical models and the development of policy-prescriptions. Unless a lifetime framework is adopted certain phenomena can be deemed irrational when, in fact, they reflect economically-rational behaviour[35]. If the processes which are internal to the employing organizations are ignored the economist is isolating only a fraction of economic behaviour.

Notes

1. The research upon which this chapter is based was undertaken while the author was a candidate for the degree of Doctor of Philosophy at the University of Oxford. He would like to thank John Corina for helpful comments on an earlier draft of this chapter.
2. There are considerable difficulties in obtaining accurate statistics for the purpose of income comparison. The most fundamental problems relate to occupation-specific differences in age–earnings profiles, the treatment of secondary incomes and the valuation of fringe benefits. Therefore Norris's figures should be treated with some caution.

3. The notion that society was witnessing mass professionalisation was contested by Wilensky (1966).

4. Hinings and Hastings (1970) indicated that training in accountancy is still based on the needs of independent practice. However, many qualified accountants move into salaried employment. Thus one would expect the role conflict between profession and organization, which has been suggested by some sociologists (e.g. Kornhauser, 1964), to be a significant factor here.

5. See Kornhauser (1964) for evidence and discussion of the first two factors.

6. This is not a new phenomenon in Britain. Reader (1966) discovered that during the latter part of the nineteenth century the 'new' professions, such as engineering, were growing at a faster rate than the 'ancient three'.

7. Addison and Siebert (1979, p.165) state that modern theorists generally abandon Smith's point about trust or translate it into a rent concept. Wood (1978, p.17) suggests that the type of approach which ignores the role of trust can be seen to date from the work of Alfred Marshall.

8. For an analysis of British evidence see Creedy (1977).

9. For examples and further discussion see Millerson (1964), Prandy (1965), and Eckstein (1955).

10. The major difference is that the capital gain on a share accrues at once whereas the income gain of, say, a recently-qualified worker will accrue over the space of 30–40 years (Fisher, 1971, p.142).

11. For evidence of the degree of substitution among individuals possessing differing types and levels of qualification in the scientific and technological area, see Wilkinson and Mace (1973, p.121).

12. The history of the Royal Institute of Chemistry (now the Royal Society of Chemistry) indicates that this professional body has varied between times when it has pressed for a system of general or partial registration/licensing for its members and times when it has seen advantages in taking an alternative course, such as maintaining a highly exclusive membership (Russell et al., 1977).

13. A further criticism of this type of approach is that it ignores the relative costs of entering differing occupations (Hansen, 1967).

14. An alternative approach is to list the market imperfections that labour markets most frequently exhibit and assess the degree to which professional labour markets are influenced by such factors (see, for example, Richardson, 1969, p.54).

15. O'Connell (1972) attempted to overcome the identification problem by estimating a simultaneous equation model. The results of his analysis are not unequivocal, however, and they show a tendency to vary from one specification to another. For a critique of his analysis see Cain *et al.* (1973, pp.44–45).

16. See above note 14.

17. The authors collected disaggregated data by social survey methods. It has been suggested that such information provides the most appropriate basis upon which to test for the existence of labour market segmentation (Loveridge and Mok, 1980, pp.399–400).

18. Alexander's figure is, however, arbitrary, as Mace acknowledged (1979, p.52).

19. The 'evidence' examined by Blank and Stigler was based upon wartime years and may therefore be atypical. One would expect a high degree of movement simply because of a high level of demand.

20. While change of industry is less likely to occur within the same organization than the other changes, it is not impossible for, say, an employee of a large diversified organization to make such a move.

21. This was pointed out by Parnes (1954, p.25). More recent research has either defined mobility extremely narrowly, for example, Burton and Parker (1969; p.200), or it has concentrated upon the analysis of turnover, for example, Parsons (1972) and Stoikov and Raimon (1968), which is but one aspect of mobility.

22. The main results of this survey are summarized in Creedy (1975).

23. Analyses of some of the results of this survey are to be found in Creedy and Whitfield (1980, 1982).

24. See Cole (1979, p.57). The problems of using the self-reporting technique in an international comparison are highlighted by his study of mobility among workers in both Detroit and Yokohama.

25. Cole (1979, p.37) notes that there is a bias in the analysis of intra-firm and inter-firm mobility. It is usual to define the former as a change of occupational category without a change of firm. The latter is usually defined as change of firm, even if there has been no change of occupational category.

26. A major component of this growing instability was increased mobility because of plant closure, redundancy and dismissal (involuntary mobility) as well as because of frustration in employment (Creedy and Whitfield, 1980, p.15). The former

reflects the worsening of economic conditions in the British economy, especially in the chemical and allied industries. The latter could reflect difficulties caused by the increasing qualification level of labour market entrants. See also the *Finniston Report* (HMSO, 1980, p.55).

27. A survey of members of the Royal Australian Chemical Institute (Whitfield, 1981, p.280) revealed that 27% of respondents had worked for only one employing organization and a further 31% for only two employing organizations at the time of the survey. The mean age of respondents was 38 years. The number of organizational changes per man year of professional experience (that is, since first qualification) was 0.085.

28. It has been usual to assume that organizations which practise promotion by seniority are simply bowing to trade union pressure. However, both Doeringer and Piore (1971, pp.54 –55) and Thurow (1975, p.84) noted that these practices are as common in non-union as in unionized sectors of the economy.

29. It has been suggested by Kornhauser (1962) that the professional scientist who is working in industry experiences a role conflict between the values of his professional association and the interests of his employing organization. However, subsequent analysis has failed to detect such a conflict and Fox (1975, pp.31–32) suggests the two roles may exhibit some congruence.

30. Leibenstein's (1976) concept of X-inefficiency, which bears much similarity to the notion of transforming labour power into labour, has been 'integrated' into the orthodox framework in just this manner. It is suggested that X-inefficiency results, in the main, from motivational deficiencies on the part of the labour force. Stigler (1980) asserted that differences in output that result from X-inefficiency reflect simply differences in technology among firms and can therefore be readily integrated into the orthodox model. However, in his review of this debate King (1980, p.9) concluded with the open question that, 'The reader will have to decide whether Stigler's treatment of work effort as merely a facet of "technology" is a valuable insight or a characteristic Chicagoan evasion.'

31. The Institute of Chemistry was so active during the 1930s that it lost its exemption from tax on the grounds that it was no longer operating as a charity (Russell *et al.*, 1977, p.226). Prandy (1965, p.70) suggested that the main reason behind this reluctance to become involved lies in the managerial

status of a large proportion of the members of professional institutions.

32. Professional unions vary in the degree to which they adhere to these characteristics. Analyses of two professional unions can be found in Dickens (1972) and Gill *et al.* (1977).

33. Thus the Executive Secretary of the APST stated that, 'About 90% of APST members have never been in a union previously, and would not have joined but for the advent of APST.' (Quoted in Gill *et al.*, 1977, p.52).

34. Of interest here is Steinberg (1975). This study found that females show higher rates of attachment to a firm but lower advancement rates within the firm than men.

35. Economic analysis should therefore take a lifetime perspective and should not ignore within-organization processes. For further analysis in relation to the labour market for professional chemists see Whitfield (1981).

References

Addison, J. T. and Siebert, W. S. (1979). *The Market for Labor: An Analytical Treatment*. Santa Monica; Goodyear

Alexander, A. J. (1974). Income, experience and internal labour markets. *Quarterly Journal of Economics* **56,** 63–86

Arrow, K. J. (1963). Uncertainty and the welfare economics of medical care. *American Economic Review* **53,** 941–973

Arrow, K. J. and Capron, W. M. (1959). Dynamic shortages and price rises: the engineer–scientist case. *Quarterly Journal of Economics* **73,** 292–308

Becker, G. S. (1964). *Human Capital*. New York; National Bureau of Economic Research

Blank, D. H. and Stigler, G. J. (1957). *The Demand and Supply of Scientific Personnel*. New York; National Bureau of Economic Research

Bosworth, D. L. and Wilson, R. A. (1980). The labour market for scientists and technologists. In *Economic Change and Employment Policy* (ed. by R. M. Lindley), pp.297–329. London; Macmillan

Burton, J. F. and Parker, J. E. (1969). Inter-industry variations in voluntary labour mobility. *Industrial and Labour Relations Review* **22,** 199–216

Byrne, J. J. (1975). Occupational mobility. *Monthly Labor Review* **98,** 53–59

Cain, G. G., Freeman, R. B. and Hansen, W. L. (1973). *Labour Market Analysis of Engineers and Technical Workers.* Baltimore; Johns Hopkins University Press

Carr-Saunders, A. M. aṇd Wilson, P. (1933). *The Professions.* Oxford; Clarendon Press

Cole, R. E. (1979). *Work, Mobility and Participation.* California; University of California Press

Creedy, J. (1975). *Careers in Chemistry: Report of a new Survey.* London; Royal Institute of Chemistry

Creedy, J. (1977). The distribution of lifetime earnings. *Oxford Economic Papers* **29**, 412–429

Creedy, J. and Whitfield, K. (1980). An analysis of the job mobility of professional chemists in Britain. *University of Monash Seminar Paper*, No. 17/80

Creedy, J. and Whitfield, K. (1982). Professional chemists: the first three jobs. *Chemistry in Britain* **18**, 352–358

Dickens, L. (1972). UKAPE. A study of a professional union. *Industrial Relations Journal* **3**, 2–12

Doeringer, P. B. and Piore, M. J. (1971). *Internal Labor Markets and Manpower Analysis.* Lexington, Mass; Heath

Eckstein, H. (1955). The politics of the British Medical Association. *Political Quarterly* **26**, 345–359

Edwards, R. C. (1975). Individual traits and organisational incentives: What makes a 'good' worker? *Journal of Human Resources* **11**, 51–68

Fisher, M. (1971). *The Economic Analysis of Labour.* London; Weidenfeld and Nicolson

Folk, H. (1970). *The Shortage of Scientists and Engineers.* Lexington, Mass; Heath

Fox, A. (1975). *Beyond Contract: Work, Power and Trust Relationships.* London: Faber and Faber

Freeman, R. (1971). *The Market for College-Trained Manpower: A Study in the Economics of Career Choice.* Cambridge, Mass.; Harvard University Press

Freeman, R. (1975a). Legal cobwebs: a recursive model of the market for new lawyers. *Review of Economics and Statistics* **57**, 171–179

Freeman, R. (1975b). Supply and salary adjustments to the changing science manpower market: physics 1948–1973. *American Economic Review* **65**, 27–39

Freeman, R. (1976). *The Over-Educated American.* New York; Academic Press

Friedman, M. (1962). *Capitalism and Freedom.* Chicago; University of Chicago Press

Friedman, M. and Kuznets, S. (1945). *Income from Independent Professional Practice*. New York; National Bureau of Economic Research

Gill, C., Morris, R. and Eaton, J. (1977). APST: the rise of a professional union. *Industrial Relations Journal* **8**, 50–61

Gintis, H. (1971). Education, technology, and characteristics of worker productivity. *American Economic Review* **61**, 266–279

Goldstein, B. (1965). Some aspects of the nature of unionism among salaried professionals in industry. *American Sociological Review* **20**, 199–205

Greenwood, E. (1957). Attributes of a profession. In *Man, Work and Society* (ed. by S. Nosow and W. H. Form), pp.208–218. New York; Basic Books

Hansen, W. L. (1967). The economics of scientific and engineering manpower. *Journal of Human Resources* **2**, 191–215

HMSO (1980). *Committee of Inquiry into the Engineering Profession; engineering our future (Finniston Report)*. Cmnd 7794

Hickson, D. and Thomas, M. (1969). Professionalism in Britain: preliminary measurement. *Sociology* **3**, 37–53

Hinings, C. R. and Hastings, A. (1970). Role relations and value adaptation: a study of the professional accountant in industry. *Sociology* **4**, 353–366

Hunter, L. C. and Reid, G. L. (1968). *Urban Worker Mobility*. Paris; Organization for Economic Cooperation and Development

Income Data Services (1979). Qualified engineers' and scientists' pay. *Study 205*, November

Johnson, W. R. (1978). A theory of job shopping. *Quarterly Journal of Economics* **92**, 261–276

Kerr, C. (1954). The balkanization of labor markets. In *Labor Mobility and Opportunity* (ed. by E. W. Bakke *et al.*), pp.92–110. Cambridge, Mass; MIT Press

King, J. (ed.) (1980). *Readings in Labour Economics*. Oxford; Oxford University Press

Kornhauser, W. (1962). *Scientists in Industry*. California; University of California Press

Lansbury, R. D. (1978). *Professionals and Management: A Study of Behaviour in Industry*. Queensland; University of Queensland Press

Lees, D. S. (1966). *Economic Consequences of the Professions*. London; Institute of Economics Affairs

Leibenstein, H. (1976). *Beyond Economic Man*. Cambridge, Mass.; Harvard University Press

Lewis, D. (1979). Comparative quit rates of men and women. *The Journal of Industrial Relations* **21**, 331–350

Loveridge, R. and Mok, A. (1980). Theoretical approaches to segmented labour markets. *International Journal of Social Economics* **7**, 376–411

Mace, J. (1979). Internal labour markets for engineers in British industry. *British Journal of Industrial Relations* **17**, 50–63

Mace, J. and Wilkinson, G. C. G. (1977). Are labour markets competitive? *British Journal of Industrial Relations* **15**, 1–17

Mackay, D. I., Boddy, D., Brack, J., Diack, J. A., and Jones, N. (1971). *Labour Markets Under Competitive Conditions*. London; George Allen and Unwin

Mincer, J. (1976). Progress in human capital analyses of the distribution of earnings. In *The Personal Distribution of Incomes*, (ed. by A. B. Atkinson), pp. 138–192. London; George Allen and Unwin

Millerson, G. (1964). *The Qualifying Associations*. London; Routledge and Kegan Paul

Monopolies Commission (1970). *A report on the general effect on the public interest of certain restrictive practices so far as they prevail in relation to the supply of professional services*. London; HMSO

Norris, K. (1980). Compulsory arbitration and the wage structure. *The Journal of Industrial Relations* **22**, 249–265

O'Connell, J. F. (1972). The labour market for engineers: an alternative methodology. *Journal of Human Resources* **2**, 191–215

Oatey, M. (1970). The economics of training: with respect to the firm. *British Journal of Industrial Relations* **8**, 1–21

Parnes, H. S. (1954). *Research on Labor Mobility*. New York; Social Science Research Council

Parsons, D. O. (1972). Specific human capital; an application to quit rates and lay-off rates. *Journal of Political Economy* **80**, 1120–1143

Parsons, D. O. (1977). Models of labor market turnover: a theoretical and empirical survey. In *Research in Labor Economics* Vol. 1, (ed. by R. G. Ehrenberg), pp. 185–223. Connecticut; JAI Press

Phelps Brown, E. H. (1977). *The Inequality of Pay*, Oxford; Oxford University Press

Prandy, K. (1965). Professional organizations in Great Britain. *Industrial Relations* **5**, 67–79

Rapoport, B. and Rapoport, R. N. (1971). *Dual Career Families*. Harmondsworth; Penguin

Reader, W. J. (1966). *Professional Men, the Rise of the Professional Classes in Mid-Nineteenth Century England*. London; Weidenfeld and Nicolson

Richardson, V. A. (1969). A measurement of demand for professional engineers. *British Journal of Industrial Relations* **7**, 52–70

Ross, A. M. (1958). Do we have a new industrial feudalism? *American Economic Review* **48**, 903–920

Russell, C. A., Coley, N. G., and Roberts G. K. (1977). *Chemists by Profession*. Bletchley; The Open University Press

Siebert, W. (1977). Occupational licensing: the Merrison Report on the regulation of the medical profession. *British Journal of Industrial Relations* **15**, 29–38

Silverstone, R. and Ward, A. (1980). *Careers of Professional Women*. London; Croom Helm

Sleeper, R. D. (1975). Labour mobility over the life cycle. *British Journal of Industrial Relations* **13**, 194–214

Smith, A. (1970). *The Wealth of Nations*. Harmondsworth; Penguin Books

Steinberg, E. (1975). Upward mobility in the internal labor market. *Industrial Relations* **15**, 259–265

Stigler, G. J. (1980). X-efficiency challenged. In *Readings in Labour Economics* (ed. by J. E. King), pp. 73–77. Oxford; Oxford University Press

Stoikov, V. and Raimon, R. L. (1968). Determinants of differences in the quit rate among industries. *American Economic Review* **58**, 1283–1298

Thurow, L. C. (1975). *Generating Inequality*. London; Macmilland and Co. Ltd.

Turkington, D. (1976). *The Forms of Industrial Conflict*. Victoria University Occasional Paper, No. 18

Whitehead, A. K. (1981). Competition in the market for chemists. *Applied Economics* **13**, 267–278

Whitfield, K. (1981). The job mobility of professional chemists in Australia and Britain. *Chemistry in Australia* **48**, 277–282

Wilensky, H. L. (1966). The professionalization of everyone? *American Journal of Sociology* **70**, 137–158

Wilkinson, G. C. G. and Mace, J. D. (1973). Shortage or surplus of engineers; a review of recent UK evidence. *British Journal of Industrial Relations* **11**, 105–123

Williams, G. L., Blackstone, T. and Metcalf, D. (1974). *The Academic Labour Market*. London; Elsevier

Williamson, O. E. (1975). *Markets and Hierarchies: Analysis and Antitrust Implications*. London; Collier Macmillan

Wood, A. (1978). *A Theory of Pay*. Cambridge; Cambridge University Press

Young, M. and Wilmott, P. (1975). *The Symmetrical Family*. Harmondsworth; Penguin

Zabalza, A., Turnbull, P. and Williams, G. (1979). *The Economics of Teacher Supply*. Cambridge; Cambridge University Press

Chapter 8

Unemployment and the labour market

8.1 Introduction

For much of the period following the Second World War the unemployment rate in the UK was of the order of 1½% of the labour force but the 1970s saw a marked rise and by 1980 the annual average number unemployed was 1.8 million or 7.4% of the labour force. In July 1981 some 2.8 million people (including school-leavers) were unemployed in the UK, which amounts to 11.8% of the labour force. Not only is this rise in unemployment of great social concern, but it has occurred at a time when the rate of inflation has been running at a high level. It used to be thought, as a basis for policy, that there was a relatively simple trade-off between unemployment and inflation (reflected in the Phillips curve discussed below). Thus policy-makers could choose between less unemployment and more inflation or between a little less inflation at the cost of more unemployment. The experience of the 1970s has shown that things are not quite so simple and that unemployment and consequently its relation with inflation is complex. This chapter will outline the main factors which affect unemployment and provide the basis for a better understanding of the operation of the labour market. As will be shown, whilst unemployment is an apparently simple concept it is misleading to think of it in this light, for without careful analysis incorrect diagnoses and prescriptions can easily be made. The first task is to provide an analysis of the nature of unemployment and the various inferences that can be drawn from official data.

8.2 The meaning and measurement of unemployment

The definition of unemployment

Unemployment is generally taken as the state of being willing and able to work but unable to find a job. Thus, the Department of Employment in a review of unemployment and vacancy statistics stated that 'it relates to those who are not at work, who want or seek a job, are capable of work and are available for work' (1980, p.499). In broad terms, therefore, it relates to the difference between the demand for and the supply of labour. Thus, if an individual is a member of the labour force but is not in either employment or self-employment then he or she would be regarded as being unemployed. In the actual measurement of unemployment there is a large conventional element. For example a person still at school or ill would not, in general, be regarded as forming part of the labour force and hence would not appear in the measurement of unemployment.

The demand for and supply of labour are not, of course, independent of the price of labour – the real wage rate. Thus, there would be some tendency for both the supply and demand sides of the labour market to change as the real wage varies; this would lead to consequences for the level of unemployment. Examining the supply side, for example, for any individual there are three basic uses to which time can be put; paid market work, unpaid non-market work (such as cooking, washing and cleaning) and leisure (Gronau, 1977). As Creedy (1981) notes, the concept of unemployment will not be unrelated to the type of society in which the individual lives, and the type most relevant to a discussion of unemployment in Western economies is that of an individualistic society with labour contracts. In this case the advantages of specialization and the division of labour are recognized and, given the advantages of the firm as a form of economic organization, the majority of individuals are employees[1].

Hence the majority of individuals in work are hired on the basis of some type of labour contract. Many individuals, however, are themselves organized with others into household units which may be regarded as a type of firm. It may be the case that it pays one or more members of the household to specialize in market work whilst others concentrate on non-market work. Those specializing in non-market work will not appear in conventional definitions of employment nor will they be regarded as unemployed. But a change in the real wage rate may lead to a re-allocation of time within the household and it may become appropriate for these persons actively to seek market employment. Likewise, the loss of job by one of the members of the unit may lead other members to seek work in compensation. The increase in the participation rate of married women is, for instance, a marked feature of the British labour market since the Second World War. On the other side of the market there is the possibility of under-utilized labour and consequent hidden unemployment. In the 1950s and 1960s such labour hoarding seemed to be substantial and firms retained labour (particularly skilled labour) during a downturn in activity in anticipation of a future recovery in the market for their products[2].

The measurement of unemployment

Issues such as those discussed in the previous paragraph can lead to changes in the level of recorded unemployment although the underlying position remains essentially the same. Thus, in interpreting unemployment statistics attention has to be paid to the precise way in which they are collected. Various different procedures and conventions are adopted both within the same country, and perhaps more importantly between countries, which is one reason why international comparisons of unemployment need to be treated with extreme caution. Particularly when unemployment rates are considered it is necessary to look carefully not only at the coverage of the unemployment statistics that are used in the numerator but also the definition and measurement of the workforce used in the denominator. The unemployment rates provided by the Department of Employment for the UK refer to the number of registered unemployed as a percentage of the total number of employees, the latter consisting of employees in employment together with the registered unemployed. Thus in the UK figures the denominator is not the total labour force but only those members of it classed as employees and as such it excludes the self-employed and members of the armed forces. It should also be noted that part-time workers are counted as equal to full-time workers.

The number of workers classed as unemployed is usually derived from one of the following two broad sources:

(1) Administrative procedures relating to unemployment benefit and social security under which unemployed workers are required to register if they are to receive the appropriate state payments;
(2) Censuses and sample surveys where the labour market status of the individual is either self-assessed, based on a judgement made by an interviewer or inferred from answers to other questions.

In the UK the principal unemployment figures are derived from a monthly count of the registered unemployed. These figures relate to unemployed persons who are registered as seeking employment and who are accepted by staff of the employment offices and careers offices as being 'capable of and available for work, whether they are entitled to unemployment benefit or not'[3]. Thus, the number who are counted depends on the propensity of those who are unemployed to register. This in turn depends on the precise regulations affecting eligibility for benefits and the success of the agencies in placing those registered in suitable employment, amongst other factors. Changes in the propensity to register contribute to the difficulties in forecasting the level of unemployment[4].

There are four categories of those registered who are, however, excluded from the count: adult students aged 18 or over seeking vacation employment; the temporarily stopped, that is people suspended by their employers on the understanding that they will shortly resume work; the severely disabled who are unlikely to obtain employment except under 'sheltered' conditions; and those seeking part-time work and not claiming unemployment benefit or credits.

Problems of measurement and the unemployment rate

As noted, the problem with using data derived from administrative procedures is that measurement does depend on the form of these procedures and the regulations under which they operate. Census or survey data, on the other hand, do generally have wider coverage and include details of other relevant characteristics of the individuals sampled but like all surveys the results are dependent upon the accuracy of the answers and the skill with which the questions are framed. Further, it is impractical to conduct surveys of the whole population other than on an infrequent basis (for example, the decennial population census in the UK) and the conclusions are therefore subject to sample bias. The main source of unemployment data for the foreseeable future in the UK will, therefore, remain the unemployment count but some survey evidence is available such as the General Household Survey[5] and the European Communities Labour Force Survey.

There are, however, limitations to the use of 'snapshot' pictures derived from both types of source which record what is happening to an individual at a particular point in time. These limitations are discussed in detail below. Many interesting questions require data based on what happens to individuals over some length of time (longitudinal data) and the principal defects of the current sources will become evident shortly.

The most commonly quoted statistics on unemployment are the total monthly count and the corresponding unemployment rate as defined above. Such statistics relate to the stock of unemployed at the appropriate date, but unemployment is also a flow concept. The pool of unemployed workers does not consist of the same individuals from month to month. There will be a number of people who remain on the register for long periods of time, but in any one month the Department of Employment records both a large inflow onto the register and a large outflow. Indeed, over a period of a year the total number of people joining the register and the total number of those leaving (although the same individual may be recorded more than once) usually amount to three or four times the average stock during the year. The flows onto and off the register are therefore large in relation to the stock. The relevant data since 1972 are shown in *Table 8.1*. Figures for earlier periods (Nickell, 1979a) confirm the impression from *Table 8.1* that the rate of inflow into unemployment has remained largely unchanged

TABLE 8.1 Monthly flow and the stock of unemployment in Great Britain, 1972–1980

	*Monthly flow into unemployment (March)**	*Stock of unemployed†*
1972	312.2	876.2
1973	285.7	640.2
1974	291.5	554.9
1975	n.a.	731.6
1976	310.9	1183.3
1977	294.2	1280.0
1978	282.6	1348.6
1979	266.7	1294.3
1980	300.6	1347.0

* Seasonally adjusted, thousands. Figures relate to employment offices only and do not cover careers offices or Professional and Executive Recruitment Service.
Source: Employment Gazette, June 1980, pp.627–635
† Seasonally adjusted, thousands.
Source: Employment Gazette, various issues

for some considerable period whilst the level of unemployment has increased markedly. There has been some increase in the rate of inflow during 1980/81 and, for example, the three monthly average for May 1981 (seasonally adjusted) was 336 000 compared with a stock of unemployed for Great Britain (excluding school-leavers) of nearly 2.5 million in that month.

The inflow does tend to rise when unemployment is increasing but there is no noticeable relationship between the level of the inflow and the level of unemployment. For example, from *Table*

8.1, in 1972 the inflow was 312 200 whilst the level of unemployment stood at 876 200; whereas in 1980 the unemployment level was over 50% higher at 1 347 000 but the inflow slightly less at just over 300 . It is therefore grossly mistaken to believe that the recent rise in unemployment is occurring simply because the flow onto the register has increased. During the middle of 1981 this undoubtedly made some contribution but it is clearly not the overriding factor.

Stocks and flows

If the inflow has not accounted for the major part of the rise, what is the explanation? What is clearly happening is that individuals on the register are becoming more likely to remain there for a longer period of time; that is, the duration of unemployment is increasing. It is the lengthening of the duration rather than an increase in the numbers who are becoming unemployed which has led to the rise in the stock. But what is equally important is that it is not simply a matter of a change in the outflow. The relationship between the stock of the unemployed and the flows onto and off the register and their associated causes are complicated. But to understand recent research work in the area and the difficulties involved, it is essential to have a firm comprehension of the role of lengthening duration. A simple analogy and simulation is helpful in this context.

Consider a supermarket chain which sets up in business and expects to (and does) sell 100 000 packets of cornflakes each day. Suppose also that the firm takes delivery each day of 100 000 packets from the manufacturer. The chain then breaks this delivery down into smaller lots and distributes them to its various outlets. Suppose that the delay between receiving a delivery and selling each packet is two days. Taking a daily count of the stock of cornflakes in these circumstances would show the numbers in column four of *Table 8.2*. Now suppose that both the inflow and outflow remain the same but there is a four-day delay between receipt of delivery and the sale of the cornflakes. The stock position is now given in column six. Allowing for the set-up period the firm soon settles down to a steady state, but it is apparent that although the steady state inflows and outflows are the same in both cases, the longer duration leads to a far higher stock. The reason is clear; each packet is counted only once for the first case but three times for the second case. Although the example is a gross simplification it does reveal the effect that a change in duration can have on the stock. Although a change in duration will be associated with some change in inflow and/or outflow (for example the outflow for the first three days in the second case is zero), *Table 8.2* does clearly illustrate that once things have settled down, the same outflow and inflow are associated with a much higher stock. In an analogous manner the increasing duration of unemployment has had a similar effect on the number of registered unemployed at the monthly count. Of course, the interesting question is to explain the reasons behind the increase in duration. But before that can be attempted a major difficulty facing the measurement of the duration of unemployment using available statistics in the UK has to be considered.

TABLE 8.2 The effect of a change in duration on stock levels   *thousands*

		Two-day delay		Four-day delay	
Day	*Daily delivery*	*Daily sales*	*Daily stocks*	*Daily sales*	*Daily stocks*
1	100	0	100	0	100
2	100	100	100	0	200
3	100	100	100	0	300
4	100	100	100	100	300
5	100	100	100	100	300
6	100	100	100	100	300

In the supermarket example all packets of cornflakes were homogeneous and all had the same shelf-life. At the stock count each packet would be observed before it had completed its shelf-life. In the two-day delay each packet would be observed to have been on the shelf for one day. With the four-day delay one-third would have been on the shelf for one, two and three days respectively; an average of two days. On average each packet will be observed half-way through its life on the shelf. It is a simple matter, therefore, to double the observed life and derive the actual length of shelf-life for each packet. Such a conclusion would occur for any homogeneous population observed in a steady state. But the unemployed are not like that; they form a heterogeneous population. Data derived from a count of the unemployed will relate to people somewhere within an incompleted spell of unemployment. It will not be possible to observe the length of completed spells. The question now is whether information on incompleted spells can be turned into estimates of the duration. This is a complicated issue and the alternatives and necessary assumptions are considered in detail in the next section.

8.3   The duration of unemployment

Measures of duration

The duration of unemployment is clearly of significance for an understanding of unemployment and its social consequences. It has already been implied that the unemployment rate is not particularly informative as to the social effect of unemployment. Thus, an unemployment rate of 10% could refer to an economy in which each member of the labour force was unemployed at random every one week in 10 or one in which every one in 10 individuals was continuously unemployed. The social implications are obviously very different for the two states. Any real economy will fall somewhere between these two extremes and labour economists have devoted considerable research effort to obtaining a better picture of the position as a guide for policy (see Bowers and Harkess, 1979 and Creedy and Disney, 1981b)

In principle there are at least three alternative and distinct measures of the length of a spell of unemployment. In the analysis that follows use will be made of the simple scheme shown in *Figure 8.1* which is an adaptation of similar illustrations contained in Salant (1977) and Main (1981). The three alternative measures are

(1) The average interrupted spell length, $(\bar{T})$. This measures the average time already spent in unemployment at the date of the survey or unemployment count. In *Figure 8.1* two survey dates are shown. Taking Survey I as an illustration the calculation would be:

$$\bar{T} = (T_2 + T_3 + T_5)/3 \tag{8.1}$$

The techniques used in the measurement of the duration of unemployment are analogous to those used by demographers in the analysis of populations and it may be helpful to give the appropriate demographic concept[6]. In population terms, the length of the interrupted unemployment spell corresponds to the average age of the current population.

(2) The average completed duration of the currently unemployed population or the experience-weighted spell length, S_{EW} (Main, 1981, p.149). This measure is equivalent to the average age at death of the current population. At the date of Survey I it would be calculated by:

$$S_{EW} = (S_2 + S_3 + S_5)/3 \tag{8.2}$$

(3) The average completed duration of all spells of unemployment occurring over a given period of time whether or not that person was unemployed at the date of the survey. This measure can be called the terminations-weighted spell length, (S_{TW}), and represents the length of time an entrant onto the unemployment register can expect to remain there (Main, 1981, p.148). In demographic terms it measures the expected life at birth. Assuming that the spells shown in *Figure 8.1* are all those occurring over the relevant time period this expected life would be given by the sum of all the spells; that is

$$S_{TW} = (1/N) \sum_{i=1}^{N} S_i \qquad (8.3)$$

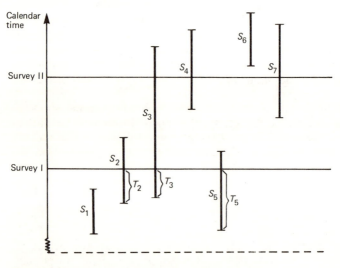

Figure 8.1 Measurement of the duration of unemployment

The last two concepts are alternative measures of the length of a completed spell of unemployment. For the individual it is clearly the length of a completed spell that is crucial, but as stressed above most unemployment data refer to the labour market position of individuals at some particular time. Hence duration data derived from these surveys will be of uncompleted spells. Using such data is it possible to derive estimates of the more interesting length of completed spell? Estimates can and have been produced and reference to these will be made shortly. But first it is important to understand the main problems involved in moving from survey data to estimates of the length of completed spells.

Measuring the length of completed spells

To analyse the factors at work it is useful initially to consider what would happen in a 'steady state', where conditions are stable. Assume also that a spell of unemployment is equally likely to commence at any time and its length is assumed to be drawn from the same distribution regardless of when the spell begins. It follows that movement from unemployment to employment is not related to calendar time in either a direct or indirect way (Salant, 1977, p.40). Assuming that *Figure 8.1* represents spells occurring in such a steady state the main problems of measurement become immediately apparent.

The length of the incomplete spell measured at the time of the survey is less than the final length of that completed spell which will be experienced by any individual. But, making use of the steady state conditions, the conclusion of a spell of unemployment is equally likely to occur at any time during the length of a spell. Thus, surveyed incompleted spells will on average be halfway through their total length – an observation which was noted in connection with the simple inventories illustration above. If this is the case why not just multiply the length of the average incompleted spell at the survey by two to obtain an estimate of the average completed spell? The problem lies in the phenomenon of sampling from a length-biased population.

Looking at *Figure 8.1* it is apparent that some individuals who experience unemployment are not picked up in the survey at all, (the spells S_1 and S_6), and one spell, S_3, is counted at both surveys. Clearly the longer the spell of unemployment the more likely it is to be recorded at the date of the survey. In a steady state the probability of an individual being recorded as unemployed at the date of the survey is proportional to the length of the completed spell. Thus, if completed spells of S weeks and $2S$ weeks are equally likely to occur, the longer spells are twice as likely to be observed in the survey. Length-biased sampling therefore introduces an upward bias for the measurement of spell length. Moreover, if the probability of leaving unemployment falls for each individual as the spell lengthens, then the expected length of an interrupted spell will exceed the expected length of a completed spell[7]. The extent of the over-estimate, as Salant (1977) notes, is likely to differ among age or occupational groups. Therefore groups that appear to be in a worse position because they have longer incompleted spells may in fact experience shorter completed spells on average. The implication is that one needs to be careful in comparing duration data among groups.

Because of these problems there is no simple way of moving from survey data on incompleted spells to estimates of the average length of completed spells over some period of time (to obtain measure 8.3). With longitudinal data the only problems in a steady state would be those associated with sampling error. It is possible, however, to use a synthetic register approach whereby survey data can be used to reconstruct the progress of individuals. This method is adopted by Bowers and Harkess (1979) in their study of unemployment duration in Britain[8].

Main (1981) has argued that in fact measure (8.2) is perhaps more appropriate for assessing the welfare consequences of unemployment. He argues that the terminations-weighted duration measure (8.3) weights all spells equally and fails to reflect how the typical week in unemployment is spent. Thus it is more concerned with the concept of the spell than with the person experiencing the unemployment. On the other hand the experience-weighted measure (8.2) weights spells by their length and thus by their contribution to the overall unemployment burden. The fact that the sample at survey date is length-biased provides an easy way of measuring S_{EW}, at least under the assumption of a steady state. In this case it can be obtained merely by doubling the length of the average of the incompleted spells at the survey date (Main, 1981). If unemployment is growing the doubling rule will underestimate S_{EW} because of the relatively larger number of recently unemployed who will have been unemployed for only a short time. Conversely, if unemployment is falling S_{EW} will be overstated.

The empirical studies on unemployment duration in Britain show a marked difference between the results for measures (8.2) and (8.3)[9]. Thus using measure (8.3) it appears that the average spell of unemployment is relatively short but has risen from about five weeks in the early 1960s to about 20 weeks in the late 1970s. On the other hand measure (8.2) shows that the average length of a spell in which a week of unemployment occurred was quite long (usually over a year) and has not shown the marked rise revealed by measure (8.3). The inference is that in recent years spells have lengthened much more at the short-end rather than at the long-end of the distribution. Evidence for the US (Akerlof, 1979) shows that during the 1950s and 1960s the average completed spell was about five to six weeks and there is some evidence of a rise, though not to the same extent as in Britain, in the mid-1970s. Measure

(8.2) shows the duration of spells of those unemployed at each survey was some four times higher at about six months.

The burden of unemployment

There are some additional factors which need to be taken into account in assessing the burden of unemployment besides the duration. First, many people in the labour market experience more than one spell of unemployment even within a short time period. As Disney (1979) stresses, a minority of people may account for a significant proportion of unemployment registrations over a given length of time. Data based on counts or intermittent surveys will only reveal information about spells and not the precise distribution of such spells across individuals. For the latter it is necessary to have access to cohort studies which record the total labour market experience of individuals from week to week. Such longitudinal data are not available for Britain but some limited cohort data are available from DHSS records. These are used by Disney (1979) to examine the concentration of unemployment among individuals in Britain[10]. It is evident from these data that unemployment is highly concentrated amongst particular people and, for example, across the three cohorts that could be distinguished, less than 5% of individuals accounted for more than 80% of the weeks of unemployment in the sample. Distinguishing among the three age cohorts he found that amongst older workers it was the duration of individual spells which was the main contributory factor, but that amongst younger workers, where there was also evidence of marked concentration, it was attributable to the repeated occurrence of spells rather than the length of a spell. It is clear that to obtain a better picture of the incidence of unemployment, attention must be paid to the recurrence of spells amongst particular groups and individuals. It has also to be recognized that employment and unemployment are not the only two possible states which are relevant to an analysis of the labour market. As Creedy and Disney (1981a) argue, leaving the unemployment register can take forms other than entering employment, such as illness or leaving the labour force completely. Little attention has been paid until recently to sickness as a labour market state although as Doherty (1979) points out, typically throughout the 1970s the loss in working days due to sickness was at least as great as that due to unemployment. Likewise, the flow out of employment into sickness may also be investigated by economic analysis[11].

Thus the term 'unemployment' is rather more complex than it appears and available statistics are not open to simple interpretation. The importance of distinguishing between the stock of unemployment and the flow into and out of that particular state cannot be over-emphasized. Having reviewed these problems it is now appropriate to examine the various causes of unemployment and the first stage in this process is to look at the different types which have been distinguished.

8.4   Types and causes of unemployment

Types of unemployment distinguished

As noted in the previous section, unemployment has a number of dimensions and any policy prescriptions are likely to differ according to the type of unemployment. Following Keynes (see Kahn, 1976) and Beveridge (1944) it has become customary to distinguish the following five types: (i) a hard core of unemployables; (ii) seasonal unemployment; (iii) frictional unemployment; (iv) structural unemployment; and (v) cyclical or demand-deficient unemployment.

The classification seems at first sight to be fairly self-explanatory. Every economy will have some group of workers who, largely because of their personal characteristics such as health and attitude to work, are likely to remain unemployed irrespective of the state of the labour market. But the size of this group may not be totally independent of economic factors. Indeed an increased duration of unemployment may not only encourage some individuals to develop undesirable characteristics, but the length of time a person has been unemployed may reduce the probability of that individual getting a job. The effect of duration on the probability of re-entering employment is an important question and will be examined further below.

Seasonal unemployment occurs mainly in certain sectors of the economy such as agriculture, construction and tourism although changes in labour contracts and more centralized hiring practices have reduced the seasonal element to some extent. Two groups which enter the unemployment register in Britain at particular times of the year are school-leavers and students. The former category are recorded separately and frequently excluded from the count for many analytical purposes, and the latter, as noted above, are excluded as a matter of course. Until recently, school-leavers appeared on the register for only a brief time, but one worrying recent feature has been the lengthening unemployment amongst young workers.

Because of these seasonal factors, the seasonally adjusted figure for unemployment is the most appropriate for many uses. Care has to be taken, however, to ensure that the seasonal adjustment process adequately reflects changes in the underlying economic conditions.

Frictional unemployment is that which occurs as workers move between jobs. In the labour market there will always be some dynamic element with workers moving from one job to another and in the course of this spending some time (usually short) on the unemployment register. Thus frictional unemployment occurs as the result of short-run changes in the labour market and the fact that labour markets do not clear instantly in response to economic factors. The duration of frictional unemployment for any individual is closely related to the concept of job search which has provided the basis for numerous insights into the operation of the labour market in recent years. This concept is developed further below.

Whilst frictional unemployment is generally regarded as being short-term, structural unemployment arises from more long-run changes in the economy and occurs because of changes in the demand for labour in particular occupations, industries or regions. Thus, with structural unemployment there is some fundamental mismatch either in terms of location or in terms of skills between the unemployed and the available job vacancies. Such a mismatch arises because of the costs of adjustment, in that re-training and re-location can be expensive, or because rigidities in the labour market can hinder mobility.

Demand-deficient unemployment occurs when the level of aggregate demand, and hence the derived demand for labour, is insufficient to provide work for the available labour force irrespective of the skills and location of its members. Some writers distinguish between that part of demand-deficient unemployment which is cyclical and that part which is more long-term – 'growth-gap unemployment'[12]. The latter can arise from the nature of technical progress and the problem that an economy's growth potential may exceed its realized rate of growth. The microprocessor revolution provides an example of this.

Unemployment–vacancy (U–V) analysis

It is all very well having a conceptual basis for categorizing unemployment, but can these concepts be turned into actual measures? Since there are different policy implications stemming from, for example structural as against demand-deficient unemployment, it is clearly desirable to have some idea of the relative magnitudes. Attempts to put numbers to the different categories have largely been based on the so-called U–V method which makes use of available data on unemployment and vacancies[13]. The U–V method attempts to distinguish among three broad types based on the categorization above, namely demand-deficient, frictional and structural unemployment. The structural element may be divided into a further three components; geographical, occupational and a mixture of the two, giving a total of five possible categories in all.

U–V analysis is essentially Keynesian in origin and was first brought to prominence in the work of Dow and Dicks-Mireaux (1958) who observed an inverse relationship between unemployment and vacancies in Britain. The theoretical basis for the relationship can be derived as follows.

The demand for labour is assumed to be determined by the planned level of output and thus both unemployment and vacancies will depend on the level of aggregate demand for home-produced goods and services. If aggregate demand increases and output rises in response, the demand for labour will rise and this will be reflected in an increase in the number of vacancies. At the same time, the level of employment will expand and the number of unemployed will fall. Such an argument leads to the suggestion of a smooth inverse relationship between U and V which will be non-linear and is depicted by the curve U–V in *Figure 8.2*. The non-linearity and convexity to the origin are easily explained in terms of the fact that whatever the level of vacancies, unemployment will not fall to zero because of frictional, structural and other elements. Similarly, frictional and structural factors will mean that whatever the level of unemployment, some vacancies will remain unfilled. Changes in factors that are held constant in the derivation of the curve will lead the curve to shift. For example, it would move towards the origin if the efficiency of information flows in the labour market reduced the average duration of frictional unemployment. On the other hand, factors that reduced the cost of unemployment to the individual such as improved unemployment benefit would work in the opposite direction shown by the curve $U_1–V_1$. (The implications of unemployment benefit are considered further below.) In Britain the relationship between unemployment and vacancies seems to have been pretty stable up to 1966 but subsequently has apparently shifted outwards on a number of occasions. The causes of these shifts have been the subject of intense debate[14].

Having looked at the theory behind the U–V curve, it remains to explain how it is possible to decompose total unemployment into its various components. Demand-deficient unemployment occurs when the supply of labour is greater than the demand for it. The U–V analysis assumes that the market is in equilibrium when total unemployment is equal to total unfilled vacancies. This is shown by point *E* on *Figure 8.2* where the 45° line intersects the *U–V* curve. Thus, demand-deficient unemployment only exists when unemployment is greater than the number of vacancies,

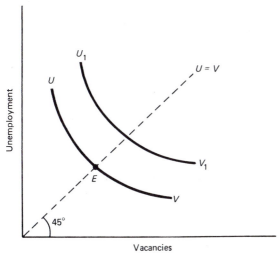

Figure 8.2 U–V analysis

taking the economy as a whole. Thus if $U > V$ the difference is taken to represent demand-deficient unemployment and correspondingly, V gives the unemployment not attributable to demand-deficiency. If $U \leqslant V$ all unemployment has non demand-deficiency causes. This procedure can give rather odd results over a cycle (Armstrong and Taylor, 1981) and an alternative somewhat preferable method is to estimate the level of unemployment that is associated with equilibrium in the labour market given the *U–V* curve; that is point *E* in *Figure 8.2*. If this equilibrium level of unemployment is denoted U^*, the amount of demand-deficient unemployment (if $U > V$) is given by $U - U^*$ and U^* represents that attributable to other factors.

Having estimated the level of non demand-deficient unemployment it is necessary to decompose this category. The details may be obtained from Armstrong and Taylor (1981), but the principle is to seek to match unemployment with vacancies such that, for example, frictional unemployment is measured as that where unemployment and vacancies occur simultaneously in both the same location and the same occupation.

There are a number of obvious problems in using U–V analysis to identify the importance of the types of unemployment including the accuracy of the statistics, the definition of occupations and areas, the order in which the components are identified and the assumption of the nature of equilibrium in the labour market. If a breakdown of unemployment into its various categories is to be useful to policy-makers, it is important that it is based on a clear and consistent conceptual foundation and can be susceptible to reasonably accurate measurement. It has to be stated that in this area the development of U–V analysis to date leaves much to be desired.

8.5   The probability of leaving unemployment

Features of the labour market

It has been noted above that the increase in the rate of unemployment in Britain in recent years has arisen from a lengthening of the average duration of spells on the register rather than from an increase in the flow onto the register. It is therefore important to analyse the factors that determine the duration of unemployment. Further, any change in the operation of the labour market which leads to an increase in duration will lead to an outward shift of the U–V curve and a corresponding increase in equilibirum unemployment. It has also been shown that to be classified as unemployed, the individual must be actively seeking work. To obtain a real understanding of unemployment it is necessary to examine the microeconomics of the labour market and in particular the nature of the job offer–acceptance decision[15]. The form and content of labour market contracts is also highly relevant[16]. One possibility, for example, is that the employer considers the qualities and attributes of each applicant and in the light of these makes a personal wage offer for a specific job. Thus the offer is associated with the characteristics of the particular individual and would vary for the same job among individuals. There is, however, a problem of asymmetric information in that before the individual is hired he or she has a greater knowledge of likely productivity on the job than the employer[17]. The recognition of the costs of acquiring information has led to the analysis of screening (Spence, 1974; Stiglitz, 1975). If labour markets operated in this way they would clear because individual wage rates would adjust; unemployment could only exist because of the inadequacies of information or misperceptions by either party. Many models of job search tend to make this sort of assumption (see for example, Phelps *et al.*, 1971), and assume that the duration of unemployment is determined solely by the cost of search[18]. Thus, anything that reduced the cost of search, such as an increase in unemployment benefit, would lead to a lengthening of the duration of unemployment. All unemployment in this case is 'voluntary' in the sense that both sides are always on their supply and demand curves and markets are in instantaneous equilibrium (Santomero and Seater, 1978).

An alternative view is that for each particular job there is a pre-determined wage and the employer simply decides whether or not to offer the job to any particular applicant. (Nickell, 1979a, 1979b; Atkinson, 1981). This assumption is more in accordance with reality and further analysis of different aspects of labour market behaviour could fruitfully be examined within this framework[19]. Thus any wage is associated not with an individual but with a particular job. Custom, equity and practice amongst other factors lead to labour markets operating in this way. Thus, the employer's decision is one of offer or not offer rather than offer and then determine the appropriate wage rate. There are at least two important implications of this assumption. First, some individuals will receive no job offers and, secondly, in the short run the wage rate for a job will be independent of the number of applicants.

As far as the unemployed are concerned it is assumed in these latter models that the individual needs to sample the available opportunities because he or she will not have full information as to the jobs and wage rates on offer. On any occasion when the individual samples from the distribution of opportunities, he or she may or may not receive an offer. If an offer is made, the individual will compare the wage of the job with a pre-determined reservation wage (see for example, Hey, 1979 and Pissarides, 1976). If the offer is greater than or equal to this reservation wage, the offer will be accepted. Thus, given that in the short run the wage is unaffected by the number of applicants it follows that the determinants of the reservation wage are crucial in analysing the behaviour of the unemployed. Similarly, if the actual wage received by an employed worker falls below the reservation wage it follows that that worker will voluntarily quit the job.

As Nickell (1979a) notes, the reservation wage will depend on such factors as the distribution of wage offers, the probability of receiving a wage offer in any period, the level of unemployment benefit and the length of time that the individual has been unemployed. The probability that an individual will leave the state of unemployment is, therefore, the product of the probality of that individual receiving a job offer and the conditional probability that the associated wage will be equal to or exceed the reservation wage. As such, the *duration* of unemployment is not a particularly suitable variable to try and explain (Lancaster, 1979; Lancaster and Nickell, 1980) and for this reason recent research has tended to examine the *probability* that an individual will leave unemployment (for example, Nickell, 1979a, 1979b; Mcgregor, 1978).

Unemployment benefit and duration

The effect of unemployment benefits on the average duration of unemployment, and hence their effect on the level of unemployment has been the subject of much controversy. For instance, the shift in the U–V relationship in the mid-1960s was attributed by some authors, at least in part, to the introduction of earnings related supplement (ERS) in 1966 (see for example, Gujarati, 1972; Mackay and Reid, 1972; Bowers *et al.*, 1970). In the model just outlined, the crucial factor is the effect of unemployment benefit on the reservation wage and, as Atkinson (1981) and Burdett (1979) have shown, there is no necessary rationale for assuming that an increase in unemployment benefit will, other things being equal, always lead to an increase in the level of unemployment[20]. In addition, it is not just the level of unemployment benefit which is important but also the tax system, and in particular the tax thresholds. These determine the tax paid on earned income and the contribution of other social security and related benefits which accrue when the individual is unemployed. These factors are encapsulated in the benefit/earnings or 'replacement' ratio (B/Y). Atkinson (1981) defines this as

$$\frac{B}{Y} = \frac{\text{National Insurance Benefit (including ERS and child benefit)}}{\text{Average gross earnings} - \text{tax} - \text{NI contribution} + \text{child benefit}}$$

Nickell (1979a) uses a wider definition of benefits and for his sample of males incorporates rate and rent rebates, free school meal allowances, wife's income and unearned income.

Time-series analyses

Most of the earlier studies of the effect of unemployment benefit used time-series data. They were either indirect, in the sense of using U–V analysis to estimate the difference between actual and predicted unemployment and then assign causes, often with little specific evidence (for example, Gujarati, 1972), or they estimated a model of the determinants of unemployment. A well-known example of the latter is the work of Maki and Spindler (1975). They produced estimates of a sizeable impact of ERS on unemployment, such that the male unemployment rate in 1966 was some 30% higher than it otherwise would have been – an increase of 110 000.

The results of the Maki and Spindler (1975) study have been criticized by Cubbin and Foley (1977), Taylor (1977), Sawyer (1979) and Atkinson (1981) amongst others, mainly on grounds of both specification and the appropriateness of the benefit/earnings ratio used. On the impact of ERS, for example, it needs to be noted that only a relatively small proportion of the unemployed actually receive ERS (less than 20%) and care has to be taken for use of the 'typical' unemployed man as a reference point leads to a marked increase in the B/Y ratio in 1966 whilst the benefits actually paid out rose by a relatively small amount (Nickell, 1979a).

Cross-sectional studies

The difficulties with time-series analysis have led a number of authors to consider the information available from a cross-section of the individuals unemployed (Lancaster, 1979; Nickell, 1979a, 1979b; Lancaster and Nickell, 1980). The data used by Lancaster relate to 479 unemployed males who were interviewed twice and thus by the second interview some had completed that particular spell of unemployment whilst for the rest it was incomplete. The data used by Nickell relate to unemployed males interviewed once as part of the General Household Survey of 1972. The importance of dealing carefully with the concept of uncompleted spells has been emphasized above and these studies discuss the statistical estimation problems involved.

Nickell argues that the factors that are likely to affect the probability of an individual leaving unemployment may be divided into four main categories: personal characteristics, family composition, local labour demand, and income variables. It has already been noted that Nickell (1979b) used an extensive measure of the benefit/earnings ratio, and he concluded that unemployment benefits did have a significant effect on the duration of unemployment but that it was much lower for the long-term unemployed (26 weeks or more). He found an elasticity of duration with respect to the household's replacement ratio of between 0.6 and 1.0. This is considerably less than that reported by Maki and Spindler (1975) and implies that ERS increased unemployment by about 10% rather than the 30% found in the time-series study. An elasticity of 0.6 was also found in the sample used by Lancaster (1979).

Thus, the general conclusion from cross-sectional evidence is that unemployment benefit has a significant but quantitatively small effect on unemployment duration. The studies are not without their limitations (see, for example, Atkinson, 1981, and the comments following Lancaster and Nickell, 1980). Thus, there are problems with the measurement of the appropriate B/Y ratio; other labour market flows such as flows into unemployment that may be benefit-induced and flows into sickness are not considered; and the data used relate to the early 1970s which pre-dates the substantial upsurge in unemployment.

Other factors

One further point is evident from these studies on the duration of unemployment. As the Nickell evidence shows, the effect of unemployment benefit seems to fall as the unemployment spell lengthens. It is also clear that the data show in aggregate a decline in the probability of leaving unemployment the higher the duration of unemployment. But it is not easy to interpret this feature. Thus, the unemployed constitute a heterogeneous population, and individuals will have different probabilities of entering employment. Individuals with higher probabilities will feature less strongly at longer durations. Hence the observation that duration has a negative effect on the probability of entering employment is consistent either with the fact that the probability facing each individual declines or that the probability facing each individual is constant but those with lower probabilities are more strongly represented at long durations. It is extremely difficult to sort out these two alternatives from the available data (see, for example, Lancaster, 1979; Lancaster and Nickell, 1980).

It also needs to be recognized that the precise terms of social security provisions are of some significance. It has already been noted that particular individuals experience repeated spells of unemployment. Under the current rules operating in Britain the question of individuals exhausting their entitlement to benefit becomes important. As Creedy and Disney (1981b) show, between one-sixth and two-fifths of the unemployed may be unemployed for more than one year and thus will exhaust their claim to national insurance benefits. Thus, as they observe, studies that assume that all the unemployed are eligible for all forms of benefit at the beginning of their spell of unemployment are likely to be misleading. The precise rules and their implications are fully discussed in Creedy and Disney (1981b) and in Disney (1981).

8.6   Unemployment and inflation

The Phillips curve

This chapter has concentrated mainly on providing an understanding of unemployment in terms of flows within the labour market. Recent work in this area has produced many useful insights which provide a greater understanding of the operation of the labour market and have important implications for public policy. It has been concerned with unemployment as a state and not so much with the repercussions of the flows into and out of that state for other macroeconomic variables. However, it is important to consider one of the key relationships which has been the subject of interest for economists and policy-makers for much of the post-war period, namely the relationship betwen unemployment and inflation. It is not possible to provide more than a brief summary of the main issues, but fortunately there have been a number of excellent surveys which provide the interested reader with a more complete statement of the arguments, contentions and empirical evidence[21].

Although not the first[22] to notice the possibility of an inverse relationship between unemployment and wage inflation, Phillips (1958) formulated the concept which now bears his name – the Phillips curve. This postulated the existence of a trade-off between the rate of inflation and the level of unemployment. Phillips was concerned with the proportionate change in money wages, or w which he argued would be related to the level of excess demand. The theoretical rationale for this view lies in the inflationary gap of standard Keynesian analysis. Thus, when excess demand for labour occurs the money wage will rise and the rate of increase will be greater the greater the level of excess demand. The problem is how to measure excess demand, and Phillips proposed the use of unemployment as a proxy. When unemployment is low excess demand will be high leading to a rise in money wage rates. Phillips proposed a non-linear relationship between the proportionate change in wage rates $\dot{w}$, and unemployment, U, of the form:

$$w = a + bU^{-c} \tag{8.4}$$

Phillips used a rather unorthodox but effective method (see Desai, 1976) to estimate the relationship for UK data from 1861 to 1913, which yielded

$$\dot{w} + 0.9 = 9.638U^{-1.3} \tag{8.5}$$

This curve is shown in *Figure 8.3* where it will be observed that as unemployment approaches 0.8% wage inflation approaches infinity, and that inflation would be zero at 5½% unemployment, with minimum wage inflation at about −1. He used an averaging procedure to obtain these results and showed that over each cycle

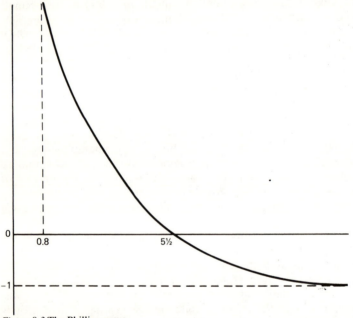

Figure 8.3 The Phillips curve

the actual observations over time described a counter-clockwise loop around the curve. Thus at times when unemployment was falling the observations were above the curve and conversely when unemployment was rising the points were below the curve. Phillips then fitted his curve to two subsequent periods, namely 1913–1948 and 1948–1957, and found that the relationship appeared fairly stable, although the loops seemed to have changed direction in the last period. The Phillips curve was attractive to policy-makers in that it appered to offer a stable choice between two of the major goals of economic policy.

The role of expectations

But the Phillips curve soon came under attack from two principal directions. First, it was criticized on theoretical grounds, initially by Phelps (1967) and Friedman (1968), and in the development of disequilibrium economics and the new macroeconomics[23]. Secondly, from the 1960s onwards the Phillips curve no longer appeared to fit the data very well; higher unemployment was associated with inflation at a higher rate that that predicted by the Phillips equation. In addition in the 1970s came the occurrence of stagflation with both unemployment and inflation rising simultaneously.

The initial important contribution of Phelps (1967) and Friedman (1968) was to argue that it was real wages rather than money wages which were responsive to excess demand and therefore expectations of the rate of price inflation should be introduced into the relationship. What results is an expectations-augmented Phillips curve and need for each expected level of inflation there is a different Phillips curve. Any trade-off can only be a short-run phenomenon. In the long run the Phillips curve is vertical and there is no trade-off. The issue revolves around the concept of the natural rate of unemployment which refers to the level of unemployment at which there is no tendency for inflation either to accelerate or decelerate. The natural rate requires that the expected rate of inflation is equal to the actual rate. The standard diagram of the expectations-augmented Phillips curve is shown in *Figure 8.4*. PC_1 represents a Phillips curve on the assumption that

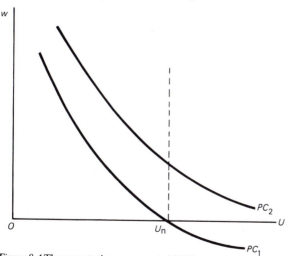

Figure 8.4 The expectations-augmented Phillips curve

the expected rate of inflation is zero. According to this curve, the expected rate of inflation will equal the actual at U_n which is, therefore, the natural rate of unemployment. Suppose that the authorities try to move along PC_1. According to Friedman (1968), they can only get away with this in the short run as people are misled by changes in money income and prices into believing that real incomes are changing. In the long run expectations will adapt and the economy will move onto a higher Phillips curve, say PC_2, reflecting the increased expectations about inflation. In the long run the Phillips curve is vertical and unemployment can only be held below the natural rate for any period by allowing inflation to accelerate at an increasing rate. The expectations-augmented Phillips curve can be represented as

$$\dot{w} = \beta_1 (U - U_n) + \beta_2 \dot{p}^e \tag{8.6}$$

where U = actual rate of unemployment
U_n = natural rate of unemployment
$\dot{p}^e$ = expected rate of change of prices.

For there to be no long-run trade-off, the coefficient β_2 must equal unity. Assuming that the natural rate is constant leads to an equation of the form:

$$\dot{w} = \beta_0 - \beta_1 U + \beta_2 \dot{p}^e \tag{8.7}$$

Thus it is possible to test whether there is a short-run trade-off by looking at the coefficient β_1; and to test for a long-run trade-off by examining coefficient β_2.

There is considerable debate in the literature about the testing of the unemployment/inflation trade-off[24]. It is certainly true that simple Phillips-curve relationships broke down in the late 1960s and 1970s even with due allowance made for expectations. One of the problems, for instance, is that the natural rate of unemployment is not in fact likely to remain constant and hence the simple scheme outlined above needs to be extended. The natural rate of unemployment has its origins in the fact that because of market frictions and structural change, unemployment will always be positive. Thus, even when the economy is in general equilibrium with no excess demand or supply in any market and all expectations are realized, there will be positive unemployment. The level of this unemployment will be determined by various real forces such as the extent of market frictions, the level of real income, unemployment benefit and tax rates (Santomero and Seater, 1978). If these real forces change, there will correspondingly be a change in the level of natural unemployment.

The factors that have been discussed in earlier sections concerning the duration of unemployment will, therefore, all have a corresponding influence on the natural rate. Further, it has been recently argued by Hargreaves-Heap (1980) that the natural rate is not independent of the actual rate of unemployment and that the tendency of governments to be cautious for fear of pushing unemployment above the natural rate may lead to decelerating employment and lower growth.

The empirical evidence

One conclusion that some authors draw from recent empirical evidence (for example, Santomero and Seater, 1978) is that there seems to be a tendency for the coefficient on the expectations variable to increase towards unity over time, implying no long-run trade-off. Similarly, in Britain there is evidence that the natural rate of unemployment has increased quite markedly over the 1970s. Thus Sumner (1978) argues that the natural unemployment rate had increased from about 2.4% in the early 1950s to 5.1% in the early 1970s. But it has to be recognized that these estimates are subject to the limitations of the measurement of the replacement ratio which have been outlined in section 8.5.

Batchelor and Sheriff (1980) in a study of the effect of unanticipated inflation in post-war Britain concluded that the rate of unemployment which is consistent with fully anticipated inflation (the natural rate) appears to have moved broadly parallel to actual unemployment and they estimate the natural rate to be around 4% at the end of the 1970s. Whilst high, this value is rather lower than the actual rates of unemployment experienced.

Further, it should be noted that the major independent forecasting units in Britain such as the London Business School and the National Institute of Economic and Social Research have emphasized an interaction between unemployment and inflation in deriving their forecasts (Allsop and Joshi, 1980).

Adaptive and rational expectations

The introduction of price expectations into the equations does require some consideration of the way in which expectations are formed. Most of the early models relied on some scheme of adaptive expectations whereby expected future prices are based on some weighted average of past prices. In times of accelerating inflation past prices will underpredict the actual rate of inflation and hence the question has to be asked as to why individuals would persist in using forecasts that are incorrect. This problem has led to interest in the concept of rational expectations where the basic idea is that people form their expectations on a rational basis, meaning (in the context of the theory) in the light of forecasts that would be given by a correct model of the economy. Thus agents are endowed with all the available information, including the correct model of the economy. Such a view removes any possibility of the authorities fooling people and has been used to reach pessimistic conclusions about the ability of governments to influence the level of unemployment. Thus, as Mayes interprets these studies:

> . . . on the whole, the use of fiscal or monetary stimuli to offset the effects of recessions in economic activity is ineffective and inflationary. Economic policy should therefore aim simply to provide conditions which, in the longer run, will enable the economy to develop at its 'natural rate', i.e. the rate of growth of real output which the unfettered economic system is thought to deliver. (1981, p.53).

The application of rational expectations to economic policy, and the underlying model which is taken to be the correct one (usually monetarist by the advocates of the system), are matters of intense debate and it is impossible to provide a realistic summary in the space available[25]. But the point is that these strands in the development of macroeconomic analysis of the labour market, from the natural rate/vertical Phillips curve analysis to the rational expectations hypothesis, point to the difficulties and possible ineffectiveness of broad macroeconomic policies in reducing the level of unemployment[26]. As a result interest increases in the use of specific labour market policies and these are considered in the next section.

8.7   Labour market policies and unemployment

The general case for labour market policies

A marked feature of British economic policy since the Second World War has been the increasing emphasis on labour market policy including the extension of labour law into collective bargaining and employee rights[27]. Many of these developments took place during and after the mid-1960s and, as has been noted, some authors have associated the apparent rise in the natural rate of unemployment with some aspects of these policies. The traditional view of labour market policies is that they are designed to make labour markets work more effectively by easing the adjustments to changing supply and demand conditions. These include alterations in the desired geographical, industrial or skill mix, and structural changes in labour supply affecting the age/sex/educational composition of the labour force. The role of labour market policy is thus seen as altering the trade-off between various objectives of government policy and in modern terms altering the rate of unemployment that is compatible with no inflation. Among the most common measures to resolve mismatches between the supply of and demand for labour are the public employment service, training and re-training schemes, redundancy and labour mobility measures, regional development aids, employment subsidies and unemployment compensation. Most countries, and Britain is no exception, have developed policies along these lines with the main objective being to 'make labour markets work'.

As Thirlwall (1972) has pointed out, there are two fairly distinct categories of labour market policy: policies concerned with the efficient use of labour at the place of work and operated at the level of the firm, and policies operated directly by national governments relating to the utilization of manpower in the national economy and its distribution among various markets – occupational, industrial and geographical.

When looking at labour market policies, there are two points to bear in mind. First, a case can be investigated for labour market policies as a contra-cyclical device designed to smooth changes in unemployment over the cycle. Secondly, the question of a general argument for labour market policies can be examined where these policies would be independent of the cycle.

Taking the second case first, it is probably fair to say that apart from references to frictions and mismatching there has been little attempt to provide a rigorous demonstration of the argument for such general labour market policies. However, recent work has provided a sounder analytical base (Johnson, 1980; Jackman and Layard, 1980). Both these papers emphasize the importance of imperfections and distortions in the labour market. Johnson, for example, considers the two following types of structural imperfection.

The first type is where the wage structure is unable to adjust sufficiently for effective supplies of and demands for some classes of labour to be equated. He cites the existence of legal or social minimum wages which can prevent the wage rates of jobs involving low skill and low human capital from adjusting to their market clearing levels and the fact that trade union power can do the same for some wage rates and classes of labour.

The second type of imperfection is distortions arising from any payments made to individuals who do not work such as unemployment benefit and the social security system. The effect of these on unemployment has already been discussed in section 8.5 above. The distortions introduced by unemployment benefit also form the basis of the analysis in Jackman and Layard (1980).

There is a further additional factor in that governments frequently provide subsidies and incentives to capital through investment grants and other devices which tends to bias production away from labour and towards capital.

Previously, if the distortions are regarded as serious it is possible to attack them directly by policies such as repealing minimum wage laws, attempting through legislation to curb union power or not paying unemployment benefit. But it is reasonable to assume that many of these policies are either not socially desirable or politically (or practically) feasible. Thus as Jackman and Layard note:

> We assume that the solution of reducing [unemployment]
> benefit is ruled out on equity and insurance grounds. Given
> whatever benefit exists, there will be opportunities for reducing
> its efficiency cost by appropriate policies on wage subsidies,
> public employment or training. (1980, p.331).

Taking the distortions as given, both papers examine the case for various labour market policies. Johnson (1980) considers subsidies for the employment of youths and low-skilled adults, training programmes for low-skilled adults and the importation of labour from low wage countries. Within a model encompassing two groups of workers, skilled and unskilled, Jackman and Layard (1980) consider wage subsidies, public employment and training policies.

Johnson (1980) shows that the policies he considers generally have a large impact on the net incomes of groups both directly and indirectly affected, and that in some cases the policies can benefit all groups in society. Taking the case of employment subsidies, for example, a subsidy on the employment of one group will increase that group's employment. What happens to other groups depends on their relationship with the subsidized group. If they are complementary factors in production their employment will increase, but if they are substitutes it will decrease. It is also necessary to consider the effect of the subsidies on real output. The change in the net income of each group depends on what happens to taxes and transfer payments as well as gross earnings. Johnson shows that it is possible for the net incomes of tax-payers to rise. He concludes that if the real wages of youths and low-skilled adults are institutionally fixed at artificially high levels, wage subsidy programmes can be introduced which will increase aggregate output and employment and may even increase the net incomes of the tax-paying groups.

Jackman and Layard show that if unemployment benefit is being paid and wages are flexible, efficiency can be increased if either the supply of workers is more elastic in one market than another or if the proportionate distortion is greater in one market than another. They note that if demand-side policies are used (wage subsidies or public employment) demand should be shifted towards the group with the higher elasticity of supply or the highest proportionate distortion. Since distortions are greatest in the low-wage market, the equity case for shifting demand towards unskilled workers is therefore reinforced by an efficiency argument. They consider both fixed and flexible wages. If the latter are relevant then it makes no difference whether the subsidy is paid to the workers or to the employer, but if wages are inflexible it is important to provide the subsidy to the employer.

These two papers are important in that they demonstrate a rigorous case for labour market intervention independent of the business cycle. The exact policy mix and the extent of policies is a matter of some dispute which requires further research, and whilst the details of the models may be criticized and alternative assumptions adopted they do provide a framework which should prove useful in formulating labour market policies.

Contra-cyclical labour market policies

It is important to turn to specific policies designed to reduce the level of unemployment, contra-cyclical labour market policies. Layard (1979) has suggested that there are three obvious questions which need to be asked in this connection:

(1) Is it better to have general reflation or to use selective measures in the labour market?
(2) If selective measures are chosen, should they aim to expand the demand for labour or reduce its supply?
(3) If it is decided to expand labour demand, should this be in the private or public sector?

He further proposes five criteria on which policies should be assessed; concerning their effects on

(1) Employment and unemployment;
(2) The government budget surplus;
(3) The balance of payments effect;
(4) Net output;
(5) The distribution of welfare.

Taking account of these five effects he argues that each possible labour market policy should be ranked in terms of the increase in inflationary pressure it would generate for any given increase in real income (adjusted for equality).

What is required therefore is a large and widespread cost-benefit analysis which has to take account both of micro and macroeconomic effects. Layard himself considers the operation of various British policies within this framework. These include the temporary employment subsidy, the small firms employment subsidy and youth employment measures. In a joint paper he has further developed the analysis of employment subsidies (Layard and Nickell, 1980).

The analysis of such labour market policies is complex and outside the scope of this chapter. Suffice it to say that interest in selective measures has increased, given the problems involved in using fiscal and monetary policies to alleviate the social problems of unemployment. Attention is likely to focus to an increasing extent on job creation and the measures that can be taken in this direction[28]. Layard concludes his summary of the various British selective measures operated during the 1970s, as compared with reflation through tax cuts, by pointing out the following two advantages possessed by such selective measures.

> First, by direct targeting of selective employment and training and indirect targeting of flat-rate wage subsidies, they produce a more equitable distribution of the burden of unemployment. Secondly, all the policies probably have lower budget deficit and balance of payments costs per man off the register than do tax cuts. (1979, p.204).

8.8   Conclusions

In the summer of 1981 the number of people registered as unemployed was almost three million, well over 10% of the labour force. This chapter has sought to provide the background and highlight the issues involved in this pressing social problem.

It has been stressed that the labour market is highly volatile and that the number unemployed at any time is a small fraction of the

total movement that takes place within the market. Such movement is essential in an economy which is to survive in a period of
rapid technical and economic change. In most of the post-war
years the average person remained in unemployment for a relatively short time. However, examination of what happens to the
'typical' man can provide a seriously misleading picture of the true
nature of unemployment. It is important to try to get the facts right
and much of the early part of the chapter places this problem in
perspective. In particular, stress was laid on an understanding of
the concept of duration and its measurement. The latest research
has shown a number of features. First, an average spell of
unemployment has been quite short for most of the period (about
five weeks) but had risen dramatically to about 20 weeks by the
end of the 1970s. This change reflects the fact that the level of
unemployment is rising not so much because more people are
being made unemployed but because once unemployed they are
remaining in that state for longer. Secondly, the burden of
unemployment is spread very unequally and in particular a minority of people account for a large proportion of the total number of
weeks spent in unemployment by the population. One important
factor here is recurrence of spells of unemployment amongst
particular groups of individuals.

The fact that particular individuals experience repeated spells of
unemployment has at least one important implication in that they
may exhaust their entitlement to National Insurance benefits.
Stories abound of the unemployed holidaying in the Swiss Alps
whilst receiving their unemployment pay over the wires. In reality,
such a view presents a grossly distorted picture. The provisions of
the unemployment benefit system may have a marked effect on
behaviour and the evidence is considered in this chapter. It is
noted that recent careful work suggests that whilst unemployment
benefit has certainly had some effect in raising the level of
unemployment since the mid-1960s there are no grounds for
claiming that it is the primary cause of the increase that has
occurred.

Unemployment and inflation are almost inexorably linked and
literature emanating from the Phillips curve in the late 1950s has
dominated the textbooks and much public discussion. Since that
time it has become clear that there is no simple relationship
between the two which offers a menu for government policy-
makers. Current debate in the profession ranges from those who
argue that monetary and fiscal policy have no effect on real
variables in the economy to those who see a much more positive
role for government intervention. In the light of this debate the

use of specific labour market policies is examined and it is demonstrated that a rigorous case can now be made for the operation of labour market policies independent of the overall state of the economy. Also consideration is given to policies such as wage subsidies designed in a specific contra-cyclical manner.

A main intention of this chapter was to stress the complexity of the labour market; even apparently simple statistics such as the unemployment rate are open to a number of interpretations and can reflect a variety of different circumstances. There are no simple diagnoses and it should not be surprising therefore if it has not proved possible to suggest a simple prescription.

Notes

The author would like to thank John Coyne for his thorough and extremely helpful comments on the original draft of this chapter.

1. See, for example, Coase (1937) and Williamson (1975).
2. For the theory of such behaviour see Oi (1962). For an analysis of adjustments in the labour market see Thomas (1981).
3. Department of Employment (1980). For further information on unemployment statistics in the UK see Lord (1981) and Garside (1981). For details of changes in the system of recording the count see Lord (1981).
4. See for example the discussion in Henry (1981).
5. For studies using these data see Nickell (1979a, 1979b and 1980).
6. See for example Salant (1977) and Akerlof and Main (1980).
7. For details see Kaitz (1970) and Salant (1977).
8. The problems involved in measuring duration are discussed in detail in Akerlof and Main (1980), Clark and Summers (1979) and Lancaster and Nickell (1980).
9. For a review of these studies and their results see Main (1981).
10. There are many other aspects relating to the burden of unemployment. For an excellent introduction see Metcalf and Nickell (1978). Much recent interesting work has been done on regional and urban unemployment; for example, Burridge and Gordon (1981), Evans and Richardson (1981), and Mair (1981). Heckman and Borjas (1980) consider the effect of a spell of unemployment on future unemployment.
11. See the studies by Doherty (1979), Fenn (1981), and Thomas (1980).
12. See for example Addison and Siebert (1979).

13. For a detailed examination of the methods involved see Armstrong and Taylor (1981).
14. See for example Mackay and Reid (1972) and Gujarati (1972).
15. For a number of important contributions in this area see the volume edited by Phelps *et al.* (1971).
16. In this connection the implicit contracts literature is of considerable importance. For a survey see Azariadis (1981).
17. For an accessible discussion of the problems raised by asymmetric information see the classic paper by Akerlof (1970).
18. For a pioneering analysis of search in the labour market see Stigler (1962).
19. For example see the application of this assumption in the analysis of discrimination in Chiplin (1981) and Chiplin and Sloane (1982).
20. For a recent survey of the literature on the effects of unemployment benefits see Topel and Welch (1980).
21. See for instance Ashworth (1981), Santomero and Seater (1978) and Trevithick (1981).
22. This honour belongs to Fisher (1926).
23. For a clear survey of this difficult literature see Casson (1981).
24. See for example Henry *et al.* (1976) and the studies in Parkin and Sumner (1978).
25. For recent surveys see Kantor (1979) and Mayes (1981).
26. For a counter-argument see Buiter (1980, 1981).
27. Sweden is perhaps the western country which has placed greatest emphasis on the role of labour market policies. For a discussion of the policies and their success see Chiplin and Sloane (1977).
28. For some of the arguments and alternatives see Baily and Tobin (1977), Johnson (1976), Kesselman *et al.* (1977) and Palmer (1978).

References

Addison, J. T. and Siebert, W. S. (1979). *The Market for Labor: An Analytical Treatment*. Santa Monica; Goodyear

Akerlof, G. A. (1970). The market for 'lemons': quality uncertainty and the market mechanism. *Quarterly Journal of Economics* **84,** 488–500

Akerlof, G. A. (1979). The case against conservative macroeconomics: an inaugural lecture. *Economica* **46,** 219–237

Akerlof, G. A. and Main, B. G. M. (1980). Unemployment spells and unemployment experience. *American Economic Review* **70,** 885–893

Allsopp, C. and Joshi, V. (1980). Alternative strategies for the UK. *National Institute Economic Review* **91**, 86–103

Armstrong, H. and Taylor, J. (1981). The measurement of different types of unemployment. In *The Economics of Unemployment in Britain* (ed. by J. Creedy), pp.99–127. London; Butterworths

Ashworth, J. (1981). Wages, prices and unemployment. In *The Economics of Unemployment in Britain* (ed. by J. Creedy), pp.186–234. London; Butterworths

Atkinson, A. B. (1981). Unemployment benefits and incentives. In *The Economics of Unemployment in Britain* (ed. by J. Creedy), pp.128–149. London; Butterworths

Azariadis, C. (1981). Implicit contracts and related topics: a survey. In *The Economics of the Labour Market* (ed. by Z. Hornstein, J. Grice, and A. Webb), pp.221–248. London; HMSO

Baily, M. N. and Tobin, J. (1977). Macroeconomic effects of selective public employment and wage subsidies. *Brookings Papers on Economic Activity* **2**, 511–541

Batchelor, R. A. and Sheriff, T. D. (1980). Unemployment and unanticipated inflation in postwar Britain. *Economica* **47**, 179–192

Beveridge, W. H. (1944). *Full Employment in a Free Society*. London; Allen and Unwin

Bowers, J. K. Cheshire, P. C. and Webb, A. E. (1970). The change in the relationship between unemployment and earnings increases. *National Institute Economic Review* **54**, 75–88

Bowers, J. K. and Harkess, D. (1979). Duration of unemployment by age and sex. *Economica* **46**, 239–260

Buiter, W. H. (1980). The macroeconomics of Dr Pangloss: a critical survey of the new classical macroeconomics, *Economic Journal* **90**, 34–50

Buiter, W. H. (1981). The superiority of contingent rules over fixed rules in models with rational expectations. *Economic Journal* **91**, 647–670

Burdett, K. (1979). Unemployment insurance payments as a search subsidy: a theoretical analysis. *Economic Inquiry* **1**, 333–343

Burridge, P. and Gordon, I. (1981). Unemployment in the British metropolitan labour areas. *Oxford Economic Papers* **33**, 274–297

Casson, M. C. (1981). Unemployment and the new macroeconomics. In *The Economics of Unemployment in Britain* (ed. by J. Creedy), pp.48–98. London; Butterworths

Chiplin, B. (1981). An alternative approach to the measurement of sex discrimination. *Economic Journal* **91**, 988–997

Chiplin, B. and Sloane P. J. (1977). *Swedish and Swiss manpower policy: its relevance for the EEC.* European Commission, programme of research and actions on the development of the labour market, Study No. 77/6

Chiplin, B. and Sloane, P. J. (1982). *Tackling Discrimination at the Workplace.* New York; Cambridge University Press

Clark, K. B. and Summers, L. H. (1979). Labour market dynamics and unemployment: a reconsideration. *Brookings Papers on Economic Activity* **1**, 13–60

Coase, R. H. (1937). The nature of the firm. *Economica* **4**, 386–405

Creedy, J. (ed.). (1981). *The Economics of Unemployment in Britain.* London; Butterworths

Creedy, J. and Disney, R. (1981a). Changes in labour market states in Great Britain. *Scottish Journal of Political Economy* **28**, 76–85

Creedy, J. and Disney, R. (1981b). Eligibility for unemployment benefits in Great Britain. *Oxford Economic Papers* **33**, 256–273

Cubbin, J. S. and Foley, K. (1977). The extent of benefit induced unemployment in Great Britain: some new evidence. *Oxford Economic Papers* **29**, 128–140

Department of Employment (1980). A review of unemployment and vacancy statistics. *Employment Gazette (May)*, 497–508

Desai, M. (1976). The Phillips curve: a revisionist interpretation. *Economica* **42**, 1–19

Disney, R. (1979). Recurrent spells and the concentration of unemployment in Great Britain. *Economic Journal* **89**, 109–119

Disney, R. (1981). Unemployment insurance in Britain. In *The Economics of Unemployment in Britain* (ed. by J. Creedy), pp. 150–185. London; Butterworths

Doherty, N. A. (1979). National insurance and absence from work. *Economic Journal* **89**, 50–65

Dow, J. C. R. and Dicks-Mireaux, L. A. (1958). The excess demand for labour: a study of conditions in Great Britain, 1946–1956. *Oxford Economic Papers* **10**, 1–33

Evans, A. W. and Richardson, R. (1981). Urban unemployment: interpretation and additional evidence. *Scottish Journal of Political Economy* **28**, 107–124

Fenn, P. (1981). Sickness duration, residual disability and income replacement: an empirical analysis. *Economic Journal* **91**, 158–173

Fisher, I. (1926). A statistical relation between unemployment and price changes. *International Labour Review* **13**, 785–792

Friedman, M. (1968). The role of monetary policy. *American Economic Review* **58**, 1–17

Garside, W. R. (1981). *The Measurement of Unemployment in Great Britain 1850–1979*. Oxford; Basil Blackwell

Gronau, R. (1977). The effect of children on the housewife's value of time. *Journal of Political Economy* **81**, 5169–5201

Gujarati, D. (1972). The behaviour of unemployment and unfilled vacancies: Great Britain 1958–71. *Economic Journal* **82**, 195–204

Hargreaves-Heap, S. P. (1980). Choosing the wrong 'natural rate': accelerating inflation or decelerating employment and growth? *Economic Journal* **90**, 611–620

Heckman, J. J. and Borjas, G. J. (1980). Does unemployment cause future unemployment? *Economica* **47**, 247–284

Henry, S. G. B. (1981). Forecasting employment and unemployment. In *The Economics of the Labour Market* (ed. by Z. Hornstein, J. Grice, and A. Webb), pp.283–309. London; HMSO

Henry, S. G. B., Sawyer, M. C. and Smith, P. (1976). Models of inflation in the UK: an evaluation. *National Institute Economic Review* **77**, 60–71

Hey, J. D. (1979). *Uncertainty in Microeconomics*. Oxford; Martin Robertson

Jackman, R. A. and Layard, P. R. G. (1980). The efficiency case for long-run labour market policies. *Economica* **47**, 331–350

Johnson, G. E. (1976). Evaluating the macroeconomic effects of public employment programmes. In *Evaluating the Labour Market Effects of Social Programmes* (ed. by O. Ashenfelter and J. Blum), pp.90–123. Industrial Relations Section Princeton University, Princeton

Johnson, G. E. (1980). The theory of labour market intervention. *Economica* **47**, 309–330

Kahn, R. (1976. Unemployment as seen by the Keynesians. In *The Concept and Measurement of Involuntary Unemployment*. (ed. by G. D. N. Worswick) pp.19–34. London; Allen and Unwin

Kaitz, H. (1970). Analysing the length of spells of unemployment. *Monthly Labor Review* **15**, 11–20

Kantor, B. (1979). Rational expectations and economic thought. *Journal of Economic Literature* **17**, 1422–1441

Kesselman, J. R., Williamson, S. H. and Berndt, E. R. (1977). Tax credits for employment rather than investment. *American Economic Review* **67**, 339–349

Lancaster, T. (1979). Econometric methods for the duration of unemployment. *Econometrica* **47**, 939–956

Lancaster, T. and Nickell, S. J. (1980). The analysis of re-employment probabilities for the unemployed. *Journal of the Royal Statistical Society* A. **143**, 141–165

Layard, P. R. G. (1979). The costs and benefits of selective employment policies: the British case. *British Journal of Industrial Relations* **17**, 187–204

Layard, P. R. G. and Nickell, S. J. (1980). The case for subsidizing extra jobs. *Economic Journal* **90**, 51–73

Lord, J. S. (1981). Unemployment statistics in Britain. In *The Economics of Unemployment in Britain* (ed. by J. Creedy), pp. 235–254. London; Butterworths

Mcgregor, A. (1978). Unemployment duration and re-employment probability. *Economic Journal* **88**, 693–706

Mackay, D. I. and Reid, G. L. (1972). Redundancy, unemployment and manpower policy. *Economic Journal* **82**, 1256–1272

Main, B. G. M. (1981). The length of employment and unemployment in Great Britain. *Scottish Journal of Political Economy* **28**, 146–164

Mair, D. (1981). Urban unemployment: a comment. *Economic Journal* **91**, 224–230

Maki, D. R. and Spindler, Z. A. (1975). The effect of unemployment compensation on the rate of unemployment in GB. *Oxford Economic Papers* **27**, 440–454

Mayes, D. G. (1981). The controversy over rational expectations. *National Institute Economic Review* **96**, 53–61

Metcalf, D. and Nickell, S. J. (1978). The plain man's guide to the out of work. *Royal Commission on Distribution of Income and Wealth: Selected Evidence for Report No. 6.* London; HMSO

Nickell, S. J. (1979a). The effect of unemployment benefit and related benefits on the duration of unemployment. *Economic Journal* **89**, 34–49

Nickell, S.J. (1979b). Estimating the probability of leaving unemployment. *Econometrica* **47**, 1249–1266

Nickell, S. J. (1980). A picture of male unemployment in Britain. *Economic Journal* **90**, 776–794

Oi, W. Y. (1962). Labour as a quasi-fixed factor. *Journal of Political Economy* **70**, 538–555

Palmer, J. L. (ed.) (1978). *Creating Jobs: Public Employment Programmes and Wage Subsidies.* Washington; Brookings Institution.

Parkin, M. and Sumner, . T. (eds.) (1978). *Inflation in the United Kingdom.* Manchester; Manchester University Press

Phelps, E. S. (1967). Phillips curves, expectations of inflation and optimal unemployment over time. *Economica* **34**, 254–281

Phelps, E. S. (ed.) (1971). *Microfoundations of Employment and Inflation Theory*. London; Macmillan.

Phillips, A. W. (1958). The relationship between unemployment and the rate of change of money wage rates in the UK. *Economica* **25**, 283–299

Pissarides, C. A. (1976). Job search and participation. *Economica* **43**, 33–49

Salant, S. W. (1977). Search theory and duration data: a theory of sorts. *Quarterly Journal of Economics* **91**, 39–57

Santomero, A. M. and Seater, J. J. (1978). The inflation unemployment trade-off: a critique of the literature. *Journal of Economic Literature* **16**, 499–544

Sawyer, M. C. (1979). The effects of unemployment compensation on the rate of unemployment in Great Britain: a comment, *Oxford Economic Papers* **31**, 135–146

Spence, M. (1974). *Market Signaling*. Cambridge, Mass; Harvard University Press

Stigler, G. J. (1962). Information in the labor market. *Journal of Political Economy* **70**, 94–105

Stiglitz, J. E. (1975). The theory of screening, education and the distribution of income. *American Economic Review* **65**, 283–300

Sumner, M. T. (1978). Wage determination. In *Inflation in the United Kingdom* (ed. by M. Parkin and M. T. Sumner), pp. 75–92

Taylor, J. (1977). A note on the comparative behaviour of male and female unemployment rates in the UK 1951–76. (mimeo) University of Lancaster

Thirlwall, A. (1972). Government manpower policies in Great Britain: their rationale and benefits. *British Journal of Industrial Relations* **10**, 161–179

Thomas, R. B. (1980). Wages, sickness benefits and absenteeism. *Journal of Economic Studies* **7**, 51–61

Thomas, R. B. (1981). Labour market adjustments. In *The Economics of Unemployment in Britain* (ed. by J. Creedy), pp. 17–47. London; Butterworths

Topel, R. and Welch, F. (1980). Unemployment insurance, survey and extensions. *Economica* **47**, 351–380

Trevithick, J. A. (1981). *Inflation*. Harmondsworth; Penguin

Williamson, O. E. (1975). *Markets and Hierarchies*. New York; The Free Press

Subject Index

Index of Authors